MW01253647

Faith, Philosophy and the Reflective Muslim

Palgrave Frontiers in Philosophy of Religion

Series Editors: **Yujin Nagasawa** and **Erik Wielenberg**

Titles include

Zain Ali
FAITH, PHILOSOPHY AND THE REFLECTIVE MUSLIM

Yujin Nagasawa (*editor*)
SCIENTIFIC APPROACHES TO THE PHILOSOPHY OF RELIGION

Forthcoming titles

István Aranyosi
GOD, MIND AND LOGICAL SPACE
A Revisionary Approach to Divinity

Gregory Dawes and James Maclaurin (*editors*)
COGNITIVE SCIENCE AND RELIGION

Trent Dougherty
THE PROBLEM OF ANIMAL PAIN
A Theodicy for All Creatures Great and Small

Aaron Rizzieri
PRAGMATIC ENCROACHMENT, RELIGIOUS BELIEF AND PRACTICE

Aaron Smith
THINKING ABOUT RELIGION
Extending the Cognitive Science of Religion

Palgrave Frontiers in Philosophy of Religion
Series Standing Order ISBN 978–0–230–35443–2 Hardback
(*outside North America only*)

You can receive future titles in this series as they are published by placing a standing order. Please contact your bookseller or, in case of difficulty, write to us at the address below with your name and address, the title of the series and the ISBN quoted above.

Customer Services Department, Macmillan Distribution Ltd, Houndmills, Basingstoke, Hampshire RG21 6XS, England

Faith, Philosophy and the Reflective Muslim

Zain Ali
Head of the Islamic Studies Research Unit
University of Auckland, New Zealand

First published 2013 by
PALGRAVE MACMILLAN

Palgrave Macmillan in the UK is an imprint of Macmillan Publishers Limited, registered in England, company number 785998, of Houndmills, Basingstoke, Hampshire RG21 6XS.

Palgrave Macmillan in the US is a division of St Martin's Press LLC, 175 Fifth Avenue, New York, NY 10010.

Palgrave Macmillan is the global academic imprint of the above companies and has companies and representatives throughout the world.

Palgrave® and Macmillan® are registered trademarks in the United States, the United Kingdom, Europe and other countries

ISBN: 978–1–137–28635–2

This book is printed on paper suitable for recycling and made from fully managed and sustained forest sources. Logging, pulping and manufacturing processes are expected to conform to the environmental regulations of the country of origin.

A catalogue record for this book is available from the British Library.

A catalog record for this book is available from the Library of Congress.

Come, come, whoever you are.
Wonderer, worshipper, lover of leaving.
It doesn't matter.
Ours is not a caravan of despair.
Come, even if you have broken your vow
a thousand times
Come, yet again, come, come.

Rumi

Contents

Series Editors' Preface   viii

Acknowledgements   ix

Introduction   1

1 A Jamesian Account of Faith   9

2 The Challenge of Al-Ghazālī's Scepticism   35

3 Al-Ghazālī's Sufi Account of Faith   54

4 A Jamesian Reading of Al-Ghazālī   78

5 The Challenge of Contemporary Evidentialism   100

6 Challenges to Religious Pluralism   123

Conclusion   152

Notes   155

Bibliography   170

Index   175

Series Editors' Preface

The philosophy of religion has experienced a welcome re-vitalisation over the last fifty years or so and is now thriving. Our hope with the *Palgrave Frontiers in Philosophy of Religion* series is to contribute to the continued vitality of the philosophy of religion by producing works that truly break new ground in the field.

Accordingly, each book in this series advances some debate in the philosophy of religion by offering a novel argument to establish a strikingly original thesis or approaching an ongoing dispute from a radically new point of view. Each book accomplishes this by utilising recent developments in empirical sciences or cutting-edge research in foundational areas of philosophy, or by adopting historically neglected approaches.

We expect the series to enrich debates within the philosophy of religion both by expanding the range of positions and arguments on offer and establishing important links between the philosophy of religion and other fields, including not only other areas of philosophy but the empirical sciences as well.

Our ultimate aim, then, is to produce a series of exciting books that explore and expand the frontiers of the philosophy of religion and connect it with other areas of inquiry. We are grateful to Palgrave Macmillan for taking on this project as well as to the authors of the books in the series.

Yujin Nagasawa and Erik J. Wielenberg

Acknowledgements

The work of John Bishop has had a deep and lasting influence on my thinking on questions of faith and philosophy. His lectures and publications on William James first drew my attention to the Jamesian account of faith. He has also influenced the approach that I have taken, namely, that of a reflective believer. This study, in part, attempts to welcome James, and Bishop's scholarship on James into the intellectual tradition of Islam.

I express my gratitude to Robert Wicks, whose door was always open to me. I have greatly enjoyed our conversations on philosophy, the meaning of life and fatherhood. I am also indebted to Glen Pettigrove for his guidance on how best to structure this study. My thanks also to Imran Aijaz and David Nickless for their stimulating comments and feedback. Thanks also to the anonymous referees for Palgrave Macmillan, who provided positive reviews and constructive feedback.

My deepest gratitude is towards my family, who have inspired me with their faith, passion and patience. I thank my parents, who have scarified much for the ideal of a better education. Many thanks also to my wife, who has stood by me throughout my studies. A note of appreciation also for my children, whose smiles are a constant source of joy – the following lines from Tagore best capture my feelings: *the smile that flickers on baby's lips when he sleeps – does anybody know where it was born? Yes, there is a rumour that a young pale beam of a crescent moon touched the edge of a vanishing autumn cloud, and there the smile was first born in the dream of a dew-washed morning.*

Introduction

I was a hidden treasure, and I wished to be known, so I created
the world.

— Hadith Qudsi

A major question in the Philosophy of Religion concerns the existence of God, and a significant portion of the literature in this field is
devoted to providing an answer to this question.[1] The question also
plays a central role in this study, though I will not attempt to provide
arguments which disambiguate in favour of, or against, the existence of
God. My approach will be to assume that the evidence leaves open the
question of God's existence, i.e., that the total relevant evidence neither
shows belief in God to be true nor false.[2] I will refer to this assumption
as the thesis of religious ambiguity or simply as the 'ambiguity thesis'.
The ambiguity thesis is open to contention, although I believe that it is
worthy of serious philosophical consideration.[3] One reason for considering this assumption is that it can be seen to explain observations
about the nature and diversity of religious commitments. For example,
Keith Ward observes that:

> Many religions claim to state truths about the nature of the universe
> and human destiny which are important or even necessary for
> human salvation and ultimate well-being. Many of these truths seem
> to be incompatible; yet there is no agreed method for deciding which
> are to be accepted; and equally intelligent, informed, virtuous and
> holy people belong to different faiths.[4]

1

In a sentiment not dissimilar to that of Ward, John Hick describes the universe as a place which elicits and sustains both religious and non-religious interpretations. His view is framed as follows:

> By the religious ambiguity of the world I do not mean that it has no definite character but that it is capable from our present human vantage point of being thought and experienced in both religious and naturalistic ways ... With the western Enlightenment of the eighteenth century, stimulated by the rapid development of the modern scientific method and outlook, a scepticism that had hitherto hovered in the background as a mere logical possibility now became psychologically present and plausible within the more educated circles of Europe and North America, and the old religious certainties began to crumble ... In this post-Enlightenment age of doubt we have realised that the universe is religiously ambiguous. It evokes and sustains non-religious as well as religious responses.[5]

I suggest that Hick and Ward are correct to observe that there exists a diversity of incompatible faith commitments and that the individuals who hold the varying commitments appear equally intelligent, informed and virtuous. This observation, if accepted as correct, invites an explanation and this is where the ambiguity thesis proves to be helpful. That is, one may contend that the ambiguity of the evidence pertaining to the existence of God is, in part, responsible for the diverse range of non-religious as well as religious responses. The ambiguity thesis, I suggest, is worthy of philosophical consideration, since it offers a potential explanation of the nature and diversity of genuinely held faith commitments.[6]

This study, as already noted, concedes the truth of the ambiguity thesis, and in doing so, we also have to consider a number of questions which this assumption elicits. For example, we may question why God would permit religious ambiguity, and whether the world has always been religiously ambiguous, or we may question whether the ambiguity thesis can be consistent with a Christian, Muslim or naturalist worldview. For the purposes of this study, our primary focus will be on the following question: can a person be entitled to hold and act on their belief in God under the condition of evidential ambiguity? We can label this question, as simply the 'question of entitlement', and it is a question that is philosophically important, as it requires us to reflect on the nature and justifiability of religious belief. The question of entitlement to believe in God, like the ambiguity thesis, also elicits a range of responses which need consideration. For instance, in reply to the question of entitlement, one may argue that believing must always be in proportion to evidence, and if the evidence is ambiguous then the appropriate course to take would be to suspend belief. One may then maintain that if the believer concedes that the question of God's existence cannot be settled on the basis of the evidence, then they should suspend their belief that God exists. As a result, a believer who concedes the ambiguity thesis will not be entitled to take it to be true that God exists. Alternatively, one may offer a Wittgensteinian inspired response which would maintain that religious beliefs are not statements of fact.[7] That is, unlike factual statements, religious beliefs do not require justification by way of proof or evidence. Thus, the question of entitlement to believe in God will be seen to be misguided, as it incorrectly assumes that religious belief is in need of justification.[8]

The view I aim to defend in this study maintains that there can, in principle, be an entitlement to believe in God under the condition of religious ambiguity. This response to the question of entitlement to believe in God, assumes that religious beliefs are statements of fact and challenges the view that one can only believe on the basis of adequate evidence. The account of faith which I aim to defend maintains that a person can be entitled to believe beyond the evidence. This view of belief is not the claim that one can believe contrary to the evidence or that evidence can be ignored. Rather, the claim is that in certain cases one can be entitled to believe even if the truth of the belief cannot be settled on the basis of evidential considerations. This account of faith draws its inspiration from William James; in particular, James's 1895 lecture 'The Will to Believe'.[9] I argue that James's account of religious faith allows us to defend the view that theistic belief can be justified under the condition of religious ambiguity. The interpretation of James which I aim to endorse is also the subject of a recent work by John Bishop, entitled *Believing by Faith: An essay in the Epistemology and Ethics of Religious Belief*.[10] I develop and refine Bishop's work by engaging with a range of philosophical and theological concerns about the Jamesian account of faith which do not feature in *Believing by Faith*.

A distinctive feature of this study is that it also has the perspective of a 'reflective Muslim' in mind. The reflective Muslim describes a person of Islamic faith who has come to acknowledge that people of other religious and non-religious persuasions are as educated and concerned with seeking truth and avoiding error as they themselves are. There are two main reasons why I have chosen to approach this study through the perspective of the reflective Muslim: (a) much of the contemporary literature within the philosophy of religion is written from Christian and secular perspectives and the introduction of a Muslim perspective offers the potential for fresh insights, and (b) there is, I believe, a growing body of Muslims who are reflective in their outlook and are seriously pondering the type of questions which this study aims to address. The reflective Muslim is also someone who is sympathetic toward those who do not share their faith commitments, and they also concede, or at least are open to the view that the total relevant evidence shows belief in God to be neither true nor false. Accordingly, the reflective Muslim is also interested in exploring the implications of endorsing the ambiguity thesis; in particular, they will be interested in seeking out a philosophically viable response to the question of entitlement to believe in God. To this end, a central aim of this study is to defend the Jamesian account of faith as offering a philosophically viable reply to the question of entitlement.

The reflective Muslim who endorses James's account will also be concerned with the relationship that the account has with the tradition of Islam. This concern is not easy to address, as there will be questions about how one is to understand and define the tradition of Islamic theism. I will not attempt to offer a definition of Islam, rather my primary gauge of the tradition will be the work and thought of Abu Hamid al-Ghazālī (c.1055–1111).[11] The main reason why al-Ghazālī can be considered a gauge of the tradition, is simply due to the fact that he is recognised as one of the most prominent and influential philosophers, theologians, jurists, and mystics of Sunni Islam.[12] Furthermore, the works of al-Ghazālī are easily accessible in Arabic and a good number of them have multiple English translations, and there is a significant body of scholarly literature which engages with al-Ghazālī's work.[13] Importantly, al-Ghazālī's discussions of faith and philosophy have strong parallels with contemporary discussions and debates on religious belief, and his discussions are also directly relevant to the questions I consider in this study. Overall, there are four specific ways in which this study will engage with al-Ghazālī's work and thought: (a) we engage with al-Ghazālī's case for scepticism, which aims to undermine the view that sense perception and reason are trustworthy; (b) we critically engage with al-Ghazālī's Sufi account of faith which promises to deliver epistemic and spiritual certainty; (c) we develop a reading of al-Ghazālī that is aligned with a Jamesian account of faith; and (d) we draw on al-Ghazālī's discussion of belief and non-belief in order to articulate a framework that is compatible with a certain understanding of religious pluralism. I should note that, in giving al-Ghazālī a prominent role in this study, I do not wish to down play the significance of great Muslim thinkers such as Ibn Sina, al-Farabi, Ibn Rushd, Ibn Arabi and Mulla Sadra. These thinkers deserve to be considered, although it is beyond the scope of this work to give each of them due regard. There are then two overarching reasons for engaging with al-Ghazālī: the first is that his thought and work provides us with a touchstone for understanding the tradition of Islamic theism, and secondly, an engagement with al-Ghazālī will provide us with resources that will be used to evaluate James's account of faith.

This study aims to address two specific concerns, namely: whether or not the Jamesian account of faith is a philosophically viable response to the question of entitlement, and whether or not the reflective Muslim can endorse the Jamesian account of faith while also being aligned with the tradition of Islam. Given these concerns, I aim to defend the view that the Jamesian account is philosophically viable, and that it offers an effective reply to the question of entitlement to believe. I also maintain that the Jamesian account can be endorsed by the reflective Muslim, and that the account can also be welcomed within the tradition of Islamic theism. With these aims in view our study begins in Chapter 1. The aim of this first chapter is to present a *prima facie* case for the philosophical viability of the Jamesian account of faith. The *prima facie* case involves defending the following claims: (a) that there are uncontroversial cases where believing beyond the evidence seems to be justified; (b) that there are a common set of features which underpin the uncontroversial cases which are outlined; (c) that James is correct to recognise these features as being necessary and sufficient conditions which justify believing beyond the evidence; (d) that James's account is relatively immune to an absolutist form of evidentialism which maintains that it is always wrong to believe upon insufficient evidence; and (e) that James's account is applicable to religious belief. I also contend that the reflective Muslim can employ the Jamesian account as a response to the question of entitlement. The reflective Muslim may be willing to endorse James's account; however, they may first want to explore the potential implications that are involved with such an endorsement. There will be a concern that James's account may, in some way, violate or deviate from the ethos of Islamic tradition; or that, there is an alternative, viable account of faith within the Islamic tradition which also addresses the question of entitlement, thus obviating the need to endorse the Jamesian account. The three chapters that follow will draw on the work and thought of al-Ghazālī in order to further elaborate and respond to these concerns.

Chapter 2 focuses on whether the religious commitments of Islam permit Muslims to evaluate their faith commitments through the use of philosophical reason. The framework of James's account of faith presupposes a reflective stance with respect to faith commitments. If we rule out the possibility of critically engaging with religious belief, then we would have to set aside James's account. An example of an argument against the enterprise of philosophy of religion can be derived from the work of al-Ghazālī. He argues that the trust we have in our cognitive abilities is misplaced, and thus the deliverances of sense perception and human reason may not guide us to truth. Accordingly, there is no motivation to critically consider faith commitments, since human reason is an unreliable guide to truth. If the Ghazālīan inspired argument is successful then we would have to abandon the enterprise that is the philosophy of religion. Given that we have taken al-Ghazālī's work as a gauge of the tradition of Islam, one may also argue that James's account, which involves engaging in philosophy of religion, deviates from the ethos of Islamic tradition. I articulate and evaluate al-Ghazālī's arguments and conclude that it would be self-defeating to interpret al-Ghazālī's position as excluding rational reflection. Thus, al-Ghazālī's sceptical concerns need not be seen to disqualify James's account, and the reflective Muslim need not abandon a critical stance with respect to their faith commitments.

Chapter 3 broadens our interpretation of al-Ghazālī's case for scepticism. We note that al-Ghazālī's sceptical stance aims to motivate a Sufi account of faith. The case for scepticism, if true, suggests that sense perception and human reason are unreliable as guides to truth. There is then doubt and uncertainty with respect to the knowledge we have of ourselves and the world. Al-Ghazālī presents us with a Sufi account of faith in order to resolve his sceptical concerns. The Sufi account posits a supra-intellectual faculty which can directly receive divinely revealed truth. That is, there exists a cognitive faculty which can apprehend truth without recourse to sense perception and human reason. If such a faculty exists, then its deliverances are 'God given': thus we can set aside concerns of a sceptical nature. Al-Ghazālī argues that there exists such a faculty and it is through the cultivation of this faculty that we can overcome doubt and uncertainty. I articulate al-Ghazālī's arguments, and I also discuss the parallels the Sufi account has with an account of faith that is endorsed by a number of contemporary Christian philosophers. My aim in this chapter is to evaluate al-Ghazālī's Sufi account of faith and argue that the reflective Muslim has good reason not to view al-Ghazālī's account as a viable alternative to the Jamesian account of faith.

Chapter 4 develops a Jamesian interpretation of al-Ghazālī's resolution of scepticism. The Jamesian interpretation aims to show that James's account provides a reading of al-Ghazālī that is philosophically and theologically more viable than al-Ghazālī's own Sufi account. I challenge al-Ghazālī's view that scepticism can be overcome by the achievement of epistemic certainty. The philosophical and theological problems associated with al-Ghazālī's view, I maintain, are remedied by a Jamesian reading. Furthermore, we observe that James's account can be successfully applied to the prophet Muhammad's reported experience of divine commission. I also note that James's account is broadly consistent with a view of faith that is endorsed by a significant number of respected Muslim scholars. Accordingly, this Chapter aims to provide the reflective Muslim with good reasons to think that the Jamesian account has a significant role to play within the tradition of Islamic theism. I do note, however, that endorsing the Jamesian account faces a number of challenges which require continued consideration. The two chapters that follow will each engage with a specific challenge of this kind.

Chapter 5 engages with a contemporary form of evidentialism which maintains that believing beyond the evidence is conceptually problematic. The reflective Muslim who endorses James's account is committed to the view that believing beyond the evidence is permissible. A person who endorses the Jamesian account must then be prepared to defend this view if it is challenged. Accordingly, this chapter engages with the work of Jonathan Adler who is a radical critic of the Jamesian account. I consider Adler's defence of evidentialism and I also consider his interpretation and critique of the Jamesian account of faith. Adler argues that James's account is guilty of violating the very concept of belief, since James seems to be endorsing the mistaken view that we can believe beyond the evidence and that beliefs can be acquired at will (doxastic voluntarism). In response to Adler's critique of James, I maintain that James need not be read as endorsing voluntarism and that Alders stance against believing beyond the evidence is philosophically inconsistent.

Chapter 6 considers the religious pluralism that is implicit in the Jamesian account of faith. The reflective Muslim who endorses James's account will also be commitment to a type of pluralism that is associated with it. First, I explain the nature of the pluralism that is associated with the Jamesian account, and then I respond to those who maintain that pluralism is philosophically inconsistent. This chapter also considers an argument which maintains that Islamic theism supports a stance that is opposed to religious pluralism. This view if true would mean the Jamesian account, which entails a pluralist ethos, would be inconsistent with Islamic theism. My focus in this chapter is to argue that the pluralism associated with the Jamesian account of faith is philosophically, psychologically and theologically viable.

The six chapters, when taken together, aim firstly to establish that, given the assumption of religious ambiguity, the Jamesian account provides us with a philosophically viable response to the question of entitlement to believe in God; and, secondly, to establish that the reflective Muslim can endorse the Jamesian account while also being aligned with the tradition of Islam.

1
A Jamesian Account of Faith

> To educate people to be more humanistic is to tell them to live
> with ambiguity and to like ambiguity – not only to live with it as
> an accident but to understand human nature as ambiguous.
> – Elhanan Naeh

Faith, according to William James, involves believing beyond the
evidence. The plan for this chapter is to first articulate a *prima facie* case
for the philosophical viability of the Jamesian account of faith. To this
end, we will engage with James's account in three distinct ways. We
will begin with an outline of the Jamesian account and then outline
the various arguments marshalled in defence of this account. The main
thrust of our initial engagement with James is to argue: (a) that there are
conditions which justify a venture beyond the evidence, and (b) that
the conditions which justify such a 'faith venture' can also be met in
everyday circumstances. A defence of these two claims lends weight to
view that the Jamesian account is philosophically viable.

The second step of our engagement with James concerns the evidentialist ethics of belief. In contrast with James's view, the evidentialist
ethics of belief, which I shall shortly consider, maintains that it is always
wrong to believe on the basis of insufficient evidence. This view of belief
would rule out believing beyond the evidence. I consider James's reply
to the evidentialist and argue that his view needs to be further refined
in order to be effective. In particular, I consider his claim that commitment to evidentialism is itself a faith commitment which involves a
venture beyond the evidence. This reply, I argue, misconstrues the
motivations of the evidentialist and fails to give due weight to the
genuine epistemic and moral concerns which underpin evidentialism.
I also argue that the epistemic and moral concerns can be adequately

9

addressed by modifying aspects of the Jamesian account of faith. Once James's account is modified, we find ourselves in a stronger position to articulate a case against the claim that it is always wrong to believe on the basis of insufficient evidence. Accordingly, our engagement with James involves responding to an absolutist form of evidentialism, and this response undermines the view that believing beyond the evidence is philosophically unjustifiable.

The third step in our engagement with James involves assuming the viability of the Jamesian account in general, but considering whether the account can be applied to religious belief. This will involve accepting the view that under certain conditions believing beyond the evidence can be justified. The question we then need to consider is whether religious belief is capable of satisfying the conditions which would justify a venture beyond the evidence. I will consider three challenges to the view that James's account can be applied to religious belief. The first challenge involves the claim that if there is religious ambiguity, then religious belief ought to be tentative. This claim, if true, would mean that James's account could only allow for tentative commitment: such a view can be seen to be problematic, since it is not the ordinary view of religious faith, according to which religious commitment must be wholehearted. We will then need to consider whether religious ambiguity only allows for tentative commitment. The second challenge involves the claim that if the ambiguity thesis is true, then religious belief cannot be momentous. Once again, this view, if true, would constrain James's account in a way that runs contrary to the ordinary view of religious faith. Thus, we will need to consider whether accepting religious ambiguity means rejecting the view that religious belief can be momentous in nature. The third challenge involves the claim that religious ambiguity undermines the notion of trust which is commonly associated with religious commitments. I critically engage with each of these challenges and develop replies to them, and if my effort is successful, then we have further strengthened the view that the Jamesian account is philosophically viable.

This chapter also aims to be cognisant of the concerns of the reflective Muslim who concedes the thesis of religious ambiguity, or is at least open to explore its implications. Accordingly, such a reflective Muslim is also concerned with responding to the question of entitlement, i.e., would a person who believes that God exists be entitled to hold and act on their belief if they also concede that the evidence leaves open the question of God's existence? So, the reflective Muslim of this kind will be acknowledging that a central tenet of Islam, i.e., the belief that God exists cannot be justified on the basis of the evidence. The challenge they will face concerns the justifiability of their commitments under the condition of religious ambiguity. I maintain that the Jamesian account of faith offers a philosophically viable resolution to this question of entitlement. That is, the Jamesian account can, in principle, be employed by the reflective Muslim. The section to follow considers the constraints that James spells out as being necessary for a justifiable faith commitment.

1.1   The Jamesian account

Faith according to James involves believing beyond the evidence, or believing while recognising that one lacks adequate evidential support for the truth of the belief. The question I intend to address is whether this account of faith is viable, i.e., can believing beyond the evidence be justified? James contends that there are conditions which justify believing beyond the evidence. We should note that James's account of faith need not be seen as relating solely to religious belief; we can view James's account as being applicable to any belief which involves a venture beyond the evidence (be it religious belief or any other type of belief). In defence of this account of faith, we can construe James as arguing for the following two claims: (a) there are conditions which justify a venture beyond the evidence, and (b) the conditions which justify a faith venture are sometimes met with in 'everyday' circumstances. In defence of the first claim, we may cite James's example of the mountaineer:

> We stand on a mountain pass in the midst of whirling snow and blinding mist through which we get glimpses now and then of paths which may be deceptive. If we stand still we shall be frozen to death. If we take the wrong road we shall be dashed to pieces. We do not certainly know whether there is any right one. What must we do? 'Be strong and of a good courage'. Act for the best, hope for the best, and take what comes … If death ends all, we cannot meet death better.[1]

James places 'us', the reader, in circumstances which require a choice to be made: we must proceed, but which path should we choose? There are many paths to choose from, and if we stand still we will be frozen to death, we must choose, but we have no evidence that will establish which of the paths open to us is a safe one. A decision has to be made, and whichever choice is made, the outcome of the decision will have significant implications. The evidence is ambiguous, but a choice has to be made, because our lives are at stake. On what basis do we make a decision? Perhaps we can decide on the basis of our physical capacity; we can choose the path which seems the easiest to follow. We could also decide on the basis of an inclination or a 'gut feeling'. None of these guarantees that our choice will be correct, but they can influence our choice. You may have a strong inclination to proceed on one of the paths, a gut feeling that this particular path could lead you toward safety. Would you be justified if you did act on your inclination or gut feeling, believing that it is the best thing to do in your circumstances? James suggests that we would be justified in acting on this belief, since the conditions impose the need to make a choice – in addition, we cannot be blamed for ignoring the evidence, as the evidence is ambiguous and does not settle which choice is the best to make. I agree with James that if the evidence is ambiguous and a choice has to be made, then believing beyond the evidence under such conditions is justifiable, or, at least, acting on the truth of such a belief is justifiable.

One drawback of the mountaineer example is that it is an extreme case and beyond the pale of everyday experience. The permissibility of faith in this extreme case, it may be argued, has little relevance to everyday life. James seems to be aware of this concern, and he cites everyday examples, which share key features with the example of the mountaineer. One case in point is the example of inter-personal relationships. James asks us to consider the person who will befriend another only if they have objective evidence that the person will be a good friend. This evidential approach to friendship seems counter-intuitive, and it is hard to imagine how a friendship could ever form if there was always a demand for prior evidence. James broadens the discussion of friendship to include courtship, and this is an important shift, since there is now an increased element of vulnerability – the willingness to trust another person wholeheartedly.

The element of vulnerability, I suggest, makes courtship a good example of an act of faith that is justifiable. We can spell this out further if we acknowledge that courtship can be linked to strong feelings – feelings which motivate the belief that another person is worthy of your wholehearted trust. While it is possible to take into account rational and empirical considerations regarding the person's character, these considerations can in no way guarantee the person as being worthy of trust. The evidence may suggest that the person has shared values, has similar interests, and in general is trusted by others, yet, this person could easily rebuff any advances that have courtship as its goal. We cannot judge how the person will react, and even though there may be much common ground, the person may not be ready or willing to recip- rocate a wholehearted trust. If the suitor believes that the right course of action is to pursue courtship, then he must first act and make his intentions clear; only then can he dispel the ambiguity. The example of courtship is an instance where it is necessary to act on a belief even before we know the belief to be justified. This example, as with the example of the mountaineer, suggests that a certain kind of venture of faith can be justified within the normal course of everyday life.

As we consider the case of the mountaineer and that of courtship as examples of justifiable faith ventures, we may note that they both share the following features: the condition of evidential ambiguity, the poten- tial for a 'non-evidential' or 'passional' cause, e.g., emotion, gut feeling or inclination, to motivate a choice, and the fact that the choices also have significant implications and require a decision to be made. When these features occur together, as they do in the case of the mountaineer and the example of courtship, they seem to provide good reasons which justify believing beyond the evidence. James regards these features as necessary conditions; accordingly, his view is that believing beyond the evidence is justified, if and only if:

(1) The justifiability of the belief in question cannot be resolved on the basis of rational and empirical considerations. This assumes that an assessment of the evidence is unable to settle the question of whether the belief is true, since the evidence available is inconclu- sive, or ambiguous.

(2) The belief, or choice, in question is passionally motivated. One important component of the Jamesian account is the view that our passional nature can be a cause of belief. We can consider the following illustrations to see how this is possible, e.g., a person is moved to believe in a higher power as they observe a beau- tiful sunset, or when reading the Quran a person is moved by its message to believe in it as a source of divine guidance. In addition to aesthetic experiences, passional causes of a belief can include emotions, desires, affection and affiliations – including cultural and religious traditions.[2] In the interest of clarity, we can define a non-evidential or passional cause of a belief as being 'any cause of a belief other than a cause that provides the believer with evidence for its truth'.[3]

(3) The belief or choice in question must settle a genuine option. According to James an option is a decision between two hypotheses,

which becomes a genuine option when it is *living, forced and momentous*. For an option to be living for a given person, the hypotheses for choice have to be 'live', in the sense that each has, in James's words, some 'appeal as a real possibility to [the person] to whom it is proposed.[4] The 'live-ness' of an option is subjective and relatively dependent on the individual and their circumstances; James uses the option of belief in the Mahdi as an example.[5] A Muslim, in general, would consider belief in the Mahdi a living option, since the character of the Mahdi is grounded in Islamic tradition. An atheist, Christian, Buddhist or Jew, on the other hand, would not regard belief in the Mahdi as a living option. The option must also be forced, in other words the two hypotheses in question must be in the form of a 'complete logical disjunction', e.g., 'either accept this truth or go without it'. A genuine option is also momentous, i.e., the decision in question is highly significant and will have considerable impact on the life of the individual.

Once the three constraints have been satisfied, James argues that believing beyond the evidence is justified, since:

> Our passional nature not only lawfully may, but must, decide an option between propositions, whenever it is a genuine option that cannot by its nature be decided on intellectual grounds.[6]

The claim being made is that we may decide a genuine option on the basis of our passional nature. We can understand James's reference to our passional nature as referring to a passionally caused belief. Thus, James argues, it is a passionally caused belief that can justifiably decide a genuine option. James's argument can be better understood with reference to the case of the mountaineer and that of courtship. These two cases can be seen to lend weight to the claim that it is justifiable for our passional nature to decide a genuine option. Let us reconsider each case in turn. The case of the mountaineer involves deciding to forge ahead along one of the many paths. The conditions which the mountaineer encounters prevent her from knowing which path is the correct one. She knows that the possibilities open to her are live, forced and momentous. It is not clear which possibility is the correct one, although, she has a strong inclination that the right thing to do is to forge ahead on one of the paths. Given these circumstances a choice based on an inclination does not seem to be objectionable. If this reading is accepted, then the case of the mountaineer illustrates the possibility that our passional nature can justifiably decide a genuine option.

Similarly, the case of courtship also illustrates this possibility. That is, strong feelings can motivate the belief that a specific person is worthy of your wholehearted trust. The evidence for the truth of this belief cannot be decided on the basis of purely rational and empirical considerations. A person who has courtship in mind will encounter a genuine option. For instance, the suitor will consider pursuing courtship as a living possibility, there is also a choice to be made as to whether courtship will be pursued or not, and the outcome of the choice will have significant implications for the suitor. As in the case of the mountaineer, the suitor's choice to act on the basis of their feelings does not seem to be objectionable. We can then view the case of the mountaineer and the suitor as being examples that give credence to the claim that our passional nature may properly be the basis on which we decide a genuine option (which cannot otherwise be resolved on the basis of evidential considerations).

The case of the mountaineer and the suitor are by no means decisive, and reflection on them gives rise to an epistemic and an ethical concern. The epistemic concern is motivated by the view that we have an obligation to always make a dispassionate choice on the basis of evidential considerations. That is, despite inclination, feelings or any other passional cause of belief, we should always decide on the basis of the evidence. Accordingly, in the case of the mountaineer, her choice, one may argue, is best guided by a consideration of the environmental conditions and her physical capacity at the time. Similarly, the suitor, one may contend, should dispassionately reflect on his own feelings and circumstances before pursing courtship. In addition, there is also a worry that James's account is not sensitive to our moral concerns. For instance, would James's account permit the suitor to pursue someone who is already in a committed relationship? Would the account also allow for ventures that were motivated by lust, envy or greed? The account, as it stands, seems silent on the moral standing of a passional cause of a belief and the content of the belief itself. This oversight could be taken to mean that James's account, in principle, allows for ventures which are morally objectionable. James is, to a limited degree, aware of these concerns, and he aims to address them by critically engaging with an evidentialist view of belief (which I shall now outline).

1.2   The Cliffordian evidentialist challenge

William K. Clifford is a proponent of the evidentialist ethics of belief. He argues that *it is wrong always, everywhere and for anyone, to believe anything upon insufficient evidence.*[7] If this maxim is true, then a belief can be justified only if there is sufficient evidence for the truth of the belief. In defence of this maxim, Clifford utilises an allegory involving a negligent ship-owner:

> A shipowner was about to send to sea an emigrant ship. He knew that she was old, and not over-well built at first; that she had seen many seas and climes, and often needed repairs. Doubts had been suggested to him that possibly she was not seaworthy... Before the ship sailed... he succeeded in overcoming these melancholy reflections. He said to himself that she had gone safely through so many voyages and weathered so many storms that it was idle to suppose she could not come safely home this trip also... he would dismiss from his mind all ungenerous suspicions about the honesty of the builders and contractors. In such a ways he acquired a sincere and comfortable conviction that his vessel was thoroughly safe and seaworthy.[8]

The allegory reveals the ship-owner as someone who has a sincere conviction in the safety of his ship, but, despite his sincerity the ship-owner is also deeply guilty. The ship-owner is guilty, since: 'he had acquired his belief not by honestly earning it in patient investigation, but by stifling his doubts... in the end he may have felt so sure about it he could not think otherwise, yet in as much as he had knowingly and willingly worked himself into that frame of mind, he must be held responsible for it'.[9] The allegory reveals a number of vices which Clifford seeks to curtail, i.e., the ship-owner accepts beliefs which reinforce his own sense of comfort, and there is no effort to evaluate whether his belief in the safety of his ship is justified. Accordingly, Clifford's evidentialist maxim can be seen as a principle which is designed as a safeguard against intellectual apathy, and against positive intellectual dishonesty. My present concern, however, is with the absolutist feature of Clifford's maxim. When Clifford declares that *it is wrong always, everywhere and for anyone, to believe anything upon insufficient evidence*, he is saying that we must not believe except on the basis of (adequate) evidence, and that there are no exceptions which would permit contravening this maxim.

This absolutist's form of evidentialism rules out ventures beyond the evidence, as they involve taking a belief to be true in our practical reasoning while acknowledging that the belief's truth is unsupported by the evidence. James recognises the evidentialist challenge and responds by arguing that commitment to the Cliffordian maxim is itself a venture beyond the evidence, as it is based on 'a passional decision ... and is attended with the same risk of losing the truth'.[10] This response needs further elaboration as it harbours two distinct arguments in response to Clifford's maxim.

The first argument relates to the alleged passional commitment that is presupposed by the Cliffordian maxim. If James is correct, in holding that commitment to Clifford's maxim is passionally motivated then he would have shown that commitment to the maxim is not based on the evidence, but rather has a passional cause. To argue his case, James suggests that implicit in Clifford's maxim is the assumption that we should avoid the risk of error, and it is on the basis of this assumption that Clifford is able to argue that we are justified in rejecting a venture beyond the evidence since such a venture risks falling into error. The Cliffordian maxim appears to endorse the view that we ought to reject believing, or committing to, anything upon insufficient evidence, so that we can guard against the risk of error. James contends that there is an alternative presumption to that of risk avoidance, namely, to believe the truth even if there is a risk of error. If you consider it sometimes acceptable to risk error so that you may know truth, then Clifford's maxim becomes less plausible. James is willing to risk error when there is a chance of attaining otherwise inaccessible truth thereby, while Clifford is unwilling to endorse such ventures due to the risk of error. We then have two competing suppositions: 'seek truth but avoid the risk of error' versus 'seek truth even at the risk of error'. If James's characterisation is correct, then the Cliffordian maxim may well have a passional cause; that is, a person's commitment to one of the two suppositions, just outlined, may depend on personal inclination. For example, a person who is optimistic in their outlook may be more willing to take a risk than the pessimist, who may resist risk altogether. If commitment to the evidentialist maxim has a passional basis, then the Cliffordian is guilty of being inconsistent. (I elaborate on this below.)

James's second argument maintains that adopting Clifford's maxim does not, in the cases he has discussed, avoid the risk of error. Consider James's case of the mountaineer, who is inclined to believe that she should take the path to her right; on reflection, she decides that since there is no evidence in favour of this decision, therefore she ought not to take this path. The mountaineer has chosen not to act on her belief, due to insufficient evidence, and in doing so has acted in accordance with Clifford's maxim. Has the mountaineer, in following Clifford's maxim, avoided the risk of error? Not so, according to James. The mountaineer has chosen not to act on her belief, but, there remains the risk of error, since she does not know which path leads to safety (and the path to her right may have been the safest one to follow). This insight forms the basis of the following argument against Clifford's maxim: If commitment to the Cliffordian maxim is motivated by an intention to avoid the risk of error, then that intention fails to do so in the case of the mountaineer, i.e., the case of the mountaineer is an example where Clifford's maxim cannot fulfil the aim of avoiding the risk of error. We can recast this argument as follows: Irrespective of how the mountaineer makes a choice, be it in accordence with Clifford's maxim or with the Jamesian account, the mountaineer cannot in practice avoid the risk of error. If the need to avoid error is held to favour adopting Clifford's maxim, then this case shows that following that maxim does not always guarantee that error will be avoided.

The Jamesian contention that commitment to the Cliffordian maxim is itself a passional decision, and is attended with the same risk of losing the truth, can now be understood as involving the following two arguments: (a) that commitment to the maxim is likely to have a passional basis and therefore Cliffordian evidentialism is self-referentially inconsistent, and (b) following Clifford's maxim, under certain conditions, is attended with the same risk of falling into error as there would be if a venture were to be made beyond the evidence. Clifford's thesis, in essence, is charged with being, at best, on an epistemic par with the Jamesian account, and, at worst, internally inconsistent.

These charges, I suggest, require closer investigation, and the reason for saying this is that there are a number of aspects of Clifford's argument which James has overlooked. The first concern I have is with James's view that commitment to the evidentialist maxim has a passional basis. I agree that commitments can have passional causes, though it does not follow that every commitment must have a passional basis. James may be correct that commitment to Clifford's maxim can have a passional cause, but I do not think such a commitment can only be passional in nature. There is the possibility that Clifford bases his commitment on rational and empirical considerations, and this is precisely what Clifford does when he employs the analogy of negligent ship-owner. The story of the ship-owner strongly conveys the view that we do have plenty of evidence that provides rational justification for endorsing the evidentialist maxim.

We can also question James's characterisation of the suppositions and motivating factors which underpin Clifford's evidentialism. James may be correct to suggest that the evidentialist maxim is motivated by a mindset which seeks to avoid risk, however, this need not be the only way to describe the Cliffordian. There may be other ways to characterise the evidentialist's motives. For example, the ship-owner in ignoring the evidence risks not only the loss of his property, but also places at risk the safety of the ship's passengers, and this suggests there is an ethical concern related to the lives and property which are put at risk. If this reading of Clifford is correct, then we have good reason to think that commitment to Clifford's maxim can be motivated by ethical concerns. We could describe Clifford as being concerned with the ethical, and this concern may well be the grounds which motivate Clifford's commitment to evidentialism. The commitment to evidentialism can be motivated in a number of ways, e.g., passionally and evidentially, and it may seem uncharitable on the part of James to speak of Clifford as being motivated purely by the fear of risking error, i.e., the fear or concern about the consequences of acting on erroneous beliefs.

1.3   The epistemic and ethical concerns of Clifford

I have suggested that James may be thought to have overlooked the underlying epistemic and ethical concerns of Clifford's case for evidentialism. These concerns are initially expressed through the case of the negligent ship-owner, though they are re-emphasised by Clifford as follows:

> ... if the belief has been accepted on insufficient evidence, the pleasure is a stolen one. Not only does it deceive ourselves by giving us a sense of power which we do not really possess, but it is sinful, because it is stolen in defiance of our duty to mankind. That duty is to guard ourselves from such beliefs as from pestilence, which may shortly master our own body and then spread to the rest of the town. What would be thought of one who, for the sake of a sweet fruit, should deliberately run the risk of delivering a plague upon his family and his neighbours?[11]

The epistemic concern, as perceived by Clifford, relates to a sense of moral duty which the negligent ship-owner has failed to live up to. The confident belief the ship-owner has in the ship's safety is a 'stolen', or perhaps dishonest, confidence. Clifford's own sense of duty, as I interpret him, relates to the way in which the ship-owner comes to grips with doubt. The ship-owner overcomes his doubt by wilfully ignoring it, and such an approach is viewed by Clifford as being negligent. The proper way to handle doubt, according to Clifford, is to investigate the matter which has come into question, and resolve or confirm the doubt on the basis of the ensuing evidence. I suggest we can agree with Clifford that if you are a ship-owner, and there arise legitimate doubts as to the safety of your ship, then the best course of action would be to investigate the matter rather than brush the doubts aside. I believe James would have no difficulty in agreeing with Clifford's judgment on the ship-owner case, but he would resist drawing a generalisation, in the form of an absolutist evidentialist maxim. I also suggest that Clifford's morally grounded epistemic concern, which James does not explicitly discuss, is in harmony with the broader Jamesian account, since according to James, one necessary condition of a permissible venture beyond the evidence is that there is evidential ambiguity. The requirement of evidential ambiguity presupposes an openness toward and engagement in rational and empirical investigation. If there are significant doubts, then an investigation of those doubts is compatible with the ethos of the Jamesian account.

Clifford's second concern pertains to the ethical significance of beliefs. He makes his case rhetorically by asking: *What would be thought of one who, for the sake of a sweet fruit, should deliberately run the risk of delivering a plague upon his family and his neighbours?*[12] This question suggests a relationship between belief and action, which, of course, also arises in the case of the ship-owner, i.e., the ship-owner believes his ship to be safe, and on the basis of that belief he will let his ship sail and thereby place at risk the lives of the passengers. A belief, as perceived by Clifford, has ethical implications, since it can inform the actions of the individual. The ship-owner, while guilty of epistemic apathy, becomes *morally culpable* when his apathy leads to him jeopardising innocent lives. If the ship-owner had properly examined the safety of the ship, then he would have known whether the ship was seaworthy. An evaluation of the evidence would have allowed the ship-owner to decide on the basis of the evidence, and such a decision would be seen by Clifford as meritorious. Accordingly, the Cliffordian maxim serves as an epistemic and ethical constraint.

I suggest that the epistemic and ethical concerns can be addressed within the Jamesian account. The Jamesian account in requiring evidential ambiguity as a condition on permissible ventures beyond the evidence, presupposes attention to the evidence and therefore accommodates decisions based on evidential considerations. Thus, the Jamesian is able to accommodate the epistemic concerns, although, a proponent of Clifford can still question whether a venture beyond the evidence is meritorious. That is, the Jamesian account appeals to our passional nature as motivating decisions as well as causing beliefs, however, there are passions which are deeply selfish, e.g., greed and lust. The concern is that such passions are flawed, and must be curtailed in order to preserve our moral integrity. An additional ethical concern pertains to the content of the beliefs in question. For example, in some historical circumstances a person may perceive belief in a racist God as live, forced and momentous. These ethical concerns require the Jamesian account to include an explicit ethical constraint on our passional nature and the content of our beliefs. The possibility of adding an ethical constraint to the Jamesian account, which I accept, has been suggested by John Bishop, who argues that a passionally motivated venture is permissible only if:

> The option and the passional motivation which settles the option is itself morally admirable, or, at least, not morally flawed.[13]

This constraint allows a proponent of James's account to address the ethical concerns which emerge from our discussion of Clifford. An ethical constraint is highly significant, especially if the Jamesian account is applied to religious belief. The question of ethics and morality is often an issue internal to a religious tradition, while the ethical constraint proposed by Bishop would require an ethical evaluation of tradition.[14] Our discussion of the evidentialist challenge suggests that James has not given enough attention to the epistemic and ethical motivations which underpin Clifford's case for evidentialism. Nevertheless, I do think that James's account can accommodate the epistemic and ethical concerns that were brought to light by our engagement with Clifford. I also suggest that James is correct to critique the absolutist nature of Clifford's evidentialist maxim. I agree with James that Clifford's maxim is mistaken, and the reasons for this view are as follows:

(1) There are exceptions, such as the example of the mountaineer and the case of courtship, where a decision has to be made on grounds other than rational and empirical considerations. These cases are examples of decisions which have to be made and require a venture beyond the evidence. If the discussion of the mountaineer and courtship are correct, then it is not always wrong, everywhere and for anyone, to believe, or decide upon insufficient evidence.

(2) A venture beyond the evidence, as characterised by James, is compatible with the pursuit of truth. If there is evidential ambiguity, then the evidence leaves open the possibility of the belief

being true, and a venture beyond the evidence would thereby be consistent with aiming to grasp truth. While there is no guarantee that such a venture does grasp truth, it does not follow from this lack of guarantee that a venture could never grasp truth. On the other hand, if a genuine option is evidentially ambiguous then following Clifford's maxim cannot avoid the risk of error, as the act of suspending belief, and not venturing beyond the evidence also incurs in practice the risk of losing truth.

(3) If we try and defend Clifford's maxim on evidential grounds, then we run the risk of circular reasoning. Consider the following dialogue, where *p* represents the believed proposition:

Alan: You should not believe that *p*.

Ben: Why shouldn't I believe that *p*?

Alan: Because there is *insufficient evidence* for *p*.

Ben: Why is *insufficient evidence* a basis to reject belief that *p*?

Alan: Because you ought to believe that *p* if and only if there is sufficient evidence to support *p*'s truth (let this response be Q).

Ben: Why should I believe that Q?

Alan: The evidence supports Q.

Ben: Why should the fact that evidence supports Q convince me to believe that Q?

Alan: Because, we ought to believe that Q only if there is sufficient evidence to support Q's truth.

This dialogue highlights the evidentialist as someone who has to assume the truth of Q, if they seek to justify Q on evidential grounds. The charge of circular reasoning does not refute the maxim, of course, though this does give us good reason to think that the evidence does not support anything quite as strong as Clifford's maxim.

There are then three good reasons to reject Clifford's maxim, namely: (a) the examples of the mountaineer and courtship suggest the justifiability of venturing beyond the evidence in some cases; (b) a venture beyond the evidence, that is in accordance with the Jamesian account, is consistent with grasping truth, and in the case of a forced option, there is no way to avoid the risk of error at the level of practical commitment; and (c) it does not seem possible to justify Clifford's maxim on the basis of evidence without begging the question. We should be careful not to overstate James's critique, as the criticisms I have discussed apply only to Clifford's defence of evidentialism. (I consider a contemporary version of evidentialism in Chapter 5.)

There are then good reasons for setting aside an absolutist form of evidentialism. The Jamesian account, as earlier noted, can also be refined to accommodate Clifford's epistemic and ethical concerns. Furthermore, the case of the mountaineer and that of courtship suggest that there are conditions which permit believing beyond the evidence. These considerations provide us with good reason to think that James's account of faith is philosophically viable. These considerations are by no means decisive and are open to question; thus, we will need to regard our case for James's account as being *prima facie* in nature. I do not intend to provide a full-blown defence of the Jamesian account of faith, although there are further considerations in favour of James's account which will emerge later in the chapter.[15] At best, the considerations highlighted thus far suggest that it is not unreasonable to endorse the philosophical viability of James's account. If we concede the *prima facie* case, we can then proceed to consider whether the Jamesian account is applicable to religious belief. To recall, we are seeking a response to the question of entitlement given the assumption of religious ambiguity. The ambiguity thesis dovetails well with the Jamesian account, since the account requires the option under consideration to be unresolvable on the basis of rational and empirical deliberations. If the remaining constraints of the Jamesian account can be satisfied, then there will be an entitlement to believe in God. There are, however, a number of challenges associated with applying James's account to religious belief. The sections to follow will consider three distinct challenges.

1.4 Challenge of tentative belief

John Hick is a notable critic of the Jamesian account. He argues that the Jamesian account, when applied to religious belief, 'is not the view of the ordinary religious believer'.[16] The ordinary believer is described by Hick as a person of faith who 'is convinced that he [or she] has met with certainty'.[17] This view of the ordinary believer is reinforced by Gary Gutting's observation that 'religious belief represents the (relative) end of a quest for emotional and intellectual satisfaction, where religious belief represents a total commitment to its implications and is incompatible with continuing reflection on its truth'.[18] James's account, by contrast, presupposes a degree of uncertainty, since a venture is permissible only if the option cannot be decided on the basis of the evidence.

There is an inconsistency, one may argue, between the common view of faith which provides 'emotional and intellectual satisfaction' and a passional venture which presupposes epistemic uncertainty. This inconsistency is further emphasised by Robert McKim, who argues that if the thesis of evidential ambiguity is true, then there is a real possibility that our religious beliefs are wrong. We should, he maintains, hold our beliefs with the awareness that we could be mistaken. Hence, the requirement that commitment entered into under ambiguity should therefore be tentative. He frames his argument as follows:

> Premise One: Disagreement about an issue or area of inquiry provides reason to think that the issue or area of inquiry is an ambiguous one.
>
> Premise Two: If an issue or area of inquiry is ambiguous, it is more likely than it otherwise would be that our views on it are mistaken.
>
> Premise Three: The more likely it is that our views on an issue are mistaken, the more likely it is that we have an obligation to examine our own beliefs and the beliefs of other groups with whom there is disagreement about an issue.
>
> Premise Four: [sub-conclusion derived from Premise Two and Three] If an issue or an area of inquiry is ambiguous, it is more likely than it otherwise would be that we have an obligation to examine our own beliefs and the beliefs of other groups about the relevant issue.
>
> Conclusion: Disagreement about an issue or area of inquiry provides reason to think that each side has an obligation to examine their beliefs about the issue under discussion.[19]

The conclusion above is termed the E-principle. McKim suggests that accompanying the E-principle is the T-principle, which requires tentative belief when faced with ambiguity, since disagreement 'about an issue or area of inquiry provides reason for whatever beliefs we hold about that issue or area of inquiry to be tentative'.[20] McKim claims that the appeal to ambiguity also provides support for the T-principle:

> ...In accordance with premise one of the argument for the E-principle...there is reason to think that a subject about which there is disagreement is ambiguous, and hence that it is a subject about which it is easy to go wrong. One strategy for coping with an awareness that your beliefs in an area may be wrong is to hold them in a tentative way, a way that involves openness to alternatives.[21]

If we accept McKim's argument that religious beliefs must be held tentatively in the face of religious ambiguity, then the question arises as to whether the Jamesian account must also require tentative belief. Given McKim's stance, it could be argued that James's account should be amended to include the need for tentative belief. If the Jamesian account were to be amended, we would encounter two specific challenges. Firstly, one may argue that the everyday view of faith, involves a form of commitment that is wholehearted, thus tentative commitment is inconsistent with the ordinary view of faith. This inconsistency need not be perceived as a critique of McKim, since the everyday view of faith is not necessarily sensitive to the thesis of religious ambiguity. One could, in fact, argue that if the thesis of ambiguity is true, then the everyday view of faith is in need of revision, and one way to do this is to recast the everyday view of faith in terms of tentative commitment.

A more significant challenge arises when we evaluate McKim's position in relation to the Jamesian account. The defining aspect of the Jamesian account is the view that belief can have a passional cause. If this view is accepted, then we also have to be open to the possibility that a belief may be held with varying degrees of commitment. A belief which is passionally caused could yield wholehearted as well as partial commitment. If we concede McKim's argument, then the Jamesian account would need to be modified to allow only for a form of faith that is partial or tentative in its commitment. But this added constraint of tentative commitment, I believe, runs counter to the spirit of the Jamesian account, since the account I have articulated endorses a view of faith that allows for wholehearted commitment.

One way to resolve the tension between McKim and James's account is to replace the term 'tentative belief' with the idea of non-dogmatic commitment. The shift in emphasis toward non-dogmatism, I believe, captures McKim's central conclusions, i.e., non-dogmatism allows for the possibility of error and an open-minded attitude. One major advantage of this shift is that non-dogmatic commitment does not rule out a form of commitment that is wholehearted. Accordingly, we can retain McKim's argument without having to forfeit the ordinary view of faith. Perhaps there is another way to interpret McKim's argument – once we accept ambiguity, there is a real possibility that our religious beliefs are mistaken, and if we realise this possibility of error, then McKim could rightly question whether we would continue to hold our beliefs with same degree of confidence that we had prior to this realisation. There is the possibility that our degree of confidence may change, however, there is no tangible way to predict how a belief's degree of confidence will change in any given individual. Moreover, even if we acknowledge the risk of error, the degree of confidence we have in the belief may remain unchanged. For example, we can raise doubts about the existence of other minds without affecting the strength of our belief in other minds.

Before I consider the other challenges associated with applying James's account to religious belief, I would like to summarise the case for non-dogmatic commitment, which I think is more fitting than tentative belief or tentative commitment. There are three reasons on which I base my case: (a) non-dogmatic commitment captures much of what tentative commitment aims to describe without ruling out a wholehearted faith; (b) we have good reason to think tentative belief is not the only outcome when we acknowledge the possibility of error; and (c) non-dogmatic commitment has an easily described practical component, i.e., being non-dogmatic means that we take the time to carefully reflect on our own beliefs and listen to the views of others. Overall, non-dogmatic commitment appears better suited to the project McKim has in mind, and I do not think the thesis of ambiguity provides good reason for religious belief to be tentative. There is, however, another implication of the ambiguity thesis which also seems to challenge the Jamesian account; this second challenge emerges from McKim's assertion that if the ambiguity thesis is true, then belief in God cannot be momentous.

1.5   Is belief in god momentous?

As part of his evaluation of the implications of religious ambiguity, McKim comes to the conclusion that belief in God cannot be momentous or important. He states that ambiguity in effect leaves the question of God's existence, or non-existence, unanswered. McKim argues that if believing in God were of momentous importance, then the facts about God would be more apparent to us. The situation we find ourselves in suggest that the facts are ambiguous, and, in effect *it is not terribly important that we believe here and now that God exists or that we enjoy any other good that is made possible (either now or later) by our presently holding such belief.* [22] To strengthen his case, McKim presents three arguments:

(1)   There is the fact that the world is religiously ambiguous [which I concede]. McKim suggests that the ambiguity surrounding God's existence and nature is, at face value, a good reason to think that

theistic belief is not important.[23] If it were, then the facts would have been much clearer.

(2) God could have created a world in which the evidence was clear. Given that he has created the actual world, a world in which there is ambiguity and non-belief, we may infer that from God's point of view the actual world is a better world than one in which the facts are unambiguous. If this is a better world then it is unlikely that belief in God is very important.[24]

(3) Even if the actual world is only on a par with a world in which the evidence was clear, then at least the disaster avoidance principle is true.[25] If this is true then God's hiddenness 'does not deprive us of any good that is essential if we are to avoid disaster, in spite of the fact that it has the result that many people do not hold theistic beliefs'.[26]

If McKim is correct, then belief in God is not momentous. This view also poses a significant challenge to the Jamesian account of faith. According to the Jamesian account, a venture beyond the evidence is permitted only if the option is a genuine option, i.e., the belief in question is live, forced and momentous. Once we concede McKim's argument, we also concede that from God's perspective, theistic belief and the goods associated with this belief are not important – if they were, then the evidence would be much clearer. The Jamesian account aims to exclude trivial options, and while McKim has not directed his argument specifically against James, his arguments suggest that theistic belief is trivial, or at least unimportant from the viewpoint of God. Should we concede McKim's argument?

There are two good reasons to think McKim has overstated his case. First, we can question whether his conclusion holds, i.e., that religious ambiguity entails that belief in God is unimportant or not momentous. On reflection, it seems more accurate to say that if God exists, then divine hiddenness suggests that God does not view it as an immediate priority that everybody should believe in God, and neither is it an immediate priority that everyone enjoys the good that is made possible by holding such a belief. In this view, belief in God and the good associated with this belief can remain important and momentous, though, from God's perspective, it is not important for every individual to believe. A second way to deal with McKim's argument is to focus on the subjective nature of a momentous option. Perhaps it is true that from God's perspective, theistic belief is not important, though for a created person, such a belief can remain momentous. For individuals who view themselves as being part of a religious tradition, belief in God can be momentous on the following grounds: (a) it serves as a link to a tradition rich in philosophy and culture; (b) the belief may strengthen the person's ability to live ethically; (c) having the belief also makes the person part of a community; and (d) the belief can also influence and guide the life and choices of an individual. On a personal level, belief in God can be momentous, irrespective of whether God views theistic belief as being important. These considerations suggest that the momentous nature of theistic belief, from the perspective of a believer, need not be undermined by religious ambiguity. The subjective experience of what is momentous also raises a broader question as to the degree to which we may trust our affections, affiliations and inclinations as a guide to truth. One may argue that given the thesis of religious ambiguity, there is a significant risk of error and the believer ought not to trust their passional inclinations – such as the inclination to believe that theistic commitment is momentous, or the inclination to believe that theistic belief is true. The section to follow considers this argument in more detail.

1.6   Can we trust our passional nature?

According to the Jamesian account, our passional nature includes emotions, desires, affection and affiliations which have the potential to give rise to beliefs.[27] One important assumption which accompanies this view is the claim that 'a passional cause of a belief is any cause of that belief other than a cause that provides the believer with evidence for its truth'.[28] This assumption draws a distinction between passional causes for a belief and evidence for the truth of a belief. This distinction is further spelled out by Bishop as follows:

> It is clearly generally true that passional ... inclinations cannot function as guides to truth. After all, they get counted as passional only because they are not evidential – not generally apt as indicators of truth. ... however ... in the very special case of a foundational faith-proposition, it can be consistent with the proper pursuit of serious epistemic goals to let ourselves follow passionate promptings. Believing by faith may thus be seen as resting on a preparedness to trust in our passional nature as a guide to truth in the limiting case where truth is otherwise inaccessible, and an important forced decision must be made at the level of practical commitment.[29]

The distinction between cause and evidence raises the following question: If passional causes of belief are not evidence for the truth of a belief, then how can we trust our passional nature as a guide to truth? If we accept that passional inclinations are not truth apt, i.e., do not count as evidence, then how can we regard our passional nature as a guide that can help us grasp truth? The arguments in the first half of this chapter, if they are accepted, provide good reason to think that there exist circumstances where a person is justified in acting on their passional inclinations. An objector may argue that even if we accept that acting and trusting our passional inclinations is permissible in certain cases, it is not so in the case of religious beliefs. We can schematise the argument as follows:

> Premise One: A person should withhold placing trust in their passional nature as a guide to truth when there is a significant risk of error.

> Premise Two: Being prepared to trust a passionally caused religious belief involves a significant risk of error.

> Conclusion One: A person should withhold placing trust in their passionally caused religious belief.

> Premise Three: Religious commitments involve a preparedness to trust in our passional nature as a guide to truth.

> Conclusion Two: (from Conclusion One and Premise Three) A person should avoid religious commitments which involve being prepared to trust their passional nature as a guide to truth.

Let us consider the details of each premise in turn. The first premise assumes that a significant risk of error is a good reason for a person not to trust their passional nature as a guide to truth. One may argue the assumption is justified, since if there is a significant risk of error, then it is possible that our passional nature may not be guiding us to truth. Given that there is a significant degree of uncertainty as to whether our passional nature is a guide to truth, one may then argue that it is better to withhold trust. A proponent of this argument can also maintain that a person may act on their passional inclinations, but there is no need to trust their inclinations in order to act on them. For example, such a proponent may say that the mountaineer, discussed earlier, can act on her inclinations to follow a particular track, but she does not have to trust her inclinations as a guide to truth. There is then a two-part argument in favour of the first premise: (a) the significant risk of error is a good reason to withhold placing trust in our passional nature as a guide to truth; and (b) withholding trust does not prevent a person from acting on their inclinations, that is, withholding trust will not undermine the Jamesian account of faith. The question is whether withholding trust in our passional nature is consistent with religious commitment.

The second premise maintains that there is a significant risk of error involved in trusting a passionally caused religious belief. There are two reasons, one may argue, why religious belief that is passionally caused incurs a significant degree of risk. The first reason relates to plurality of theistic and non-theistic beliefs, e.g., atheism, Buddhism, Christianity, Islam and Judaism, If, at most, only one of these belief-systems can be true, then it follows that our passional nature generally produces false religious beliefs, and that it is thus a generally unreliable cause for the formation of religious belief.[30] If this argument is correct then being prepared to trust our passional nature involves trusting a belief forming mechanism that generally produces false beliefs. Therefore, trusting our passional nature involves taking a significant risk. A second reason why one can regard the degree of risk as being significant relates to the stakes involved with religious commitment. The stakes are not very high when we take it to be true beyond one's evidence, e.g., that another person is trustworthy. But in such a case, one is trusting non-evidential inclinations only for the truth of a single hypothesis. In the religious case, one trusts such inclinations *for the foundations of one's entire practical orientation to the world as a whole!*

If one accepts the view that a person should withhold placing trust in their passional nature as a guide to truth when there is a significant risk of error, and that the case of religious belief involves a significant risk of error, then it seems reasonable to conclude that a person should withhold placing trust in their passionally caused religious belief. The conclusion, if true, rules out religious commitments which require a preparedness to trust our passional nature as guide to truth. This is problematic since authentic religious commitment seems to require a preparedness to trust.[31] If we are to maintain that we can be entitled to trust our passional nature, then we will need to respond to the argument just outlined.

I acknowledge that trusting our passional nature in the case of religious belief does involve a significant risk of error. The risk of error, however, does not justify withholding trust altogether. At best, the risk of error is a caution against 'blind-faith' and against forms of trust which take our passional nature as being an infallible guide to truth. There is room, I believe, for wholehearted trust which recognises the significant risk of error. We can draw a distinction between unquestioning trust and a form of trust which is reflective. Consider the example of a child who unquestioningly trusts their parents to make choices on their behalf, e.g., which school they attend, which subjects they should study at school, which sports they participate in. Now consider an adult who also unquestioningly trusts their parents to make choices on their behalf, e.g., which clothes to wear, which career path to follow, which political party to vote for. The case of a child having total trust in their parents does not seem unreasonable, as the child is not in a position to be able to evaluate the choices available to them. In the case of the adult, however, there is cause for concern in the level of trust they have placed in their parents. An adult can trust their parents, but they do not need to do so unquestioningly, and there are two reasons for this: (a) it is possible for one's parents to be mistaken; and (b) even if one's parents make good choices, there is value in being able to think for oneself. On the basis of these examples, we note that there exist degrees of trust, and often the degree to which one trusts turns on the cognitive capacities of the individual concerned. It seems to be the case that a person who is mature and able to properly exercise their cognitive capacities seems best advised to exercise trust in a way that is reflective, i.e., by taking into account the risk of error. If this view is correct, then there is no inconsistency in acknowledging the risk or error while also being prepared to trust.

We are now in a position to maintain that a significant risk of error, at best, motivates an added degree of caution as to how a person exercises trust. One can also argue that a person is culpable only if they uncritically exercise trust, especially under conditions where there is a significant risk of error. If this claim is correct, we can then challenge the assumption which underpins the first premise, namely, that it is always better to withhold trust under conditions of uncertainty. This assumption can be challenged on the grounds that uncertainty due to the risk of error does not undermine the right to exercise trust altogether; rather, uncertainty simply reinforces the need for a form of trust which is reflective in nature. Accordingly, we may argue that there is good reason to reject the claim made in Premise One, i.e., that a person should withhold placing trust in their passional nature as a guide to truth when there is a significant risk of error. Once we concede that Premise One is implausible, then the argument for withholding trust is thereby undermined. This response also brings us to the end of the *prima facie* case for the Jamesian account of faith.

1.7   Summary

The Jamesian account permits a venture beyond the evidence if and only if the following conditions are fulfilled:

(1)   The option cannot be resolved on evidential grounds.
(2)   The content of the option, and the passional commitment to the option is itself morally admirable, or, at least, not morally flawed.
(3)   The option is genuine, i.e., living, forced and momentous

The *prima facie* case for the philosophical viability of the Jamesian account of faith is based on the following considerations:

(1)   The constraints imposed by the account are motivated by cases where believing beyond the evidence seems to be justified.
(2)   The requirement of evidential ambiguity presupposes the need to consider the evidence if available; thus, what is recognised is that, in general, not only belief but also practical commitment to the truth of a given claim should be based on adequately supporting evidence. There is also an implicit recognition that the Jamesian account would not endorse a venture which went against the available evidence, though the account does permit a venture beyond the evidence. The requirement of evidential ambiguity is then a safeguard to ensure epistemic integrity.
(3)   The moral constraint of the Jamesian account emphasises the need to morally evaluate: (a) the passionally caused belief in question, and (b) the passional cause of the belief. This condition serves as a safeguard to ensure moral integrity.
(4)   The commitment to engage in an evidential and moral evaluation of a passionally caused belief and its contents helps to counteract forms of commitment which are arbitrary and wishful.
(5)   The account is resistant to an *absolutist* form of evidentialism which maintains that it is always wrong to believe upon insufficient evidence.
(6)   There is no claim of epistemic privilege associated with the Jamesian account, and there is an acknowledgment of the possibility of error, and in doing so, the account requires an attitude of non-dogmatic commitment from anyone who makes a faith venture. In being

non-dogmatic, there would need to be an openness to engage in dialogue. The openness to dialogue may also enhance a person's ability to reflect critically on their own point of view.

(7) The account does not undermine the importance of seeking truth. At no point does the account endorse the view that there is no truth, or that all beliefs are true in some relativist sense. Rather, the account is committed to the claim that the search for truth, under certain conditions, is compatible with a venture beyond the evidence.

These considerations do not conclusively prove the Jamesian account to be philosophically viable. The seven considerations only aim to establish a *prima facie* case; i.e., the case aims to establish that there are good reasons to think the Jamesian account is philosophically viable. There is also a need to be cautious, since the *prima facie* case does not address every possible criticism that may be directed at James's account. We will need to concede that the *prima facie* case can be challenged, although, it would be a mistake to think that the viability of James's account can be proved only if the account is shown to be immune to every possible criticism. Such a requirement would be unreasonable, since it is not feasible to consider every possible criticism. It would also take us beyond the scope of this study if we were to set out to identify and respond to the entire range of criticisms that may be directed at James.[32]

In light of the discussions above, I believe the reflective Muslim can employ the Jamesian account in order to respond to the question of entitlement. To recall, the question is whether the reflective Muslim is entitled to hold and act on their belief in God under the condition of evidential ambiguity. In reply, the reflective Muslim may contend that they satisfy the Jamesian constraints: (a) belief in God is a live hypothesis which cannot be resolved on the basis of evidential considerations; (b) the option is forced – they face a choice on whether or not they want to continue to live in accordance with their belief in God; and (c) the option is also momentous, as on it turns whether they will fulfil a major requirement for living as a Muslim and being part of the Muslim *ummah* or community. The final requirement, which I believe can be fulfilled, is that the kind of God a Muslim believes in, and the passional cause which motivates belief in God need not violate accepted moral norms. Accordingly, if the reflective Muslim maintains that their belief in God is passionally caused, then they are entitled to decide the option in accordance with their passional nature. That is, once the reflective Muslim can satisfy the Jamesian constraints, they are then entitled to hold and act on their belief in God, under the condition of evidential ambiguity. This response can also be employed by a reflective theist from other religious traditions as well, and this may be troubling for some Muslims. Accordingly, we will consider in later chapters whether the pluralism associated with the Jamesian account is consistent with the tradition of Islam.

Nonetheless, even if it appears that the reflective Muslim can satisfy the Jamesian constraints, there will be concerns involving the implications associated with endorsing James's account. There will be a concern that James's account may, in some way, violate or deviate from the ethos of Islamic tradition or that there is an alternative, viable account of faith within the Islamic tradition which also addresses the question of entitlement, thus undermining the need to endorse the Jamesian account. My preferred response is to welcome the Jamesian account and employ it within the tradition of Islamic theism. First, however, it will be important to articulate and evaluate objections and alternatives to the Jamesian account that arise within the tradition of Islamic theism. Accordingly, the chapters to follow will consider these objections and alternatives.

2
The Challenge of Al-Ghazālī's Scepticism

> If man is able to doubt, this is because certitude exists.
>
> – Frithjof Schuon

We have engaged with James's account of faiths in three distinct ways. First, I articulated James's argument which suggests that a person can, under certain conditions, be entitled to believe beyond the evidence. Second, we engaged with Cliffordian evidentialism, which maintains that it is always wrong to believe anything based upon insufficient evidence. This absolutist form of evidentialism was found to be weak. There were three considerations in support of this conclusion: (a) it begs the question against the example of the mountaineer and courtship which suggest the justifiability of venturing beyond the evidence; (b) the case of the mountaineer suggests that in some cases, Cliffordian evidentialism and the Jamesian account are on a par with respect to grasping truth and avoiding error, i.e., in the case of the mountaineer, when a choice is made, be it in accordance with Clifford's maxim, or with the Jamesian account, the mountaineer cannot avoid the risk of error; and (c) it does not seem possible to justify Clifford's maxim on the basis of evidence without begging the question. Third, we considered and responded to three distinct challenges which questioned the applicability of James's account to the case of religious belief. In response to these challenges, I argued that: (a) acceptance of the ambiguity thesis is consistent with an attitude of non-dogmatic commitment and does not require tentative commitment; (b) it is also possible to accept ambiguity yet continue to view faith commitment as being momentous and important; and (c) ambiguity, uncertainty and the risk of error do not undermine the right to exercise trust; instead, we need a form of trust which is reflective in nature. Our engagement with Clifford also helped to strengthen a *prima facie* case in favour of the philosophical viability of James's account. The *prima facie* case, as outlined at the end of the previous chapter, is open to contention; however, it serves to undermine the view that endorsing the Jamesian account is unreasonable or irrational.

The current chapter assumes that the constraints of the Jamesian account will not prevent the reflective Muslim from endorsing the account. The reflective Muslim may concede the ambiguity thesis, and they may also believe in the existence of God on passional grounds; furthermore, the passionally caused belief in God may also decide a genuine option. If there are no ethically motivated objections to believing in God, then the reflective Muslim is in a position to offer a reply to the question of entitlement to believe in God. The reflective Muslim, who decides to endorse James's account, may argue that once they have satisfied the Jamesian constraints, they are entitled to hold and act on the belief that God exists. We need to be cautious, since it is possible that the reflective Muslim who satisfies the constraints of James's account may yet reject the account. The reflective Muslim may contend that aspects of the tradition of Islam block acceptance of the Jamesian account of faith. This chapter considers an objection to the Jamesian account of faith that emerges from within the intellectual tradition of Islam. To this end, I focus primarily on an objection that is motivated by al-Ghazālī's case for scepticism. The scepticism of al-Ghazālī involves the claim that the deliverances of sense perception and human reason are unreliable and therefore cannot be trusted. If successful, this form of scepticism would rule out any philosophical approach which assumes that the deliverances of sense perception and human reason can be trusted. The conclusion that the deliverances of our cognitive capacities are not trustworthy would serve to undermine our motivation for philosophically reflecting on religious belief. The motive for philosophical reflection is to seek truth and avoid error through the use of our cognitive capacities; if, however, we cannot trust our cognitive capacities, we then have to abandon the pursuit of our epistemic goals.

I have drawn on the tradition of analytic philosophy of religion to articulate and defend a Jamesian account of faith. The Jamesian account of faith also presupposes a significant degree of trust in our cognitive capacities. If al-Ghazālī's case for scepticism were to succeed, it would involve abandoning the enterprise of philosophical reflection altogether, thus ruling out any attempt at a philosophical justification of an entitlement to faith including the Jamesian account. Given that we have taken al-Ghazālī's views as a gauge of how we may understand the tradition of Islam, one may argue that the Jamesian account is inconsistent with the ethos of Islam.

I should note that al-Ghazālī's sceptical attitude is not typical of Muslim philosophers or theologians. One good example of a Muslim thinker who embraces the tradition of philosophical thought is Abu Yusuf al-Kindi (d. 873),[1] the first Muslim philosopher.[2] According to al-Kindi, philosophy is 'knowledge of the true nature of things, insofar as is possible for man', and commenting on the pursuit of truth, he notes: 'We should not be ashamed to admire the truth or to acquire it, from wherever it comes. Even if it should come from far-flung nations and foreign peoples, there is for the student of truth nothing more important than the truth, nor is the truth demeaned or diminished by the one who states or conveys it; no one is demeaned by the truth, rather all are ennobled by it'.[3] There are also a number of Muslim thinkers who are critical of philosophy and philosophers.[4] For example, the poet Rumi writes, *The leg of the syllogisers is a wooden one, A wooden leg is very infirm.*[5] Another example is Abu Sulayman Ahmad ibn Muhammad al-Busti al-Khattab (d. 998), who suggests that the success and popularity of speculative theology and philosophy was due to demonic influences. He believed that Satan had caused the clever people to think that if they were content with tradition, they would be no better than the masses. As a result, they began to deal with speculative theology – which employs philosophical speculation in matters of faith – in order to distinguish themselves from the masses.[6] There also appear to be deeper motivations which underlie the pessimism of Rumi and Abu Sulayman. For example, Oliver Leaman observes: 'the difficulty of accepting the main principles and techniques of...philosophy is that this would seem to imply that the Islamic sciences are not up to the task of handling theoretical questions, so one has to import a methodology from an entirely different culture, one which pre-dates the arrival of Islam'.[7] If Leaman is correct, then critics such as Abu Sulayman may view the philosophical turn among Muslims as stemming from an inferiority complex.

I do not intend to dwell on the varying criticisms Muslims have had, and continue to have, of philosophy and philosophers.[8] The central aim of this chapter is to engage with al-Ghazālī's case for scepticism. To this end, this chapter is divided into four sections. The first section explores the challenge of defining what we mean when we speak of philosophy of religion. Once we have adequately clarified questions of meaning,

I then argue that there are good reasons for engaging in the philosophy of religion. This argument will also help to clearly identify how al-Ghazālī's scepticism threatens the enterprise of philosophy of religion. In the second section, I will consider and respond to al-Ghazālī's general criticisms that he directs toward philosophers he had studied. The third and fourth sections will involve critically engaging with the details of al-Ghazālī's case for scepticism.

2.1   Defining philosophy of religion

An initial challenge involves defining what we mean when referring to philosophy of religion. Consider Brian Davies, who writes:

> It is difficult to say what the philosophy of religion is. One might define it as philosophizing about religion. But many people disagree when it comes to what philosophy is. They also disagree about the meaning of the word religion. Philosophy of religion is a recognized branch of philosophy. Yet it would be rash to conclude that we can quickly explain its nature.[9]

Among those who do offer a definition are Beverly and Brian Clack, who note that philosophy of religion involves evaluating the rationality of theistic belief.

> It would seem, then, that philosophers of religion have been concerned with seeking explanations (and possible justifications) for the kinds of things that a religious believer believes. So rational proofs for the existence of God are offered in response to the question of: 'why believe in God?' When philosophy of religion is done in this way its chief concern is with the rational basis for religious belief.[10]

We encounter an alternative formulation in the work of Muslim philosopher of religion Shabbir Akhtar. His definition involves three assumptions, which he says any philosophy of religion must necessarily make:

> Firstly, one needs to assume that religious belief is not *sui generis*: it can be subsumed under a subsection of belief in general in the same way as historical or political or moral belief.
> Secondly, it has to be assumed that even if religious belief is indeed a special gift of grace, it is at another level simultaneously a purely

human conviction whose content is subject to ordinary appraisal and scrutiny. Thus, even if it is true that authentic revelation is the only source of true religious ideas, the thinker may still reasonably assess the truth and plausibility of revealed claims once these appear on the mortal plane.

And, thirdly, I take it that the actual existence of God is not a necessary condition of the very possibility of entertaining belief in God or belief that there is a God. Some religionists have, mistakenly, thought that the very fact that people actually believe in God implies that the human mind is an arena for the direct causal activities of God, Gabriel, or the Holy Spirit. [11]

The views outlined above suggest that the overarching endeavour of philosophy of religion involves evaluating the rational basis and justifiability of religious beliefs. We may adopt this overarching view as a working definition of the enterprise that is the philosophy of religion. One initial concern the reflective Muslim may have with this definition it that is seems to subsume religion under philosophy. The assumption which underpins this concern is that to philosophise about religion is to admit the superiority of philosophy over religion. In response to such concerns. the philosopher-poet Muhammad Iqbal writes:

> ...to rationalize faith is not to admit the superiority of philosophy over religion.
>
> Philosophy, no doubt, has jurisdiction to judge religion, but what is to be judged is of such a nature that it will not submit to the jurisdiction of philosophy except on its own terms. While sitting in judgement on religion, philosophy cannot give religion an inferior place among its data. Religion is not a departmental affair; it is neither mere thought, nor mere feeling, nor mere action; it is an expression of the whole man. Thus, in the evaluation of religion, philosophy must recognize the central position of religion and has no other alternative but to admit it as something focal in the process of reflective synthesis. Nor is there any reason to suppose that thought and intuition are essentially opposed to each other. [12]

There are two important insights from Iqbal's response. The first is that philosophising about religion need not devalue religion; in fact, one's motivation for engaging in philosophy of religion may be precisely because one considers the subject matter of religion as being of significant importance. This insight is expanded on by atheist philosopher of religion J. L. Mackie, who writes:

> ...the question of whether there is or is not a god [arguably 'the' central question in the philosophy of religion] can and should be discussed rationally and reasonably...This is a genuine, meaningful question, and an important one – too important for us to take sides about it **casually or arbitrarily.** Neither the affirmative nor the negative answer is obviously right, but the issue is not so obscure that relevant considerations of argument and evidence cannot be brought to bear upon it.[13] (emphasis added)

The second insight we may derive from Iqbal involves the relationship between philosophy and religion, and here I think he is right to point out that philosophy and religion need not be viewed as inherently opposed to each other. We could, following in the footsteps of Alfred North Whitehead, maintain that religion is best understood as the longing for justification. Whitehead writes:

> Religion is the longing of the spirit that the facts of existence should find their justification in the nature of existence. 'My soul thirsteth for God', writes the Psalmist...science can leave its metaphysics implicit and retire behind our belief in the pragmatic value of its general descriptions. If religion does that, it admits that its dogmas are merely pleasing ideas for the purpose of stimulating its emotions. Science (at least as a temporary methodological device) can rest upon a naive faith; religion is the longing for justification. When religion ceases to seek for penetration, for clarity, it is sinking back into its lower forms. The ages of faith are the ages of rationalism.[14]

If Iqbal and Whitehead are correct, then the significance and nature of religious belief provides good reason to think that the enterprise of philosophy need not devalue or subvert religion or religious faith.

There might still be a concern, however, that the characterisation of philosophy of religion I have endorsed does not assume the truth of Islamic theism. Accordingly, it may be claimed that philosophy of religion is an anathema to Islamic theism. This concern can be motivated by the following Quranic verse:

> Do you not see that God has subjected to your (use) all things in the heavens and on earth, and has made his bounties flow to you in exceeding measure, (both) seen and unseen? Yet there are among

men those who dispute about God, without knowledge and without guidance, and without a Book to enlighten them![15]

On the basis of this verse, one may argue that engaging in philosophy of religion undermines the authority of the Quran. The claim would be that God alone has total knowledge, some of which is revealed in the Quran, and one may question whether we are in a position to make judgements of our own concerning ultimate reality. But this line of critique is offset to a degree by the Quran itself, since it claims that God offers humanity a standard to judge between right and wrong, so that we may guard ourselves against evil.[16]

So, in response, we may clarify that the aim of philosophy when applied to religion involves critically reflecting on theistic belief. The need to reflect critically is also morally important. Consider, for example, Hannah Arendt's observation that a lack of critical self-reflection often leads to moral degeneration.[17] If we accept Arendt's observation, then we may argue that the process and outcomes of critical thought serve to complement the Quranic injunction to seek truth and avoid falsehood. With these considerations in mind, I believe we are now in a position to formalise an argument in favour of philosophy of religion:

Premise One: Religious commitments have significant existential import.

Premise Two: We (or at least the reflective individual) ought to guard against casual and arbitrary commitments, especially when they are of significant existential import.

Premise Three: Evaluating the justifiability of religious commitment through the use of philosophical reason is a way to guard against casual and arbitrary commitment.

Conclusion: There is good reason to engage in philosophy of religion, namely, as a way to guard against casual and arbitrary religious commitment.

The first two premises of the argument strongly cohere with the Quranic ethos, in that religious beliefs, especially belief in God and the afterlife, are regarded as being of ultimate existential import, requiring a deep level of critical self-reflection. Consider the following verses:

Now let man but think from what he is created! He is created from a drop emitted... Surely (God) is able to bring him back (to life)! The day that (all) things secret will be tested. Man will have no power and no helper. Behold this is the Word that distinguishes (Good from Evil): It is not a thing for amusement... [18]

If there is to be criticism of the argument, just outlined, then it is Premise Three which will have to be contested. One could argue that philosophising about religion does not adequately guard against casual and arbitrary commitment. The strongest challenge to Premise Three that I sense within the Islamic tradition arises from the work of al-Ghazālī.

2.2 Al-Ghazālī's critique

Al-Ghazālī's critique of philosophy is primarily directed toward the *falasifa*. During al-Ghazālī's intellectual milieu, the *falasifa* described a group who were committed to the legacy of Greek philosophy, mainly a Neoplatonic interpretation of Aristotelianism.[19] Al-Ghazālī's critique is based on the view that certain beliefs of the *falasifa* contradict the principles of Islamic orthodoxy. In his work entitled the *Incoherence of the Philosophers*, he writes that his intention is to:

> ...refute the philosophers [*falasifa*], to show that, contrary to their claims, their theories contradicting religious principles have not been demonstrated; they have failed to fulfil the condition for demonstration which they themselves had set down in their logical works.[20]

The central theme of al-Ghazālī's approach concerns the justifiability of those beliefs which, according to him, contradict the principles of Islam. Irrespective of the scope and success of al-Ghazālī's arguments, his approach appears to fit in well with my overall description of philosophy of religion. If we understand philosophy of religion as involving the use of philosophical reason to evaluate the justifiability of theistic commitments, then it appears that al-Ghazālī's critique of the *falasifa* is in harmony with the philosophy of religion – that is, al-Ghazālī is using philosophical reason to evaluate the religious commitments of the *falasifa*. Accordingly, I do not have objections to al-Ghazālī's general approach, which seems consistent with the one we have taken in this study. Al-Ghazālī's critique of the *falasifa*, however, threatens to undercut our case for the philosophy of religion. Consider the following two arguments:

(1) The first argument, which we may term al-Ghazālī's sociological critique of the *falasifa*, aims to question the uncritical acceptance of Greek philosophy. He writes:

> I have seen a group who, believing themselves in possession of distinctiveness from companion and peer by virtue of a superior wit

and intelligence, have rejected the Islamic duties regarding acts of worship ... [and] belittled the devotions and ordinances prescribed by the divine law ... The source of their unbelief is their hearing of high-sounding names such as 'Socrates', 'Hippocrates', 'Plato', 'Aristotle', and their likes ... They have done this thinking that the show of cleverness in abandoning the traditional imitation of what is true by embarking on the imitation of the false is a beauteous thing, being unaware that moving from one mode of imitation to another is folly and confusedness. What rank in God's world is there that is lower than the rank of one who adorns himself with the abandonment of the truth that is traditionally believed by the hasty embracing of the false as true, accepting it without reliable report and verification? [21]

The charge here levelled against the *falasifa* is that they are guilty of absorbing philosophical doctrines without critical reflection. If we set aside the accuracy of al-Ghazālī's observation, his mode of critique sets a significant benchmark. In essence, his critique concedes that we ought to guard against casual and arbitrary commitments, especially with regard to religious belief. He also mentions the need for verification, which dovetails well with our definition of philosophy of religion – that is, a philosophical evaluation of the justifiability of religious commitments. In response to al-Ghazālī's broader concerns, I believe we can agree with him that we need epistemic vigilance, although we ought surely to reject his overarching claim that every philosopher merely absorbs the conclusions of other philosophers without critical reflection.

(2) The second argument, which we may term the deficiency argument, arises from al-Ghazālī's philosophical critique of the *falasifa*. One major target of al-Ghazālī's attack is their belief in the pre-eternity of the universe. The majority of the *falasifa* adhered to the view that the world had existed eternally without beginning.[22] As part of his critique, al-Ghazālī questions whether the *falasifa* could in fact demonstrate the impossibility of a world created in time by an eternal will; furthermore, in order to strengthen his case against the *falasifa*, he argues against the existence of an actual infinite. [23] I do not intend to investigate the details of the arguments involved; nevertheless, we may note that al-Ghazālī's purpose is to show that the *falasifa*:

... have not rendered their opponents unable to uphold belief in the connectedness of the eternal will with the act of temporal creation except by invoking [rational] necessity and that they are unable to disengage from those who [in turn] invoke [rational] necessity against them in those matters opposed to their own belief.[24]

The reason I think these arguments are important is that they reveal a perceived deficiency in philosophy. The nature of this deficiency is expressed by al-Ghazālī as follows:

They [the philosophers who apply logic] draw up a list of the conditions to be fulfilled by demonstration which are known without fail to produce certainty. When, however, they come at length to treat of religious questions, not merely are they unable to satisfy these conditions, but they admit an extreme degree of relaxation.[25]

The preceding critique can be construed as offering two kinds of arguments, which can be interpreted as challenges to the case for the philosophy of religion. Let us consider each argument in turn:

(1) A key premise [Premise Three] in the argument presented earlier states that philosophising about religion is a way to guard against casual and arbitrary commitment. The accusation, however, is that many philosophers fail to reason in the proper manner. Al-Ghazālī notes that when philosophers discuss religious questions, they allow for an 'extreme degree of relaxation' in the rules of reason. If al-Ghazālī is correct, then he would have shown that philosophers, even in the act of philosophising, are not immune from casual and arbitrary commitments. One response to this criticism is to concede the fallibility of human reason, yet maintain that the proper exercise of philosophical reason does allow us to pursue and safeguard our epistemic interests. In other words, a philosopher can discuss religious questions in a way that accords with the proper exercise of philosophical reason. Al-Ghazālī's critique does not challenge philosophical reason *per se*; rather, it challenges the way in which some philosophers exercise philosophical reason.[26]

(2) A more substantial critique that one may draw from al-Ghazālī relates to whether religious beliefs and commitments are open to philosophical evaluation. Until now, we have implicitly assumed, along with Akhtar, that religious belief is not *sui generis* and thus open to evaluation. This assumption commits us to the view that religious belief can be evaluated in much the same way as historical, political and moral beliefs. There are two ways one may challenge this assumption: first, one may argue that philosophy is an inadequate tool to evaluate the

rationality and justifiability of theistic beliefs; and, second, one may argue that religious belief is formed in a way that is different from all other beliefs, thus requiring an alternative method of evaluation. I suggest that al-Ghazālī can be read as pursuing both strategies – that is, his work reveals a sceptical attitude toward the reliability of human reason, and the conviction that religious belief is *sui generis*. The remaining portion of this chapter will aim to articulate and evaluate al-Ghazālī's sceptical challenge as I understand it.

2.3 The challenge of scepticism

The roots of al-Ghazālī's scepticism can be traced to his youth when the realisation dawned on him that within his society there was parity among the different faiths. He noted that the tendency was for Christian children to grow up as Christians, young Jews to grow up in Judaism, and young Muslims in Islam.[27] The observation of parity among the varying faith traditions had the effect of loosening the grip of tradition and conformism. Al-Ghazālī then describes an upsurge of a powerful 'interior force' within him, desiring only certainty about the essence of knowledge. As he explains:

> Certain knowledge is that in which the thing known reveals itself without leaving any room for doubt or any possibility of error or illusion, nor can the heart allow such a possibility. One must be protected from error, and should be so bound to certainty that any attempt, for example, to transform a stone into gold or a stick into a serpent would not raise doubts or engender contrary probabilities. I know very well that ten is more than three. If anyone tries to dissuade me by saying, 'No three is more than ten', and wants to prove it by changing in front of me this stick into a serpent, even if I saw him changing it, still this fact would engender no doubt about my knowledge. Certainly, I would be astonished at such a power, but would not doubt my knowledge... Thus I came to know that whatever is known without this kind of certainty is doubtful knowledge, not reliable and safe; that all knowledge subject to error is not sure and uncertain.[28]

The quest for certainty motivates al-Ghazālī to embark on an epistemological odyssey. His desire for certainty also drives him to physical and mental paralysis. He notes his inability to continue with his teaching and his inability to overcome his sceptical frame of mind. Eric Ormsby, in his biography of al-Ghazālī, suggests that his crisis 'was caused not by the doubt which had tormented him as a young man, but by something more devastating: he had discovered the truth [the Sufi Path] but could not act on it. He was effectively paralysed by the truth'.[29] I agree with Ormsby that al-Ghazālī was aware of the 'Sufi path' and had much trouble acting on it; however, his awareness of 'the truth' did not resolve his epistemological concerns. It would be his experience of the Sufi path that would dissolve his doubt and restore him to health. The crisis as I perceive it was both epistemological – that is, dealing with the intellectual challenges of scepticism – and existential – that is, generating the will power to pursue the Sufi Path. My intention is to focus on al-Ghazālī's epistemological crisis, and I will do so by evaluating his case for scepticism. The reasons for doing so are as follows: (a) al-Ghazālī articulates clear arguments in favour of scepticism, and given the time and space which he devotes to these arguments, it would seem that they serve as a cornerstone in his intellectual defence of a Sufi inspired epistemology (which I will detail in the chapter to follow),[30] and (b) the Ghazālīan arguments for scepticism also challenge the possibility of a philosophy of religion. (I elaborate on this shortly.)

Al-Ghazālī's case for scepticism begins with the observation that sense perception is at times misleading, and that it is only through reason that we are able to correct these misperceptions. He writes:

> ... how can one trust the evidence of one's senses? Sight is the most powerful of our senses, and we could stare at a shadow and judge that it is fixed and not moving at all. Yet, at the end of an hour's watching we find that the shadow has moved ... This and similar cases exemplify how the evidence of one's senses leads one to a judgement which reason shows irrefutably to be totally erroneous.[31]

The thrust of this argument focuses on reason as moderating and correcting perceptual beliefs. Al-Ghazālī broadens his argument to include the principles of reason. He notes that in the example of the shadow, reason took 'epistemic priority' over sense perception. Correspondingly, if a supra-intellectual faculty exists, it would take epistemic priority over reason. Al-Ghazālī explains his argument as follows:

> ... just as sense perception was proven wrong by the intellect, perhaps the intellect can be proven wrong by a supra-intellectual

apprehension. Perhaps there is something beyond reason which would show that reason in turn is in error, just as reason showed the error of the evidence of the senses. The fact that this further intelligence is not manifest does not prove that it is impossible.[32]

Al-Ghazālī's case can be articulated in two parts: first, if we had access to a supra-intellectual faculty then we would regard it as having epistemic priority over reason, and if there exists a supra-intellectual faculty, then reason and sense perception cannot alone give us full epistemic access to the world we occupy. These considerations allow for a context where our cognitive abilities can be brought into question. The second element of al-Ghazālī's case aims once again to target the trustworthiness of sense perception and human reason. Al-Ghazālī appeals to our experience of dreams to argue his point. He observes that when in a state of sleep we have experiences which at that moment appear very real, but when we wake up, we realise it was just a dream. He writes:

> When one is asleep one believes all sorts of things and finds oneself in all sorts of situations; one believes in them absolutely, without the slightest doubt. When one wakes up, one realises the inanity of the phantasms of the imagination. In the same way one might ask oneself about the reality of beliefs one has acquired through one's senses or by logical thought. Could not one imagine oneself in a state which compares to being awake, just as wakefulness compares to being asleep? Being awake would be like the dreams of that state, which in turn would show that the illusion (of certainty) of rational knowledge is nothing but vain imagination.[33]

We note that Descartes, approximately five hundred years after al-Ghazālī, makes a similar argument:

> Nevertheless, I must remember that I am a man, and that consequently I am accustomed to sleep and in my dreams to imagine the same things that lunatics imagine when awake... But I am speaking as though I never recall having been misled, while asleep, by similar illusions. When I consider these matters carefully, I realise so clearly that there are no conclusive indications by which waking life can be distinguished from sleep that I am quite astonished, and my bewilderment is such that it is almost able to convince me that I am asleep.[34]

The insight of the 'argument from dreams' is that there is no guarantee that being 'awake' immunises our cognitive capacities from error, and once again we are forced to question the trustworthiness of our epistemic apparatus. We can formulate al-Ghazālī's overall challenge to the case for philosophy of religion as follows: in order for us to evaluate the justifiability of our beliefs and commitments, we must be sure that human reason which underpins philosophical reason is a reliable investigative tool. Until such time as our cognitive capacities are shown to be trustworthy, we do not have a basis for trusting the arguments and conclusions which arise from philosophical reasoning. We may agree that theistic beliefs are of great existential import, and that we need to exercise a high degree of epistemic vigilance with regard to theistic belief; however, in order for us to accept philosophy as a tool of epistemic vigilance, we need first to establish the trustworthiness of our cognitive capacities.

2.4   Evaluating al-Ghazālī's scepticism

In response to al-Ghazālī, we could cite the Quranic endorsement of the use of reason. However, we need to keep in mind that his scepticism began with reflections on religious diversity. Accordingly, even if the Quran affirms the use of reason, one may still question the basis of this affirmation. Given religious diversity, not everyone accepts the Quran and its commands as authoritative. If al-Ghazālī chose to base his trust in reason on the authority of the Quran, he would run the risk of begging the question.[35]

A stronger line of argument in response to al-Ghazālī is to note that once we reject the reliability of human reason, we effectively terminate the possibility of further dialogue. To reject human reason as wholly unreliable would call into question the reasoning which the sceptic must rely on to argue for scepticism. So, a global form of scepticism is quite unhelpful and self-undermining, leaving us with no means of resolving the existentially important question of commitment to the truth of theistic belief. For, global scepticism entails that we doubt all our thoughts, beliefs and intuitions, and reject our cognitive and critical capacities as being in any way trustworthy.

Perhaps our characterisation of al-Ghazālī should be more charitable, since he does wish for ongoing critical dialogue on religion. All he has questioned is the reliability of our cognitive faculties; while his arguments tend toward global scepticism, he is not a global sceptic. In order to evaluate the force and extent of al-Ghazālī's scepticism, we have to consider the degree to which his arguments undermine trust in our cognitive faculties. We may draw on al-Ghazālī's thoughts and articulate his case for scepticism as follows:

> Premise One: If there are grounds for doubt that our cognitive faculties are absolutely trustworthy, then we are entitled to withhold trust in the deliverances of our cognitive faculties.
>
> Premise Two: If it is possible that our present state of consciousness is a dream state, then we have grounds to doubt that our cognitive faculties are absolutely trustworthy.
>
> Premise Three: It is possible that our present state of consciousness is a dream state.
>
> Conclusion 1: We have grounds for doubt that our cognitive faculties are absolutely trustworthy (from Premise Two and Premise Three).
>
> Conclusion 2: Given Conclusion One and Premise One, we are entitled to withhold trust in the deliverances of our cognitive faculties.

A further consequence of this argument involves the justifiability of our beliefs. If we do not trust the deliverances of our cognitive capacities, *ipso facto* we will also doubt the justifiability of beliefs formed through the exercise of these capacities. This form of scepticism shifts our critical focus away from the content of our beliefs toward our belief-forming capacities. If we accept this form of scepticism, we not only question the justifiability of theistic beliefs, but we challenge all our beliefs. This form of scepticism is thus a threat to the Jamesian account of faith I have set out and defended in Chapter 1. The viability of the Jamesian account rests on the assumption that the deliverances of human reason can be trusted. If al-Ghazālī's scepticism is justified, then the deliverances of reason are not worthy of our trust. Conversely, al-Ghazālī may argue that the arguments marshalled in defence of the Jamesian account can have no force unless it is first shown that we are entitled to trust human reason. If we are to maintain that our rational capacities are trustworthy, then we will need to respond to al-Ghazālī's scepticism.

One way we may respond is by utilising al-Ghazālī's sceptical strategy against his case for scepticism. We note that al-Ghazālī's sceptical strategy rests on the assumption that the mere possibility of being in a dream state is reason enough to take this possibility seriously. This assumption can be seen to underpin Premise Two of the argument outlined above. That is, the dream hypothesis is given credence, since it is possible that our present state of consciousness may actually be a dream state. We may contest this assumption with the following counter-claim: it is possible that our cognitive faculties are, in general, trustworthy. We can then use al-Ghazālī's own strategy and argue that this possibility is a good reason to doubt scepticism. The argument against scepticism can be formalised as follows:

> Premise One: If it is possible that our cognitive faculties are, in general, trustworthy, then we are entitled to trust in the deliverances of our cognitive faculties.
>
> Premise Two: It is possible that our cognitive faculties are, in general, trustworthy.
>
> Conclusion: We are entitled to trust in the deliverances of our cognitive faculties.

Al-Ghazālī's sceptical strategy can thus be employed to defend an attitude of trust that is contrary to his case for scepticism. Nevertheless, the sceptic may argue that the dream hypothesis remains a real possibility. They may further concede that our cognitive capacities can function to bring us truth, but maintain that we ought to doubt them because they cannot be relied on to do this. In reply to these considerations, we may concede the possibility that our present state or our everyday consciousness may in fact be a dream state. But the mere possibility of being in a dream cannot be taken as a good reason to think that we actually are in a dream. At best, the possibility of being in dream at best undermines the naïve view that we can at all times wholeheartedly trust in the deliverances of our cognitive faculties. This study does not aim to defend the naïve view, and we may accommodate the possibility of the dream hypothesis by acknowledging that our cognitive capacities are fallible. We may also maintain that the trust we have in our cognitive capacities can be undermined only if it can be shown to be true that our present state of consciousness is in fact a dream state.

The underlying concern which motivates al-Ghazālī's sceptical stance, I believe, relates to the possibility for error. That is, the possibility of error is seen as a reason to distrust, or even suspend judgement on whether we can trust our cognitive faculties. Given the significant existential import of theistic belief, there should to be no room for error. Al-Ghazālī can be interpreted as someone who seeks to eliminate doubt. While we may be able to undermine his sceptical conclusions to a significant degree, we have yet to justify an attitude of trust. According to Jeffery Whitman, sceptics, like al-Ghazālī and perhaps Descartes, are not alone when they question our common-sense view of the world:

> The skeptic does not dogmatically accept this common sense assumption. However, he is not alone in rejecting this sort of dogmatism. Most philosophers working in the field of epistemology reject this assumption as well. They, like the skeptic, endeavour to critically examine the assumption of common sense.[36]

We also note that Whitman's line of thought is developed by Stewart Cohen, who observes that while most philosophers question the common-sense view of the world, most philosophers also reject scepticism and embrace fallibilism.[37] Cohen defines fallibilism as the view that: S can know P on the basis of R, even if there is some alternative to P, compatible with R, [where]...an alternative to P [is] any proposition incompatible with P.[38] At the core of fallibilism is the rejection of the entailment principle: *S knows P on the basis of (reason or evidence) R only if R entails P*. Fallibilism allows for the common-sense view that we have knowledge without having to strictly adhere to the entailment principle.[39] The following example will help clarify the argument being made:

> Max and his son Adam are at the zoo visiting the various animal enclosures. They arrive at the enclosure marked zebra, Max then points out to his son that the animal they are looking at is a zebra, noted for its black and white banding patterns. At this point Adam turns to father and says the zebra looks just like a mule, but with different colours.

Among the reasons Max has for believing he is looking at a zebra are that: (a) in the past, other people have pointed out to him what a zebra is; (b) he has read books which describe zebras; (c) the enclosure at the zoo is marked with a sign advising visitors that the animal is a zebra; and (d) he believes that the zoo administration will not deceive its patrons with a cleverly disguised mule. None of the reasons just mentioned strictly entails that the animal Max is looking at is actually a zebra. Yet, while there is room for doubt, on a fallibilist view Max is entitled to claim that he knows that the animal before him is a real zebra. But al-Ghazālī, in his sceptical mode, would maintain that Max cannot claim to know, since his experience of seeing the zebra may be illusory.

Al-Ghazālī's case for scepticism entails that we cannot trust our cognitive capacities as long as there is the possibility of error. On a fallibilist view, however, it is possible to trust in the deliverances of our cognitive capacities while acknowledging the possibility of error. The possibility of fallibilism thus gives rise to an additional counter-argument in our response to al-Ghazālī's scepticism, and this is to argue that al-Ghazālī begs the question against a fallibilist view of knowledge. In order to undermine fallibilism, a proponent of al-Ghazālī's scepticism would have to defend the highly questionable view that an attitude of trust can be justified only if there is no possibility of error. We should note, however, that al-Ghazālī presents scepticism as a challenge to be overcome, and not as a philosophical position one might reasonably adopt.[40] Al-Ghazālī endorses the Sufi path, which he claims allows for a mode of consciousness which eliminates altogether the possibility of error. We will consider the details of the Sufi account in the chapter to follow.

2.5 Summary

The central aim of this chapter was to critically engage with al-Ghazālī's case for scepticism. Our study of al-Ghazālī's scepticism was motivated by the concern that it had the potential to prevent the reflective Muslim from endorsing the Jamesian account of faith. I maintain the view that philosophising about religion enables us to guard against casual and arbitrary commitment. The crux of the argument lay in the follow proposition: *Evaluating the justifiability of theistic belief, through the use of philosophical reason, is a way to guard against casual and arbitrary commitment.* The initial set of criticisms directed at this premise involved the claim that philosophy may devalue religion, and the act of philosophising may contravene the ethos of Islamic tradition. In response to these concerns, we emphasised that the act of philosophising need not devalue theistic belief, since philosophising about religious belief is in fact motivated by a deep concern for truth with respect to religion. In addition, philosophising, it was argued, took to heart the Quranic imperative to reflect on the question of theistic belief. The subsequent introduction of al-Ghazālī raised the challenge of scepticism, and our chief response to the sceptical argument involved a *tu quoque*, whereby the sceptic's strategy is used to undermine the sceptical argument. The sceptic's strategy assumes that the possibility of being in a dream state is enough to doubt our cognitive capacities. In reply, we noted that it is also a possibility that our cognitive capacities are, in general, trustworthy. Moreover, al-Ghazālī's sceptical strategy assumes that an attitude of trust is justified only if there is no possibility of error. This assumption is problematic, since it is possible to exercise trust while acknowledging the possibility of error, e.g., fallibilism – a view which a majority of philosophers endorse. Thus, al-Ghazālī's case for scepticism need not be seen to undermine James's account – which presupposes a reflective ethos.

The sceptic and fallibilist can agree that it is imperative to guard against casual and arbitrary commitments. The point of difference arises when we consider the best way to evaluate the justifiability of our commitments. One essential premise of our case assumes that the process of philosophising about religion – that is, evaluating the justifiability of theistic beliefs – is a way to guard against casual and arbitrary commitment. Al-Ghazālī's case for scepticism questions the trust we have in our cognitive capacities. As noted above, the Ghazālīan-inspired case for scepticism is self-undermining. In addition, the enterprise of philosophy of religion, on the fallibilist view, is practicable, since our cognitive capacities, when properly functioning, are viewed as trustworthy. However, we should not completely dismiss al-Ghazālī's case, since we can interpret his case as a means by which a Sufi account of faith is motivated.[41] That is, the case for scepticism allows al-Ghazālī to cast doubt on the trustworthiness of our cognitive capacities, and if we accept his view, there arises the question of whether we could ever grasp truth. In response, he proposes a supra-intellectual faculty which transcends sense perception and reason. He contends that the supra-intellectual faculty grasps truth in a way that allows no room for doubt. This account of faith, which I term al-Ghazālī's Sufi account of faith, can be construed as a possible alternative to the Jamesian account of faith. The chapter to follow will explore and evaluate al-Ghazālī's Sufi account of faith.

3
Al-Ghazālī's Sufi Account of Faith

Reason is God's shadow; God is the sun. What power has the
shadow before the sun.

– Rumi

Al-Ghazālī's case for scepticism aims to challenge the common-sense
view of the world. He maintains that the deliverances of sense perception and human reason are not trustworthy. If we concede this form of
scepticism, then we must also be prepared to suspend the enterprise of
philosophy of religion. The philosophy of religion involves engaging
with theistic belief through a process of critical reflection, thus assuming
a degree of trust in sense perception and human reason as guides to
truth. Consequently, if we do not trust our cognitive capacities to grasp
truth, then there would be little motivation to critically reflect on our
faith commitments. Once we concede that truth is beyond our grasp,
it would be pointless either to seek truth or to guard against casual
and arbitrary commitment through a process of critical reflection. In
response to this view, I have argued that the Ghazālīan strategy assumes
that the possibility of being in a dream state is reason enough to withhold trust in our cognitive capacities. This approach can in turn be
used against the sceptic; that is, we can be entitled to trust, since it is
also possible that our cognitive capacities are in general trustworthy.
We can also adopt an attitude of fallibilism, which is the view that
we can, in general and for the most part, trust the deliverances of our
cognitive capacities. An attitude of fallibilism does not require that we
dogmatically trust our cognitive capacities; rather, it is an open-minded
commitment where there is room for critical reflection. Fallibilism also
rejects the assumption that an attitude of trust is justified only if there
is no possibility of error.

The Jamesian account of faith presupposes a degree of trust in the deliverances of our cognitive capacities. This is evident as we reflect on the evidential and moral constraints of James's account. For example, the evidential constraint requires us to reflect on whether the truth of the belief in question can be decided on evidential grounds, and the moral constraint requires us to reflect on whether the content of a passionally caused belief is morally acceptable. Satisfying these constraints assumes a significant degree of trust in the deliverances of our cognitive capacities. So, these constraints could not be satisfied had we conceded al-Ghazālī's case for scepticism. Fortunately, al-Ghazālī's case can be defused, and the reflective Muslim need not view al-Ghazālī's scepticism as a reason to reject the Jamesian account, or the enterprise of philosophy of religion.

There is good reason to set aside al-Ghazālī's case for scepticism, however, his case can also be interpreted as a component of a broader argument,[1] one in which he claims that 'anyone who believes that the unveiling of truth is the fruit of well-ordered arguments is guilty of disparaging the mercy of God'.[2] If God is all-powerful and all-merciful then God can disclose, or allow access to, the truth in a variety of ways (perhaps through inspiration, revelation, or through other passional inclinations). Thus, God's mercy is disparaged when attaining truth is regarded as being solely the domain of human reason. The mercy of God, as understood by al-Ghazālī, would allow for a number of pathways to truth, and if you accept this understanding of divine mercy, then the Sufi path – as a mystical rather than a rational account of faith – becomes worthy of serious consideration.

The central aim of this chapter is to articulate and evaluate al-Ghazālī's Sufi account of faith. There are three reasons which motivate the study of al-Ghazālī's Sufi account: (a) al-Ghazālī's crisis, to recall, began when he took to heart the reality of religious diversity, and the Sufi account can be seen as being a resolution to his crisis; (b) the Sufi account of faith is significantly different from the Jamesian account. Since both accounts can be interpreted as responses to religious diversity, and perhaps religious ambiguity, I will need to engage with al-Ghazālī's Sufi account; and (c) we also have al-Ghazālī's testimony that his experience of the Sufi path returned him to physical and mental health, and this in itself suggests that the Sufi account is worthy of consideration. In addition, al-Ghazālī's Sufi account can be interpreted as an alternative to the Jamesian account. As a result, the reflective Muslim will need to weigh up the Sufi account of faith with reference to the ambiguity thesis and the question of entitlement to believe in God. This chapter will engage with al-Ghazālī's Sufi account in five steps: the first step will involve detailing al-Ghazālī's account; the second step will involve providing an outline of the arguments which can be deployed in defence of the Sufi account; the third step will critically engage with the metaphysics that underpins al-Ghazālī's Sufi account; the fourth step will involve aligning al-Ghazālī's Sufi account with the school of 'Reformed epistemology', and for the purposes of this study, I will focus of the work of Alvin Plantinga, a leading figure in the reformed epistemology movement; and the fifth step will critically engage with the 'Reformed' version of al-Ghazālī's Sufi account.

3.1 A Sufi account of faith

The understanding of faith preferred by al-Ghazālī rests on the view that there exists a mode of perception which transcends sense perception and human reason, namely a supra-intellectual faculty, and it is this mode of perception, according to al-Ghazālī, which has the capacity to overcome doubt. Al-Ghazālī's work reveals a number of arguments in defence of this position, and we can summarise his view with the following conditional: *If there exists a supra-intellectual perceptual faculty, then it would allow us to judge the reliability of our rational and sensory perceptual cognitive capacities.* In the interests of clarity, I offer my own formulation about what I take to be al-Ghazālī's overall case for a supra-intellectual faculty:

Premise One: If there is a mode of perception which has epistemic priority over sense perception and reason, then we cannot rely exclusively on sense perception and reason to arrive at truths (or, in other words, we cannot regard sense perception and reason as altogether reliable sources of true belief).

Premise Two: If divine inspiration is possible, then there is a mode of perception which has epistemic priority over sense perception and the human reason.

Premise Three: According to Islamic tradition it is possible to experience divine inspiration.

Conclusion One: There is a mode of perception which has epistemic priority over sense perception and human reason. (from Premium Two and Premiun Three)

Conclusion Two: We cannot rely exclusively on sense perception and reason to arrive at truths (or, in other words, we cannot regard sense perception and reason as altogether reliable sources of true belief). (from Premium One and Conclusion One)

We draw one further conclusion if we add the following sub-premise:

Sub-Premise: If there is a mode of perception which has epistemic priority over sense perception and human reason, then we ought to take it into account when judging the extent to which those cognitive capacities are reliable.

Conclusion Three: We ought to take it, i.e., the supra-intellectual faculty, into account when judging the extent to which those cognitive capacities are reliable. (from Conclusion One and Sub-Premise)

The argument presented above represents my understanding of al-Ghazālī's broader justification of the Sufi path. At the core of al-Ghazālī's conception of the Sufi path is his defence of the supra-intellectual faculty. His case for the supra-intellectual faculty utilises a number of supporting arguments which buttress the claim made in the first premise of the argument above. The remaining two premises can be reinforced with a general appeal to the tenets of Islamic theology. My intention, in the sections to follow, is to evaluate al-Ghazālī's case, but first, I believe, it is crucial that we present his argument in its strongest form.

3.2 Defending the Sufi account

Al-Ghazālī's case for scepticism aimed to put pressure on the view that sense perception and human reason are reliable guides to truth. If we concede al-Ghazālī's case, then we also concede that the deliverances of sense perception and human reason are unreliable. However, if there exists a supra-intellectual faculty which can deliver divinely revealed truth, then there is a way to overcome scepticism. The Sufi account of faith affirms the existence of a supra-intellectual faculty, and it also involves a programme of cultivating that faculty. The Sufi account provides a way to overcome scepticism, since the supra-intellectual faculty directly delivers divinely revealed truth, so a programme of cultivating that faculty is the route to arriving at indubitable truth. The aim of the argument outlined above is to secure the conclusion that we ought to take into account the deliverances of the supra-intellectual faculty when judging the extent to which sense perception and human reason are reliable.

3.2.1 Defence of premise one

We may divide al-Ghazālī's defence of this premise into the following considerations:

(1) As part of his case for scepticism, al-Ghazālī argues that our cognitive capacities may be prioritised. The example he uses to make his case involves the relationship between sense perception and reason. For example, a shadow at first glance appears stationary. On reflection, however, we realise that the shadow actually moves. Our faculty of reason, in the case of the shadow, corrects sense perception. Thus, reason takes epistemic priority over sense perception. This argument serves to introduce the idea of epistemic prioritisation as a feature of our cognitive capacities.

(2) Building on the insight that there can be epistemic prioritisation of our cognitive faculties, al-Ghazālī argues that if there exists a supra-intellectual faculty, it would take priority over reason. This second insight involves the recognition that there exist levels of disclosure, depending on the mode of perception. If a supra-intellectual faculty exists, then it would provide a superior form of disclosure, and therefore take epistemic priority over reason and sense perception. One possible response to this view would be to claim that reason and sense perception are generally reliable and collectively provide an adequate level of disclosure. A critic of al-Ghazālī who makes this response may also suggest that the reliability of sense perception and reason would not be affected by any consideration about the possibility of a supra-intellectual faculty. In reply, a defender of al-Ghazālī may re-employ the argument from dreams, whereby doubt is cast on the reliability of our cognitive faculties. One may argue that the intuitions associated with ordinary, everyday consciousness may in fact be mistaken. For example, our intuitions of space and time may not reflect reality as it is; rather, we may be in a dream state where space and time represent properties that are constructions of our mind and not properties or relations of things as they are in themselves.[3] If the dream argument is accepted, then it would serve to undercut the claim that human reason and sense perception alone provide adequate epistemic disclosure. The aim of this second argument is to establish the following possibility, i.e., if a supra-intellectual faculty exists, then it can be given priority over human reason, in much the same way as reason can take priority over sense perception.

The above considerations aim to increase the plausibility of Premise One, which states that if there is a mode of perception which has epistemic priority over sense perception and reason, then we cannot rely exclusively on sense perception and reason to arrive at truths (or, in other words, we cannot regard sense perception and reason as altogether reliable sources of true belief).

3.2.2 Defence of premise two

Premise Two involves the claim that if God chooses to reveal truths to, or inspires, a person, then such a process can operate independently from the operations of reason and sense perception. This view does not rule out the possibility that inspiration could complement a process of reasoning or the deliverances of sense perception. The claim, however, is that divine inspiration, if there is such a thing, need not be restricted to operating through processes of reasoning or sense perception. There is the possibility that there exists a quasi-perceptual supra-intellectual faculty distinct from the faculties of reason and sense perception, which is receptive to divine inspiration. Consequently, divine inspiration, if possible, allows for modes of perception which are independent of reason and the five senses. One may also maintain that the supra-intellectual faculty may yield a greater degree of disclosure and a greater degree of reliability. This argument reinforces the claim that the supra-intellectual faculty can take priority over the senses and reason – and in so doing, bring us closer to truth. In addition, we are able to draw once again on the dream argument in order to undercut the claim that the feeling of certainty is a reliable indicator of truth. For example, a vivid dream, or perhaps a nightmare, can feel very real, yet upon waking we realise the experience was illusory. Similarly, it may be argued that there is a mode of consciousness – supra-intellectual consciousness – which we attain when we awaken from our everyday consciousness and realise that our senses and reason were caught up in illusion. This argument would support the claim that the supra-intellectual faculty – which is the locus of divine inspiration – has epistemic priority over sense perception and human reason.

3.2.3 Defence of premise three

The claim of Premise Three is that divine inspiration is possible. From the perspective of Islamic tradition this premise is relatively uncontroversial. At the core of Islam is belief in Muhammad as a messenger of God, and the Quran makes note of this:

> We have sent thee inspiration, as We sent it to Noah and the Apostles after him: we sent inspiration to Abraham, Isma'il, Isaac, Jacob and

the Tribes, to Jesus, Job, Jonah, Aaron, and Solomon, and to David
We gave the Psalms.[4]

There is, for Muslims, a deep commitment to the truth that Muhammad
was inspired by God and thus experienced divine inspiration. We note
also that the Quran describes Muhammad as belonging to a distinguished lineage of individuals who, within the Judaeo-Christian tradition, are understood to have received divine inspiration.

Given these three premises, which are well supported within the
tradition of Islamic theism, we arrived at the following conclusions: (a)
there is a mode of perception which transcends sense perception and
human reason; (b) we cannot rely exclusively on sense perception and
reason to yield knowledge of reality in order to judge the reliability
of our cognitive capacities; and finally (c) we must take into account
the mode of perception which has epistemic priority over sense perception and human reason when judging the reliability of those cognitive
capacities, i.e., reason and sense perception.

These conclusions, if true, also constitute a response to al-Ghazālī's
scepticism. The scepticism of al-Ghazālī is motivated by the view that
the deliverances of human reason are fallible and therefore do not
provide the certainty that is needed for knowledge. If, however, there
exists a supra-intellectual faculty, then there exists a mode of perception which, according to al-Ghazālī, allows for epistemic certainty. This
view, if true, would serve to resolve al-Ghazālī's sceptical crisis, since the
achievement of epistemic certainty also entails, for him, the achievement of knowledge. Such a view is significantly different to James's
account, which embraces epistemic uncertainty – I plan to elaborate
more on this shortly.

The sections to follow will critically engage with the case for the Sufi
account of faith. First, however, I intend to further outline al-Ghazālī's
Sufi account, which introduces the concept of a prophetic faculty as a
supra-intellectual faculty.

3.3 Al-Ghazālī's metaphysics

The challenge of scepticism involves questioning the reliability of
our cognitive capacities. In response to the question of cognitive reliability, al-Ghazālī posits a supra-intellectual faculty available to all
human beings, which he terms the 'prophetic faculty'. The details of
the prophetic faculty are embedded within al-Ghazālī's metaphysics.[5]

Ghazālīan metaphysics has two central components: first, the distinction between the visible world and the unseen world (the world of Dominion), and second, the Quranic parables of light (24:35) and of darkness (24:40). This first component focuses on the visible world, which is the world of everyday experience. For al-Ghazālī, the world of experience, of which we are a part, is but a shadow of, or an effect that proceeds from, the world of Dominion (the unseen world). Thus, the world of experience exists as an effect of the world of Dominion while the world of Dominion is said to emanate directly from God. As al-Ghazālī explains:

> For when someone is in the world of Dominion, he is with God ... from God the secondary causes of existent things descend into the visible world, while the visible world is one of the effects of the world of Dominion. The visible world comes forth from the world of Dominion just as the shadow comes forth from the thing that throws it, the fruit comes forth from the tree, and the effect comes forth from the secondary causes.[6]

Al-Ghazālī's emphasis is on the visible world as a reflection of the unseen world of Dominion: 'the visible world acts as a similitude for the world of Dominion'.[7] To clarify the nature of this semblance, al-Ghazālī presents an exegesis of two Quranic parables, that of light and of darkness. We begin with the parable of light: the 'Light Verse' reads as follows:

> God is the light of the heavens and the earth; the likeness of his light is as a niche wherein is a lamp, the lamp in a glass, the glass as it were a glittering star kindled from a blessed tree, an olive that is neither of the East nor of the West, whose oil well-nigh would shine, even if no fire touched it; light upon light; God guides to His light whom He wills.[8]

Al-Ghazālī perceives each of the five features mentioned in the parable as representative of the five 'faculties of the human soul'. David Buchman summarises al-Ghazālī's view as follows:

> ...the lamp, the niche, the glass, the tree and the olive of the Light Verse are all visible, existent things whose characteristics point to the attributes of these five faculties; senses, imagination, reflection, the rational faculty, and the prophetic faculty.[9]

Buchman notes that al-Ghazālī envisions true believers as people who aim to purify their souls. Thus, he says that the 'greater the soul's purification, the more one is able to perceive God's light and gain true knowledge of things'.[10] Hence, for al-Ghazālī, the essence of knowledge resides in perception of the divine light. Importantly, the prophetic faculty is equated with the oil of the lamp.[11] Like oil, the prophetic faculty symbolises purity which is distilled and thus becomes a source of light. The oil can itself be luminous or ignited to produce illumination. Al-Ghazālī describes prophets as light-giving lamps.[12] The rational faculty has the task of selecting and adopting as exemplars those who have already been illuminated. According to al-Ghazālī, the parable of light is meant to reveal the nature of the soul and its path to illumination. God is seen as the Light of lights, and our journey toward the divine can only be through illumination of the various aspects of the soul. Once we have begun the journey toward illumination, we get closer to God and the essence of knowledge.

The second parable concerning darkness is also interpreted as revealing the nature of the soul. The parable of light gives an insight into the faculties of the soul, whereas the parable of darkness diagnoses the state of the soul. The parable reads:

> [The unbelievers state is like] a fathomless ocean covered by a wave, above which is a [further] wave, above which are clouds, darkness piled one upon the other.[13]

As with the parable of light, Al-Ghazālī elucidates the symbolic nature of each component of the parable. For example, the 'fathomless ocean' symbolises the world, since 'within it are destructive dangers, harmful occupations and blinding murkiness'.[14] The first wave symbolises the bestial attributes, such as preoccupation with sensory pleasures, 'so that people will eat and enjoy just as cattle eat and enjoy'.[15] The second wave symbolises the predatory attributes, such as anger, enmity, malice, vainglory and arrogance.[16] The clouds symbolise loathsome beliefs, lying opinions, and corrupt imaginings, which veil 'knowledge of the Real'.[17] The soul is said to be veiled in darkness if it is covered (consumed) by the waves and clouds. The spiritual standing of a person corresponds to his or her position on the spectrum of light and darkness. Al-Ghazālī considers this spiritual spectrum as consisting of three broad categories: those 'veiled in darkness alone, those veiled by sheer light, and those who are veiled by light along with darkness'.[18] Al-Ghazālī also describes the various character types depending on their position within the spectrum. As an example, those veiled by total darkness may suffer from various vices such that their 'ultimate end of searching in this world is to achieve wishes, to obtain objects of appetite, and to obtain bestial pleasures by means of women, food, and clothing'.[19] The person who is veiled by sheer light encounters the august glories of the face of God. This person will encounter the ruling authority of majesty and thus become 'extinct from themselves, so that they cease observing themselves'.[20]

Given this account of al-Ghazālī's metaphysics, we are able to highlight a number of key epistemological points: the prophetic faculty is available to all humans, and if properly cultivated the prophetic faculty is able to receive divine illumination. In addition, faith is seen as a process whereby believers aim to inculcate their souls with virtue. It is only when a person begins the process of seeking virtue that apprehension of the divine becomes possible, and it is this apprehension that leads to an experience of illumination. Commenting on his own experience, al-Ghazālī writes:

> My disease grew worse and lasted almost two months, during which I fell prey to scepticism, though neither in theory nor in outward expression. At last, God the Almighty cured me of that disease and I recovered my health and mental equilibrium. The self-evident principles of reason again seemed acceptable; I trusted them and in them felt safe and certain. I reached this point not by well-ordered or methodical argument, but by means of a light God the Almighty cast into my breast, this light is the key to most knowledge.[21]

Al-Ghazālī's illumination experience is an event which restores in him the ability to trust reason, and he is therefore able to overcome scepticism. The solution to al-Ghazālī's scepticism does not come in the form of a syllogism; rather, al-Ghazālī experiences a change of heart that was made possible by following the Sufi path. This experience, if we take al-Ghazālī's account at face value, dissolved completely the psychological and physiological impact of scepticism. A proponent of al-Ghazālī's account of faith, who wishes to challenge the Jamesian account can reason as follows: It might not be possible to completely rule out rationally the challenge of scepticism, but we can overcome the epistemological challenge of scepticism by following the Sufi path, i.e., we can achieve epistemic certainty by following the Sufi path. The

Ghazālīan account of faith is a challenge to the Jamesian account on the grounds that it promises the achievement of epistemic certainty. The Jamesian account, however, embraces epistemic uncertainty. I suggest that al-Ghazālī and James would have agreed that the evidence of reason and sense perception is not sufficient to provide us with knowledge of the truth of religious belief. The difference of opinion, however, relates to: (a) the diagnosis of why we lack this knowledge, and (b) the way in which we may respond to the lack of knowledge. The lack of knowledge in view of the Jamesian account relates to the nature of the relevant evidence – i.e., the relevant evidence leaves open the question of God's existence. Al-Ghazālī, however, would have viewed the evidence as tending toward theism, but, he would have questioned whether the deliverances of our cognitive capacities could be trusted – hence, the denial of knowledge. In response to the evidential ambiguity and the lack of knowledge of the truth of religious belief, James defends the possibility of a venture beyond the evidence. Such a venture embraces epistemic uncertainty and involves practical commitment to the truth of religious belief; while al-Ghazālī's Sufi account is an epistemological framework which has the achievement of knowledge as its aim. The Jamesian account and al-Ghazālī's Sufi account are equally concerned with faith commitments and the lack of knowledge, but they differ radically on how we should respond. Given these differences, the reflective Muslim will most likely want to know whether al-Ghazālī's Sufi account is a viable account of faith.

I do not believe that Ghazālī's account is viable; I contend the account is deeply problematic, and there are five reasons for this view:

(1) The prophetic faculty, as described by al-Ghazālī, is a faculty of the human soul. If al-Ghazālī believes that the faculty of reason and sense perception are prone to error, then how can we be sure the prophetic faculty is immune from error? We can re-employ the dream argument to suggest the prophetic faculty may itself be caught up in an illusion. Once again we may question the basis on which it would be justified to trust in the deliverances of the prophetic faculty. Perhaps an appeal can be made to the overwhelming feeling of 'trustworthiness' that arises in those who experience illumination.

(2) If the Ghazālian proponent appeals to the feeling of 'trustworthiness', then they must respond once again to the argument from dreams. The dream argument, to recall, also questioned whether the feeling of certainty was sufficient to ensure the reliability of our perceptions. As formulated by al-Ghazālī, the dream argument serves to decouple the feeling of certainty from the justifiability of a belief. This argument also

seems applicable to the Sufi account, since it may very well be the case that following the Sufi path inspires trust in human reason, but, on al-Ghazālī's own terms, the feeling of certainty is insufficient to justify the truth of the belief or attitude in question.

(3) The scope of al-Ghazālī's Sufi account is restricted to those who presuppose the truth of Islam, e.g., believe in the existence of God, the prophetic faculty and divine inspiration. On a less charitable reading, al-Ghazālī can be accused of begging the question, as he interprets his experience as a genuine instance of divine inspiration. That is, one may offer a naturalistic interpretation whereby al-Ghazālī's experiences are interpreted as a purely mental phenomenon. Such an interpretation need not appeal to God, the prophetic faculty or divine inspiration in order to explain his experience. Al-Ghazālī assumes that Islamic theism is the correct framework within which to interpretation his experience, but this view is easily contested.

(4) We can also contend that in the light of our knowledge of religious pluralism, al-Ghazālī's experience can strengthen the thesis of religious ambiguity. For example, al-Ghazālī's experience can be added to numerous experiences of illumination within the Jewish, Buddhist and Christian traditions. This plurality of experiences across varying traditions should not be taken to discredit al-Ghazālī's experience; rather when taken as a whole these experiences require an explanation. To this end, we could ask the following questions: Why do people have such experiences, or why do these experiences arise within certain traditions, and why is there such diversity within these experiences? The diversity of illumination experiences serves to reinforce the phenomenon of religious diversity and does not necessarily help to disambiguate in favour of one particular view.

(5) Lastly, the Sufi account presupposes God's existence, but that does not entail that it 'undercuts the thesis of ambiguity': one may (by a passionally motivated venture) make a commitment while recognising the truth you commit yourself to is evidentially ambiguous. That is, we can speak of the Sufi path as allowing for a change in our passional nature, i.e., it allows for a shift in our inclinations. The Sufi path can inspire a change in passional inclinations whereby doubt can be replaced with trust, and in the case of al-Ghazālī, the Sufi path also allowed him to regain trust in human reason.[22] Accordingly, al-Ghazālī's experience need not be seen as a challenge to the Jamesian account, since in Jamesian terms, what breaks through al-Ghazālī's scepticism is his coming to have trust in his reason and senses on passional, rather than rational, grounds. (I plan to further develop a Jamesian reading of al-Ghazālī in the chapter to follow.)

The five reasons discussed above, I suggest, shift the burden of proof back onto the person who wants to argue that al-Ghazālī's account is a viable account of faith. There is, however, the possibility of a more robust Ghazālīan inspired challenge, and this becomes possible when we ally al-Ghazālī's Sufi account of faith with the school of 'Reformed epistemology'.

3.4   Reforming al-Ghazālī

The fundamental link between al-Ghazālī's epistemology and Reformed epistemology is the claim that we can be entitled to beliefs even if we lack propositional evidence or arguments for those beliefs. The argument presented by al-Ghazālī draws on the notion of divine mercy, which he claims liberated him from scepticism. Al-Ghazālī's insight is that God has the ability to disclose truth and knowledge in ways that need not involve the believer making inferences from propositional evidence. Similarly, proponents of Reformed epistemology also argue that the justifiability of theistic belief need not depend on propositional evidence. One case in point is Alvin Plantinga, a key figure in the Reformed epistemology movement, who employs the following, twofold strategy: (a) to undercut the evidential challenge of classical foundationlism to theistic belief, and (b) to defend the rationality of theistic belief. The foundationalist challenge to the rationality of theistic belief asserts:

(1)   If there is no sufficient propositional evidence for theism, then theistic belief is irrational or unreasonable.
(2)   There is no sufficient propositional evidence for theism.

Conclusion: Theistic belief is irrational and therefore unjustified.[23]

In response, a number of theists have taken issue with the second premise of the above argument by maintaining that there is sufficient propositional evidence in favour of theism. Reformed epistemologists, however, argue that foundationalism fails to live up to its own standard of rationality by questioning whether the foundationalist criterion, which specifies the need for propositional evidence, is itself supported by propositional evidence. Plantinga argues that foundationalism, if it is to live up to its own standards of rationality, must be believed on the evidential basis of other propositions; propositions that are properly basic, i.e., self-evident, incorrigible, or evident to the senses, and that evidentially support it. Yet, he maintains, 'No classical foundation-alist has produced any such arguments or proposed some properly basic proposition' which demonstrate that foundationalism satisfies its own criteria for justification.[24]

I do not intend to pursue this argument any further, as there is a deeper issue which I think is worthy of further consideration. The deeper issue concerns Plantinga's observation that the vast majority of our beliefs do not conform to the foundationalist criterion. Plantinga argues that once we assume the foundationalist criterion, we are then committed to the claim that for any beliefs to be rational, or justified, they must be:

> ... believed on the evidential basis of propositions that are self-evident or evident to the senses or incorrigible for [the believer]. Furthermore they must be probable and seen to be probable with respect to prop-ositions of that sort; there must be good arguments, deductive, inductive, or abductive to these conclusions from those kinds of propositions.[25]

But if we consider our everyday beliefs – for example, the belief that I had cornflakes for breakfast – we find that they usually fail to meet the requirements of the foundationalist criterion and so would not qualify as rational. The truth of the proposition 'I had cornflakes for breakfast' is neither self-evident, evident to my five senses, nor incorrigible for me. Plantinga also maintains that there are no propositions of that sort with respect to which this belief is probable, nor are there good deductive, inductive or abductive arguments for its truth. A person simply knows that they ate cornflakes this morning. The foundationalist criterion thus fails to account for everyday beliefs which we regard as rational, i.e., the truth of such beliefs is usually taken as being evident in our everyday experience. For example, the belief that *there exist other minds*, and that *the world was not created ten minutes ago with all its dusty books, apparent memories, crumbling mountains, and deeply carved canyons*, as Plantinga puts it, are regarded as rational beliefs, though they appear to fail the foundationalist criterion. With this insight in mind, Plantinga's objection to the foundationalist critique of theism is that even if theism lacks sufficient propositional evidence, it does not follow from this that theistic belief is irrational – that is, the truth of theistic belief is claimed to be something that is directly evident in experience, just as our everyday perceptual and memory beliefs are directly evident. [26] Before we evaluate Plantinga's argument, we should first consider how he formulates his case using the concept of a *basic* belief and the notion of *warrant*, and then consider how he understands these terms.[27]

Plantinga maintains that religious beliefs can be *basic* in the same way perceptual beliefs are basic. In order to explain how theistic beliefs are *basic*, he presents an account of faith inspired by Thomas Aquinas and John Calvin – labelled the A/C account. The A/C account proposes 'a kind of faculty or a cognitive mechanism, what Calvin calls a *sensus divinitatis* or sense of divinity, which in a wide variety of circumstances produces in us beliefs about God'.[28] Plantinga explains:

> The *sensus divinitatis* is a disposition or set of dispositions to form theistic beliefs in various circumstances, in response to the sorts of conditions or stimuli that trigger the working of this sense of divinity.[29]

The claim is that if humans have been created by God, then it is possible that there has been placed within us a cognitive faculty, or set of dispositions, capable of producing beliefs about God. This *sensus divinitatis* is capable of being stimulated by certain conditions which yield theistic beliefs. For example, the *sensus* may be triggered in an individual who contemplates the vastness of the night sky and finds within herself an overwhelming sense of the glory and power of God. Plantinga also notes that such an experience does not serve as the premise for an argument:

> It isn't that one beholds the night sky, notes that it is grand, and concludes that there must be such a person as God; an argument like that would be ridiculously weak... It is rather that upon the perception of the night sky... these beliefs just arise within us.[30]

So, belief in God, made possible by the *sensus divinitatis*, would thus count as a *basic* belief, since the belief arises non-inferentially, and does not rest on the evidential basis of other beliefs.[31] The *sensus divinitatis* can be said to resemble sense perception, since when I see a tree or hear music, the experience of seeing and hearing yield the belief that I see a tree or can hear music. I do not attempt to justify my perceptual beliefs; such beliefs are *basic*, and the experience of my five senses is enough to ground my beliefs and secure their rationality. If there is a mode of perception such as the *sensus divinitatis*, then beliefs that arise when this faculty is properly functioning must also be regarded as *basic* and *prima facie* rational.

The second key term in Plantinga's argument is the notion of warrant. According to Plantinga warrant is:

> ... that property or quality enough of which is sufficient to transform true belief into knowledge. A belief is warranted ... if it is produced by cognitive faculties functioning properly in a congenial environment according to a design plan successfully aimed at truth.[32]

So, a belief that God exists will be warranted (and thus count as knowledge) if it is produced by the *sensus divintatis* functioning properly in a congenial environment according to a design plan successfully aimed a truth. With these considerations in mind, Plantinga's overall argument can be summarised as follows:

> According to PRE [Plantinga's Reformed Epistemology], some theistic beliefs – those foundational to the theistic 'noetic framework' – will be *basic* beliefs, in the sense that they are not held through inference from other, more inferentially fundamental, warranted beliefs. And it follows from PRE's central claim that, if theistic belief is true, these basic beliefs will be *properly* basic – i.e., basic *and warranted*. Now, though these beliefs are basic it does not follow that they are *evidentially groundless*. It does follow from their status as basic that they are not evidentially grounded *by inference from other beliefs*. But they may still be evidentially grounded since they may be (non-inferentially) grounded *in the believer's experience*. That is, the believer may find their truth to be *simply evident in experience* – which is not to say that she finds them *self-evident*, but just that some of her experiences have the character that they reveal or disclose the truth of (certain) theistic beliefs.[33]

The above summary provides three important insights: (a) theistic belief can be evidentially grounded in a believers experience, as opposed to being grounded by inference from other beliefs; (b) if theistic belief is directly evident in the believers experience, then theistic belief counts as basic belief; and (c) if God exists, then it is assumed that humans have been created with a cognitive capacity that is designed to produce true beliefs about God.[34]

These three insights are also useful in linking Reformed epistemology with al-Ghazālī's epistemology. To recall, al-Ghazālī commits himself to the claim that there exists within us a prophetic faculty, much like the *sensus divinitatis*, which is capable of receiving divine illumination. He notes that through the prophetic faculty, we have access to knowledge without inference from other beliefs – hence his claim: 'anyone who believes that the unveiling of truth is the fruit of well-ordered argument is guilty of disparaging the mercy of God'. Overall, there appear to be four broad areas of agreement between al-Ghazālī's account and Plantinga's Reformed epistemology:

(1) If God exists, then it is possible that God has placed within us a faculty or disposition which is capable of causing theistic beliefs.
(2) Theistic beliefs can be basic beliefs and need not be arrived at through inference from other beliefs.
(3) Theistic beliefs, even if basic, are evidentially grounded since they are grounded in the believer's experience (e.g., an illumination event).
(4) Theistic beliefs which are basic are highly likely to be warranted if and only if theistic belief is true, and therefore qualify as knowledge.

Given these strong epistemological parallels between al-Ghazālī and Plantinga, a critique of Plantinga's epistemology will also have implications for al-Ghazālī. In the section to follow, I evaluate a recent series of objections to Plantinga's epistemology and consider their impact on al-Ghazālī's Sufi account of faith.

3.5   Evaluating reformed epistemology

In their critical assessment of Plantinga's Reformed Epistemology (PRE), John Bishop and Imran Aijaz argue that the 'PRE does not provide a categorical answer to the *de jure* question about Christian belief'.[35] When discussing this *de jure* question, Bishop and Aijaz have Christian belief in mind, but their findings are applicable to theistic belief in general. The *de jure* question about theistic belief may be framed as follows: *Are reflective theists, who give some weight to the evidentialist principle, within their rights in continuing to hold and act on their theistic beliefs?*[36] The *de jure* question with regard to theistic belief, whether it is Islamic or Christian theism, arises for:

> ... the reflective ... believer who has come to give some weight to an evidentialist claim that one should hold and act on beliefs ... only to the extent that their truth is supported by their evidence; i.e., that one is within one's rights to hold and act on Christian [or Islamic] belief only with evidential support for its truth.[37]

The *de jure* question is, in effect, a restatement of the question of entitlement with which the reflective Muslim is also concerned, i.e., can reflective Muslims be within their rights in continuing to hold and act on their beliefs under the condition of evidential ambiguity? Given that al-Ghazālī's epistemology has strong parallels to that of PRE, a proponent of al-Ghazālī may contend that the *de jure* question, which parallels the question of entitlement, can be answered as follows: belief in God is non-inferentially evident in a believer's experience and is also warranted (provided theism is true) and is thus properly basic. Moreover, if basic perceptual beliefs are warranted, then by parity, basic theistic belief may also be warranted. If this argument is correct, then the reflective Muslim does not need the Jamesian account of faith, since al-Ghazālī's epistemology provides a reply to the *de jure* question (and the question of entitlement to believe in God). Accordingly, we will need to further consider the 'parity' argument as on it turns the success of the Ghazālīan-inspired reply to the *de jure* question.

The parity argument may be better understood if we first consider the *de jure* question as it would apply to perceptual beliefs: that is, are we within our rights in continuing to hold and act on our perceptual beliefs? Bishop and Aijaz observe that perceptual beliefs are basic beliefs, not inferred from other beliefs.[38] They contend:

> We are within our rights in holding and acting on basic perceptual beliefs only because *we simply have no real choice about whether we do so or not, and we must be entitled to do what we cannot avoid doing* (ought implies can)... The *de jure* question about basic perceptual beliefs does not arise as a genuine question bearing on how we live our lives; acting confidently on their truth is 'hard-wired' in us...[39]

In response to the *de jure* question about perceptual beliefs, it is maintained that we are within our rights in holding and acting on basic perceptual beliefs, since we are hard wired to do so. Working with this insight, a proponent of PRE can argue that theistic belief is basic in the same way as perceptual belief, and we refer to this claim as the 'parity argument'. In regard to this argument, Bishop and Aijaz concede that:

> If our...believer does indeed find that taking her foundational [theistic or religious]...beliefs to be true is as practically unavoidable for her as taking basic perceptual beliefs to be true, then, we agree, she is by default epistemically entitled to those beliefs.[40]

But they question whether the antecedent condition is likely to be satisfied. There is the logical possibility that theistic belief may be basic in the same way as perceptual belief. The question that a proponent of PRE faces is whether theistic belief *actually* is basic in the same way as perceptual belief. Bishop and Aijaz formulate two arguments for the negative answer to this question:

> theistic beliefs are not taken as evident in experience by human beings generally (otherwise attempts to give reasons for our epistemic entitlement to basic theist belief would be seen as equally esoteric as the parallel attempts with respect to basic perceptual beliefs)... plenty of people who do believe in God do not take that belief to be on par with a basic perceptual belief in respect of being basically evident in experience.[41]
>
> Many... who do have religious experiences... recognise that they are choosing to interpret their experiences in a religious way when that interpretation is not unavoidable for them... Here it may be observed that all perceptual experience involves active interpretation by the mind... [but] when it comes to basic perceptual beliefs the mind's activity is both subconscious and involuntary; whereas, in the case of basic religious beliefs we may become conscious that we are placing a religious construal on our experience.[42]

Bishop and Aijaz appear to be advancing two arguments here. The first argument concerns the number of believer's who experience theistic belief as directly evident in experience in the way that basic perceptual beliefs are. Bishop and Aijaz maintain that the majority of theists do not experience their theistic beliefs in the same way as perceptual beliefs, but rather they recognise that they involve placing a certain interpretation on their experience. Their second argument elucidates this last point; unlike perceptual experiences, religious experiences involve an element of conscious interpretation.

I agree with Bishop and Aijaz that PRE is problematic, however, I do not feel that their arguments get to the nub of the problem. For example, in reply to these arguments quoted above, proponents of PRE may note that they are not committed to the claim that all theists will take theistic belief to be basically evident in experience. Their central claim is that there is the potential to experience theistic belief as being on par with perceptual beliefs. A proponent of PRE is able to concede that for perhaps the majority, religious belief involves an act of interpretation. This admission does not undercut PRE, as it is only committed to the claim that there exists the potential for individuals to experience theistic belief as basic, i.e., subconscious, involuntary and religious in nature. This criticism of PRE is also supported by Duncan Pritchard, who notes that the parity argument overstates the parallels between religious belief and perceptual beliefs. Pritchard states:

> It was noted ... that religious beliefs, like perceptual beliefs, can sometimes seem to have the same sort of 'directness' that one might find in the perceptual case, as if one were directly responding to a religious being in the way that one directly responds to objects in the physical world through perception. It was this spontaneity of perceptual belief that made it apt for a radically non-evidentialist construal since evidence seemed to play no essential warranting role as regards standard perceptual belief. *The problem, however, is that whereas this sort of 'directness' is the norm in the perceptual case, it is more naturally thought of as the exception to the norm in the religious case.*[43] (emphasis added)

The proponent of PRE can concede that for a number of believers, theistic belief may not be basic in the same way as perceptual belief is. They may also concede the disparity between perceptual belief and religious belief, since *basicality* is the norm for perceptual belief, but an exception to the norm for theistic belief. This concession in no way weakens PRE, since the parity argument was never intended to establish the *basicality* of theistic belief as the norm. The parity argument establishes the possibility that if theistic belief is experienced as a basic belief, then we would be entitled to these beliefs in the same way we are entitled to our perceptual beliefs. Bishop and Aijaz think it unlikely that theistic belief can be directly evident in experience; they also note that theists, in general, do not envision religious belief in the same way as Plantinga. We must note, however, that even if the majority of believers do not regard their beliefs as basic, the claim that religious belief can be experienced as basic remains unscathed. Bishop and Aijaz are aware their arguments may not eliminate this possibility:

> We are not, however, able to entirely exclude the possibility that, for some ... the truth of basic Christian [or Islamic] belief is as inevitably compelling as the truth of basic perceptual believe ... if there are such Christians [or Muslims], then for them the *de jure* question has an affirmative answer by default.[44]

The question we face relates to whether theistic belief can be directly evident in experience as perceptual belief. This question is difficult to answer, since if a person were to say, *Yes, for me religious belief is as compelling as perceptual belief,* there would be no way to prove that this was the case. The phenomenology of religious experience is limited to the individual's experience; unless a person is able to step into the mind of the believer, the experience is purely that of the individual. If a person says, *No, for me religious belief is not as compelling as perceptual belief,* we run into a similar difficulty. A person's experience limits their understanding of the phenomenology of a belief, and it is always possible that a person who says, *Theistic belief is basic for me* is correct – the problem is that, if we do not have such experiences ourselves, we can never step beyond our minds to know what such an experience is like. We do have access to testimony. We know that for the majority, religious belief is not held in a basic way. This should not blind us to the presence of significant figures within the tradition of theism that do confirm the experience of theistic belief as basic in nature. For example, within the tradition of Islam, there is al-Ghazālī, and given his testimony, there exist modes of perception, intimately linked with theistic belief, which are more compelling than perceptual belief.[45]

3.6   Reflections on al-Ghazālī's Sufi account

Al-Ghazālī's Sufi account of faith, in part, serves as a response to scepticism. He claims that beliefs which arise through sense perception and reason are open to doubt – on the basis of the shadow and dream argument. The problem of scepticism has added poignancy within the Islamic tradition, which, according to al-Ghazālī, affirms the supra-intellectual faculty or the prophetic faculty. Al-Ghazālī regards the prophetic faculty as being available to all human beings and argues that it would take epistemic priority over sense perception and reason. The discussion of al-Ghazālī's Sufi account has already highlighted areas of concern when the account is construed as disambiguating in favour of Islamic theism. These concerns, I argue, will also impact on PRE. An initial concern arises from al-Ghazālī's sceptical attitude toward sense perception and reason. Even if we concede that for al-Ghazālī theistic belief is basic, his account of faith remains susceptible to his sceptical arguments. For example, the dream argument attempts to decouple the feeling of certainty from the question of justifiability. When in a dream state, we have a number of experiences, e.g., seeing a fire-breathing dragon, which appears real at the time, though upon waking we realise the perceptions were illusory. Similarly, the feeling of immediacy that al-Ghazālī says is involved in an illumination event does not necessarily entail its truth. There may be other modes of perception al-Ghazālī is yet unaware of, which could show that his illumination was perhaps illusory in nature. The possibility that a person experiences theistic belief in a basic way cannot rule out the possibility of error. If, as al-Ghazālī argues, our basic beliefs can be doubted (e.g., scepticism toward our perceptual beliefs), then irrespective of how compelling a belief is to us, there always remains room for error. A proponent of PRE may note that this line of argument cannot apply to Plantinga's account, since, unlike al-Ghazālī, PRE does not endorse scepticism toward our cognitive capacities. We may, accordingly, concede that on the question of scepticism, one can draw a distinction between PRE and al-Ghazālī, although there is a deeper concern which undercuts both al-Ghazālī and PRE.

The major concern relates to the challenge of religious diversity. For example, there exist irreconcilable differences among those who may, with equal justification, claim that their religious beliefs are properly basic. For example, Plantinga is Christian, while al-Ghazālī is Muslim, now both may state that belief for them is properly basic. If there exists within both individuals a *sensus divinitatis*, or prophetic faculty, and both appeal to this faculty to explain the origin of their beliefs, then why are their beliefs in certain respects mutually incompatible? This observation suggests that belief, even if subjectively compelling, may yet be mistaken. One could imagine a meeting between al-Ghazālī and Plantinga where both agree that justified theistic belief need not require propositional evidence. The sticking point would arise when they come to discuss whether it is Islamic or Christian theism that is warranted. The fundamental concern is that the status of religious belief as basic belief does not entirely settle the *de jure* question. All is not lost; there are a number of important insights we can garner from PRE and al-Ghazālī, namely that theistic beliefs have the potential to be properly basic beliefs and need not be arrived at by inference from other beliefs, and that basic beliefs can be justified in the believer's experience.

This insight helps to partially answer the *de jure* question with regard to theistic belief. The *de jure* question takes into account *the evidentialist criterion and questions whether believers can be within their rights in continuing to hold and act on their theistic beliefs*. If theistic belief is experienced as being basic, then the *de jure* question appears, in part, to have an affirmative answer – i.e., if a person experiences theistic belief as a basic belief, then they would be entitled to that belief – in the same way as they are entitled to other basic beliefs. This is not to say that all *basic* beliefs are true, especially if we keep in mind al-Ghazālī's example of the shadow which, at first glance, appears stationary. There is the possibility that theistic belief, even if basic, may in fact be mistaken. The possibility of error is heightened when considering the diversity of religious beliefs which have been experienced as basic. Accordingly, the possibility of error and the observed diversity of basic beliefs raises the question of whether religious commitment is justified under conditions, where there appears to be evidential ambiguity.

3.7   Summary

Given our discussion and evaluation of al-Ghazālī's Sufi account, there are two significant conclusions we may draw. The first is that al-Ghazālī's Sufi account cannot be, and need not be, construed as a philosophical refutation of scepticism. His case for scepticism relies on arguments which aim to decouple the compelling nature of basic beliefs from the question of justification. The concern is that even if a supra-intellectual faculty exists, there would remain room for doubt since the compelling nature of a belief is not sufficient to establish its truth. There was also a concern that the supra-intellectual faculty may itself be caught up in a dream-like state; thus, we re-encounter the possibility for error. Moreover, there remains the possibility of a higher perceptual faculty, the supra supra-intellectual faculty, and if we concede this possibility, then the deliverances of the supra-intellectual faculty are open to doubt. We also noted earlier that the purported deliverances attributed to the supra-intellectual faculty could also be explained in naturalistic terms, and it would be presumptuous to think that Islamic theism provided the best, or the only, explanation of an illumination experience. Accordingly, al-Ghazālī's Sufi account does not adequately resolve the sceptical concerns which he raised.

The second conclusion relates to the distinction that can be drawn between the feeling of immediacy and trustworthiness, and the question of justifiability. One reason why we can decouple the feeling of immediacy from the question of justifiability is due to the challenge of scepticism, i.e., the argument from dreams suggests that the feeling of immediacy and trustworthiness can attach to a belief that is, in fact, false. A stronger reason in support of the decoupling is the fact of religious diversity, i.e., there are individuals who subscribe to epistemologies that parallel PRE, yet they adhere to mutually exclusive belief systems. Clearly, such fundamental disagreement suggests that religious ambiguity persists even if religious belief is directly evident in experience in the way that basic perceptual beliefs are.

In summary, al-Ghazālī's Sufi account is not a philosophically viable alterative to the Jamesian account. We note that al-Ghazālī's Sufi account, including PRE, serves to reinforce, not resolve, the question of entitlement to believe in God. That is, we encounter a range of individuals who experience religious belief as being evident in experience, yet the beliefs in question are at times mutually incompatible, e.g., believing that God is tri-personal, and believing that God is uni-personal. Given this diversity, the reflective individual will question whether we can be entitled to make a commitment to take such beliefs to be true. Accordingly, the reflective Muslim has good reason to think that al-Ghazālī's Sufi account cannot adequately respond to the question of entitlement. The chapter to follow will once again consider al-Ghazālī's Sufi account, but this time we will interpret his experience and narrative from the perspective of the Jamesian account. A Jamesian reading of al-Ghazali will focus on his illumination experience as involving a passional cause of belief, thus setting aside the claim that such an experience provides us with knowledge. The task of the chapter to follow will be to align al-Ghazālī's narrative and illumination experience with the Jamesian account of faith.

4
A Jamesian Reading of Al-Ghazālī

At the root of great awakening is great doubt.

– Zen Proverb

The aim of this chapter is to consider an alternative reading of al-Ghazālī's narrative and enlightenment experience. Our reason for seeking an alternative reading is motivated by the weaknesses of the Sufi account which were highlighted in the previous chapter. To recall, there were three significant deficiencies associated with al-Ghazālī's Sufi account. The first deficiency relates to the concern that al-Ghazālī's account is susceptible to the arguments which he employed against sense perception and reason; that is, there exists a supra-intellectual faculty which must be given epistemic priority. If such a mode of perception did exist, then the deliverances of sense perception and reason could be open to reinterpretation. The problem with this view was that it did not rule out a supra-supra-intellectual perceptual faculty, which, if it were to exist, would take epistemic priority. Accordingly, the deliverances of the supra-intellectual faculty, if such a faculty indeed were to exist, need not be seen as a mode of perception that is wholly immune to doubt. The second deficiency arose from al-Ghazālī's concession that the feeling of certainty can be decoupled from the truth of a belief. As a consequence, al-Ghazālī's Sufi account is also undermined, since the Sufi account is said to secure certainty. If, however, al-Ghazālī is correct, then the feeling of certainty does not guarantee that the belief, or experience, is aligned with truth. The third deficiency concerned Reformed epistemology, which closely parallels the epistemological framework of al-Ghazālī's Sufi account. Our concern related to the mutually exclusive beliefs which were associated with the frameworks in question. It would appear that a proponent of Reformed epistemology and al-Ghazālī's account could endorse the claim that theistic belief is properly basic; however, the beliefs which are purported to be properly basic turn out to be mutually exclusive, e.g. monotheism vs. Trinitarian monotheism. Accordingly, we re-encounter the phenomenon of religious diversity, and if there is no apparent way to disambiguate between the competing beliefs, then we also encounter the phenomena of religious ambiguity. The persistence of religious ambiguity is problematic, especially if al-Ghazālī's Sufi account is construed as an epistemology which is meant to disambiguate in favour of Islamic theism. In light of these deficiencies, we can maintain that al-Ghazālī's account does not provide an adequate resolution to the epistemological challenge of scepticism. There are a number of additional concerns associated with al-Ghazālī's account, especially with the demand for certainty that motivates it, and I intend to discuss these concerns later in this chapter.

There are good reasons, then, to think that al-Ghazālī's Sufi account is problematic and does not offer us a viable account of faith. A way forward can be found if we draw a distinction between al-Ghazālī's narrative and al-Ghazālī's Sufi account of faith. The Sufi account of faith can be seen as a way of interpreting al-Ghazālī's narrative. For the reasons, I have already discussed, the Sufi account is problematic; however, that is not to say that al-Ghazālī's narrative is itself problematic. In principle, al-Ghazālī's narrative is open to alternative readings, and one such reading is in accordance with the Jamesian account of faith. A Jamesian reading of al-Ghazālī's narrative will be distinct from the Sufi account for the following reasons: (a) the Jamesian account defends faith without requiring certain knowledge; thus, James's account does not link the achievement of knowledge with adequate faith commitment; (b) the account sets out a number of constraints which, if met, justify a venture of faith in the face of epistemic uncertainty; and (c) the Jamesian reading will interpret al-Ghazālī's enlightenment experience as involving a passional cause of belief.[1] I maintain that al-Ghazālī's narrative can be read in a way which satisfies the Jamesian constraints. Thus, a Jamesian reading of al-Ghazālī's narrative will reveal it as recounting a personal transformation in the face of doubt and uncertainty, as opposed to the Sufi reading which recounts a transformation in which certainty is achieved. I will argue that the Jamesian reading allows us to avoid the philosophical problems associated with al-Ghazālī's Sufi account, and I also will contend that James's account has some theological advantages over al-Ghazālī's Sufi account.

We have already noted that the reflective Muslim can, in principle, satisfy the constraints of the Jamesian account. However, there remained a concern as to whether the account could be welcomed within the tradition of Islamic theism. Accordingly, giving al-Ghazālī's narrative a Jamesian reading, if successful, will serve two important functions: (a) it will provide a reading of al-Ghazālī's narrative that is immune to the philosophical and theological weaknesses of the Sufi account, and (b) if James's account provides a viable reading of al-Ghazālī's narrative then the reflective Muslim will have good reason to think the account may have a place, and a role to play, within the tradition of Islam. Furthermore, I will also compare the Jamesian account and al-Ghazālī's Sufi account in light of an oral tradition which describes the prophet Muhammad's reported experience of divine commission. I will argue that, given the details of the oral tradition, it is the Jamesian account and not al-Ghazālī's Sufi account, which offers an adequate reading of the tradition. The final portion of this chapter will have the concerns of the reflective Muslim firmly in mind, and we will consider the degree to which the Jamesian account is aligned with the tradition of Islam.

4.1   A Jamesian reading

The Jamesian reading will attempt to align al-Ghazālī's narrative with the constraints of the Jamesian account. To recall, the central feature of al-Ghazālī's narrative is the purported experience of God casting a light into his heart. This experience, according to al-Ghazālī, helped him to overcome scepticism. Al-Ghazālī notes that his experience restored in him the ability to trust in the self-evident principles of reason. He also notes that the experience allowed him to recover his physical and mental equilibrium. Al-Ghazālī does not describe the moment or the circumstances of his experience; we are only given an insight into the effects of the experience. What we do know is that al-Ghazālī's experience resolves what is for him a profound existential crisis. The experience restored in al-Ghazālī the belief that reason is trustworthy, and this is existentially significant, since the belief also helped him recover his mental and physical health. A Jamesian reading of al-Ghazālī's narrative will aim to establish that: (a) al-Ghazālī faces a genuine option, and that he possesses a passionally caused belief which can decide the genuine option; (b) the passional cause of the belief and the associated belief is morally acceptable; and (c) the truth of the passionally caused belief in question is subject to evidential ambiguity.

With this in mind, we can now consider the first constraint of the Jamesian account which requires a genuine option. A genuine option, to recall, is a choice between two hypotheses; where the option would have to present a real possibility (living); the hypotheses in question must form a complete logical disjunction (forced); and, the option must be highly significant to the individual concerned (momentous). We can assume that in the case of al-Ghazālī the hypotheses which constitute the option are: (a) believing that the principles of reason are trustworthy, and (b) withholding belief that the principles of reasons are trustworthy. Given al-Ghazālī's narrative, the option he faces is clearly a living possibility, the hypotheses also form a complete logical disjunction, and given his existential crisis, the option is also momentous. Accordingly, al-Ghazālī's narrative suggests that he faced a genuine option, and if this reading is correct, there is the possibility that the option could be decided by a passionally caused belief. If we interpret the illumination event as involving a passional cause of belief, then we can also suggest that the belief, in question, was the belief that human reason is trustworthy. This interpretation does fit with what al-Ghazālī's tells us, namely:

> ...God the Almighty cured me of that disease and I recovered my health and mental equilibrium. The self-evident principles of reason *again* seemed acceptable; I trusted them and in them felt safe and certain. I reached this point not by well ordered or methodical argument, but by means of a light God the Almighty cast into my breast, this light is the key to most knowledge.[2]

This passage suggests that al-Ghazālī did at one point believe that the principles of reason were in fact trustworthy; however, this belief was subsequently undermined in the course of his philosophical reflections. The illumination experience had the effect of restoring the belief that human reason was indeed trustworthy. This reading, if accepted, suggests that al-Ghazālī's illumination experience motivated a belief – which can decide the genuine option we have just sketched out. Accordingly, al-Ghazālī's narrative can be seen to satisfy the first constraint of the Jamesian account.

The second constraint requires the passional cause of the belief and the belief itself to be of a morally acceptable type. We may argue that the passional cause of belief, which involves the illumination event, is existentially and morally significant. That is, in being able to trust in human reason, al-Ghazālī was able to live a life that was in accordance with reason. If his scepticism had persisted, there may have been a danger that al-Ghazālī would have abandoned the pursuit of epistemic goals, e.g., seeking truth and avoiding error. The passional cause in question is existentially significant, since it helped him to overcome his scepticism and allows him to live and think in accordance with reason, and this may be seen as morally admirable.

One might, however, argue that al-Ghazālī cannot satisfy the moral constraint, since he does not adopt a reflective stance toward his experience. Moreover, al-Ghazālī seems to interpret his experience within a Sufi epistemology, which allows him to view his experience as conferring to him a level of certainty that was beyond any doubt. An argument can then be made that al-Ghazālī's experience is not conducive to a reflective stance, and it seems that his experience subverts such a stance. Perhaps his experience had an intensity that overwhelmed any desire to take a reflective stance, i.e., the divine light acts to extinguish his critical perspective. If his experience was of such a nature, then it would run counter, not only to the moral constraint, but also to the ethos of the Jamesian account which presupposes a reflective stance with respect to our commitments and their underlying motivations.

There is a more plausible view of al-Ghazālī's experience. It is clear from al-Ghazālī's narrative that his experience itself did not overwhelm his capacity for critical reflection. The experience, according to al-Ghazālī, only helped him to trust in reason. It is only on reflection that the experience is contextualised within a Sufi framework. If this was the case, then the experience did not overwhelm his critical capacities, since he clearly sought an epistemological framework within which his experience could be explained. We could speculate on the reasons that motivated al-Ghazālī's wholehearted endorsement of the Sufi account, but the important point to note is that his stance involves a conscious choice. We may then argue that al-Ghazālī's experience did not subvert his critical capacities, rather he made a conscious choice to endorse the Sufi account. Given this reading of al-Ghazālī, we can maintain that the enlightenment experience did not subvert his critical capacities.

There is, however, another aspect of al-Ghazālī's narrative which, if true, would suggest that his experience is morally admirable. Consider the following quote from al-Ghazālī's friend, Abd al-Ghafir al-Farisi:

> I visited him many times, and it was no bare conjecture of mine that he, in spite of what I saw in him in time past of maliciousness and roughness towards people, and how he looked upon them contemptuously through his being led astray by what God had granted him of ease in word and thought and expression, and through the seeking of rank and position, had come to be the very opposite and was purified

from these stains. And I used to think that he was wrapping himself in the garment of pretence, but I realized after investigation that the thing was the opposite of what I had thought, and that the man had recovered after being mad.[3]

The quote gives us two contrasting portraits of al-Ghazālī. The first is of a man who is well respected, wealthy and deeply self-centred, while the second picture is of a man who is humble and kind. Al-Farisi speaks of the changes in al-Ghazālī as being a recovery from madness. The transformation of al-Ghazālī's character can also be seen as a change in his moral disposition. It is not clear whether the enlightenment experience was the sole event that brought about this change, but we may contend that the experience did play a significant part. The experience is reported to have restored al-Ghazālī to mental and physical health. This is significant especially if we assume that prior to this point, al-Ghazālī was deeply self-centred. Given al-Ghazālī's crisis, he would have realised that his mental and physical health could not be restored by his learning, status or wealth. These factors only seemed to compound his crisis. Importantly, the cure was experienced as a light entering his heart, that is, the cure came from a source external to him. This experience could have had a deeply humbling effect on him, since it was not something of his own making. He would have had to acknowledge that his crisis was a period of weakness, and he overcame it through seeking the assistance of others and turning ultimately to God. The cure in the form of his enlightenment experience initiated a turning away from self-centredness. If this reading is correct, then the passional cause of al-Ghazālī's belief is morally admirable.

We can argue that the passional cause of al-Ghazālī's belief is morally admirable. There are two reasons for this view: the first is that the passional cause of belief can be seen to represent a positive transition in the moral character of al-Ghazālī, and second, the passional cause in question broadens our discussion of morality, since it indicates a possible link between passional causes of belief and character traits. Importantly, what I hope to have shown is that the passional cause of al-Ghazālī's belief satisfies the moral constraint of the Jamesian account. If we recall, the moral constraint requires a passional cause of a belief to be morally acceptable, and given our discussion thus far, the passional cause in question seems morally acceptable and even admirable. In addition, the moral constraint requires the content of the passionally motivated belief to be morally acceptable. Unfortunately, al-Ghazālī does not say whether his experience motivated a belief. However, we may contend that his experience motivated the belief that the principles of reason were trustworthy; hence, his ability to trust in reason. If this is the case, we then need to consider whether the passionally caused belief has morally acceptable content. For current purposes, the belief in question is the belief that human reason is trustworthy, and given that such a belief is widely taken for granted, I do not anticipate that such a belief would be accused of being morally deficient. Thus, the moral acceptability of such a belief is uncontroversial.

The view just outlined can be concerning, since the uncontroversial nature of the belief may also be taken to indicate that the truth of the belief is not evidentially ambiguous. One may argue that if the belief were evidentially ambiguous, then there would be widespread disagreement over this belief, and since there is a lack of disagreement, the belief is therefore not evidentially ambiguous. This argument, if successful, would rule out satisfying the third constraint of the Jamesian account, i.e., that the truth of the belief in question cannot be resolved on evidential grounds. In reply, we can argue that believing in the trustworthiness of reason is not necessarily the result of having reflected on evidence. The belief can be motivated by factors such as social and cultural upbringing. If, however, a decision were to be made to evaluate the belief on evidential grounds, then we quickly get caught in an epistemic circle. That is, the process of evaluating whether believing in the trustworthiness of reason is justified presupposes the use of reason. Such an approach will involve assuming the very thing we are seeking to evaluate. It is difficult to think of an evaluative process that does not involve the use of reason. The threat of being caught up in an epistemic circle is also a good reason to think that the truth of the belief cannot be decided on purely evidential grounds. This view, I suggest, is consistent with the claim that believing in the trustworthiness of reason is subject to evidential ambiguity, thus we are in a position to satisfy the third and final constraint of James's account.

In light of the above discussion, we can claim the following: (a) al-Ghazālī faces a genuine option concerning the trustworthiness of human reason; (b) the belief in the trustworthiness of human reason is subject to evidential ambiguity; (c) the illumination experience can be interpreted as involving a passional cause of the belief that reason was worthy of trust; (d) the belief decides the genuine option in question; and (e) the illumination experience and the associated belief are not morally objectionable. The reflective Muslim may, at this point, acknowledge that al-Ghazālī's narrative can satisfy the constraints of the

Jamesian account. They may note, however, that it remains to be seen whether this new reading is true to al-Ghazālī's narrative and whether it is a better reading than the Sufi account. The section to follow will aim to address these concerns.

4.2 Evaluating the Jamesian reading

We now need to evaluate the viability of the Jamesian reading, and we will do this in light of the following considerations: (a) deciding whether the Jamesian reading is 'true' to al-Ghazālī's narrative; (b) considering whether the Jamesian reading is susceptible to the weaknesses that were associated with the Sufi account; and (c) evaluating the standing that al-Ghazālī's Sufi account and the Jamesian reading have with reference to the ethos of Islamic theism.

The first consideration relates to whether the Jamesian reading is consistent with al-Ghazālī's narrative. There are two contestable claims which underpin the Jamesian reading: the claim that al-Ghazālī's enlightenment experience involves a passional cause of a belief, and the claim that the trustworthiness of human reason is subject to evidential ambiguity. Al-Ghazālī does not explicitly say whether his experience was the cause of a belief, and neither does he explicitly affirm any type of ambiguity thesis with regard to the trustworthiness of human reason. One may then argue that since al-Ghazālī does not explicitly endorse these claims, the Jamesian reading is not viable. We may challenge this line of thought by arguing that the two claims are consistent with al-Ghazālī's narrative. That is, even though the claims are not explicitly endorsed by al-Ghazālī, they are consistent with his narrative. For example, al-Ghazālī's enlightenment experience allowed him to trust in human reason, and this is consistent with the view that the experience motivated the belief that reason is trustworthy. Similarly, al-Ghazālī notes that it was not reason and argument which brought about his enlightenment; now, such a view is consistent with a type of ambiguity thesis, since al-Ghazālī acknowledges that his sceptical crisis could not be resolved on intellectual grounds. Accordingly, we can concede that while al-Ghazālī does not explicitly endorse the claims discussed, it would not follow from this that the Jamesian reading is inconsistent with his narrative. We can thus set aside the concern that the Jamesian reading is not viable, since it involves assumptions that are not explicitly endorsed in al-Ghazālī's narrative.

The second consideration relates to whether the Jamesian reading is susceptible to the weaknesses of al-Ghazālī's Sufi account. One major concern with al-Ghazālī's Sufi account stemmed from his case for scepticism in which he aimed to decouple the feeling of certainty from any truth claim. I argued that such a claim would rule out any epistemology that linked the experience of certainty with the truth of a belief. This is problematic, since al-Ghazālī's central claim is that he came to know the truth through an experience which gave him certainty. Even if we are charitable and set aside the sceptical concerns of al-Ghazālī, there remains the issue of religious diversity. I used Plantinga as a case in point, and I argued that Plantinga has developed an epistemology very similar to that proposed by al-Ghazālī. The problem is that Plantinga and al-Ghazālī claim that theistic belief can be properly basic, yet the beliefs they endorse are at times mutually exclusive. This helps to reinforce the view that the experience of certainty cannot be proof that the belief in question is aligned with truth. Given these concerns, we may then question whether the Jamesian reading of al-Ghazālī fares any better. The issue which needs to be considered is whether the Jamesian reading can succeed as an interpretation of the resolution of al-Ghazālī's crisis, while also accommodating the concerns raised by scepticism and religious diversity. To recall, al-Ghazālī's case for a Sufi account is motivated by his inability to intellectually overcome scepticism; accordingly, we may question whether a Jamesian reading can be of help. If we concede that al-Ghazālī's belief in the trustworthiness of reason is a passionally caused belief, then we can speak of a passionally caused belief in the trustworthiness of reason as deciding a genuine option. The Jamesian reading does not eliminate the epistemic concerns raised by scepticism, and neither does it yield the epistemic certainty which al-Ghazālī so desperately sought;[4] instead, it gives al-Ghazālī an entitlement to act. That is, on the Jamesian account, al-Ghazālī would be entitled to act on the belief that human reason is worthy of trust even if he did not possess epistemic certainty. The Jamesian account explains the resolution as pertaining to the level of practical commitment. This resolution involves understanding the illumination experience as strengthening al-Ghazālī's will so that he could take the belief to be true in his practical reasoning. A proponent of al-Ghazālī's view may note that the Jamesian reading it is not the kind of explanation that would have satisfied al-Ghazālī. The problem is that the Jamesian account lacks the epistemic certainty which al-Ghazālī regards as an absolute requirement. This concern seems justified given al-Ghazālī's narrative; however, the requirement for certainty is deeply problematic. (I plan to elaborate on this point shortly.)

The third consideration concerns the standing that al-Ghazālī's Sufi account and the Jamesian reading have with reference to the ethos of Islamic theism. One area of concern associated with the Jamesian reading relates to the concept of a passional cause of belief. The concern is that the concept of a passionally caused belief has not been explicitly endorsed or identified within the intellectual tradition of Islam. It may then be argued that the concept of a passionally caused belief does not fit comfortably with the tradition of Islam. In reply, we may appeal to al-Ghazālī's view of divine mercy. According to al-Ghazālī, God, in his mercy, has made available a number of mechanisms through which truth can be grasped. This variety of mechanisms allows for a number of pathways through which truth is made available. If passional causes of belief are seen as mechanisms through which divine mercy can act, then such causes can be accommodated within the tradition of Islam. The link between passionally caused belief and divine mercy also suggests the possibility for an epistemological framework not unlike al-Ghazālī's Sufi epistemology. If passional causes of belief are a divinely sanctioned pathway to truth, then the passionally caused belief will be veridical. We need to be cautious, since the believer who gives weight to the thesis of religious ambiguity will likely question whether a passionally caused theistic belief is in fact veridical. If we accept the ambiguity thesis, then there is only *the possibility* that such a belief is veridical, but for now it remains an open question, which may be settled only at the level of practical commitment. Thus, we need not view the concept of a passionally caused belief as being foreign to the tradition of Islam; rather, if what al-Ghazālī says about divine mercy is true, then passionally caused beliefs do have a place within the tradition. Significantly, the concession that passionally caused beliefs can have a place within the tradition also threatens to undermine al-Ghazālī's demand for certainty. Once we acknowledge that there is a place for passionally caused beliefs within the tradition of Islam, then we will also have to allow room for doubt. This is not to say that a passionally caused belief is false, rather, the truth of the belief remains an open question. The decision of how to respond to the belief is left to the subject. We may then argue that if al-Ghazālī's view of divine mercy allows for passionally caused beliefs, then al-Ghazālī's demand for certainty is inconsistent with his view of divine mercy.

There are two further ways in which the demand for certainty can be seen to be inconsistent with al-Ghazālī's own understanding of Islamic theism. As part of his study of al-Ghazālī's criteria for knowledge, Imran

Aijaz argues that the criteria express expectations that are unreasonable. Aijaz's assessment is insightful and worth quoting at length:

> One of the requirements of al-Ghazālī's criteria for knowledge is that our beliefs must be infallibly justified in order for them to constitute knowledge. But, given our cognitive limitations as finite and fallible human creatures, such a demand is unreasonable. It is unreasonable not only because of our finitude, but also because it appears to elevate the powers of human cognition to the same level as those of the Divine mind. Indeed, al-Ghazālī himself... recognises important differences between Divine and human cognition... God's knowledge he writes, is 'the most perfect possible, with respect to its clarity and its disclosure'. But, he says 'man's disclosure, while clear, does not reach beyond the goal beyond which no goal is possible; rather his seeing of things is like seeing them behind a thin veil'. Given this disparity... it seems more reasonable to maintain that out beliefs are, or have to be, fallibly justified rather than infallibly justified.[5]

We can identify two arguments from the above quote; the first relates to al-Ghazālī's expectations as being unreasonable in light of the finite and fallible nature of human cognition; and the second relates to the inconsistency between al-Ghazālī's expectations and his theological views on the finite and fallible nature of human knowledge.

In addition to the challenges raised by Aijaz, there is a concern that the demand for certainty runs the risk of cognitive idolatry. Paul Moser explains that cognitive idolatry involves imposing a cognitive standard 'whether empiricist, deductivist, rationalist, or some hybrid' to which we expect God to conform.[6] The problem with cognitive idolatry is that 'we seek to control the terms for knowing God's reality in a way that devalues God's preeminent authority'.[7] Moser's argument also has resonance with the tradition of Islamic theism which also seeks to guard against idolatry. We may argue that the demand for certainty risks being a form of cognitive idolatry; that is, the demand imposes a cognitive standard to which divine reality is expected to conform.

There are then two main considerations which undermine the reasonableness of al-Ghazālī's demand for certainty: the first is that the demand runs counter to his view of human cognition; and secondly, the demand runs the risk of cognitive idolatry. These considerations also challenge the cogency of al-Ghazālī's Sufi account; that is, if it is unreasonable to demand certainty, then the mechanism that purportedly makes this possible must also be regarded with an equal degree of suspicion.

I believe, however, that the Jamesian reading is in a better position than al-Ghazālī's Sufi account. The main reason why the Jamesian reading is better placed is due to it being immune to the challenges faced by al-Ghazālī's Sufi reading. If the Jamesian reading were to be adopted then there would be no demand for certainty; accordingly, al-Ghazālī's narrative would no longer be inconsistent with his understanding of divine mercy and human cognition. Furthermore, once we resist the demand for certainty, al-Ghazālī's narrative would no longer run the risk of cognitive idolatry. In addition, there are a number of virtues explicitly associated with a Jamesian reading that make it a more admirable reading. For example, the Jamesian account and the associated reading require an attitude of humility, an acknowledgement of fallibility, and a significant degree of empathy. Humility is prompted by the realisation that one has not grasped the whole truth and that one's beliefs are corrigible.[8] Similarly, fallibility is prompted by an acknowledgement that one does not have epistemic certainty, and that one's venture involves taking a risk. The feeling of empathy is prompted by the recognition that others are also taking a risk. These qualities are also valued within the tradition of Islamic theism, and the Jamesian account can be seen to be admirable, since it is so closely linked with these qualities.[9] The Jamesian reading of al-Ghazālī has the effect of shifting attention away from the deeply problematic demand for certainty and instead directs attention toward morally admirable character traits.

In light of the preceding discussion, we can maintain that the viability of al-Ghazālī's Sufi account is undermined by a number of philosophically and theologically inspired considerations. On the other hand, the Jamesian reading proves to be a more viable reading of al-Ghazālī's narrative, and there are five reasons for this: (a) the Jamesian reading provides a practical resolution to al-Ghazālī's sceptical crisis; (b) the reading does not aim to achieve epistemic certainty and thus avoids the inconsistencies that are associated with the demand for certainty; (c) it is not susceptible to the charge of cognitive idolatry; (d) it is a reading that is closely associated with a set of qualities and character traits that are morally admirable; and (e) the reading brings to light character traits that are central to the tradition of Islamic theism. These reasons, I suggest, strongly favour the view that the Jamesian reading is viable and preferable. Accordingly, al-Ghazālī's enlightenment experience need not be interpreted as a transformation that is made possible through the achievement of epistemic certainty; rather, we may interpret the event as involving a transformation and strengthening of his will in the face of epistemic uncertainty.[10] The idea of a personal transformation in the face of epistemic uncertainty is also an important theme in the life of Muhammad – the prophet of Islam. In the section to follow, I argue that Muhammad's experience of divine commission can add further weight to the Jamesian account of faith.

4.3 Doubt and personal transformation

Al-Ghazālī's Sufi account of faith seeks a transformation of a person's will through the achievement of epistemic certainty. The Jamesian account, on the other hand, allows for a personal transformation in the face of uncertainty. The theme of personal transformation in the face of uncertainty, as I shall argue, is evident in the life of Muhammad. The event which dramatically brings out this theme reportedly occurs as Muhammad is engaged in a prolonged period of meditation. According to a number of oral traditions, it is reported that Muhammad would regularly retreat to the seclusion of a cave in the mountains surrounding Mecca. On one particular retreat, Muhammad is said to have had an experience which deeply unsettled him. It is reported that while he was in the cave, a divine agent in the form of an angel approached him and asked him to read:

> The Prophet replied, 'I do not know how to read [recite]'. The Prophet added, 'The angel caught me (forcefully) and pressed me so hard that I could not bear it any more ... There upon he caught me for the third time and pressed me, and then released me and said, 'Read in the name of your Lord, who has created (all that exists) [and] has created man from a clot. Read! And your Lord is the Most Generous'. Then Allah's Apostle returned with the Inspiration and with his heart beating severely. Then he went to [his wife] Khadija and said, 'Cover me! Cover me!' They covered him till his fear was over and after that he told her everything that had happened and said, 'I fear that something may happen to me'. Khadija replied, 'Never! By Allah, Allah will never disgrace you. You keep good relations with your kith and kin, help the poor and the destitute, serve your guests generously and assist the deserving calamity-afflicted ones'. Khadija then accompanied him to her cousin Waraqa bin Naufal bin Asad bin 'Abdul 'Uzza, who, during the Pre-Islamic Period became a Christian and used to write with Hebrew letters. He would write from the

Gospel in Hebrew as much as Allah wished him to write. He was an old man and had lost his eyesight. Khadija said to Waraqa, 'Listen to the story of your nephew, O my cousin!' Waraqa asked, 'O my nephew! What have you seen?' Allah's Apostle described whatever he had seen. Waraqa said, 'This is the same one who keeps the secrets (angel Gabriel) whom Allah had sent to Moses. I wish I were young and could live up to the time when your people would turn you out'. Allah's Apostle asked, 'Will they drive me out?' Waraqa replied in the affirmative and said, 'Anyone (man) who came with something similar to what you have brought was treated with hostility; and if I should remain alive till the day when you will be turned out then I would support you strongly'.[11]

The report cited above proves to be of interest for two reasons: the first is that Muhammad is in fear of being injured by a divine agent; and the second is Khadija's and Waraqa's reassuring responses. Muhammad's initial reaction suggests that he sensed danger, hence his concern that something bad may happen to him. His wife Khadija, however, expresses confidence in his character and in the goodness of God; she reassures Muhammad that he is a good person and that God would not disgrace a good person. Similarly, Waraqa expresses confidence in the experience of Muhammad as being in accordance with the experience of biblical prophets. The tradition in question indicates Muhammad's willingness to obey the divine commission; however, he is also concerned as to whether he can trust God to safeguard his well-being.[12] Thus, the experience can be seen to motivate two competing hypotheses: (a) to obey the divine commission with confidence and trust in God, or (b) to obey the divine commission without explicitly having confidence or trust in God. These hypotheses can be seen to present a forced option as they constitute a logical disjunction. The hypotheses in question also present themselves as a live option in that both hypotheses would have been living possibilities in the mind of Muhammad. Furthermore, the option, from Muhammad's perspective, is also momentous, since the hypotheses are seen to be highly significant to his life. If we take into account Khadija's response, then the experience cannot be dismissed for fear of moral or cognitive deficiency in the person of Muhammad. This reading of Muhammad's experience suggests that he faced a genuine option that did not seem resolvable on the basis of purely evidential considerations. Muhammad would eventually resolve to trust in God and not see the experience as being a sign of danger. The reading I have offered satisfies the constraints of Jamesian account without, I hope, distorting the details of tradition in question. Let us now consider the tradition from the perspective of al-Ghazālī's Sufi account.

The Sufi account seeks epistemic certainty through a perceptual experience of the divine, and the tradition cited above presents Muhammad's experience as a perceptual experience. In spite of the experience being perceptual in nature, Muhammad does not achieve epistemic certainty; rather, Muhammad's response is heavily tinged with fear and uncertainty. Fear and uncertainty seem inimical to the ethos of al-Ghazālī's account; accordingly, his Sufi account could not apply to this experience, since the experience is not accompanied by epistemic certainty. However, the experience, as I have endeavoured to show, easily satisfies the constraints of the Jamesian account. We may then maintain that unlike al-Ghazālī's account, James's account provides a viable reading of a defining moment in the life of Muhammad; and in the mind of the reflective Muslim this would count in favour of the Jamesian account. The reflective Muslim may then concede that with reference to the tradition cited above, the Jamesian account has a distinct advantage over al-Ghazālī's Sufi account.

I noted earlier that the Jamesian reading of al-Ghazālī provided a reading of al-Ghazālī's narrative that was philosophically and theologically more viable than that provided by the Sufi account. The Jamesian reading of al-Ghazālī can also provide the reflective Muslim with a reason to think that James's account can have a role to play within the tradition of Islamic thought. Our case for James's account is further strengthened by a Jamesian reading of Muhammad's reaction to his encounter with a divine agent. The experience of Muhammad, as related by the tradition in question, lent itself to an interpretation that easily satisfied the constraints of the Jamesian account, as opposed to the Sufi account. Accordingly, the reflective Muslim is provided with an additional reason to think that James's account has a role to play within the tradition of Islamic thought. The reflective Muslim may agree that the Jamesian account provides us with a philosophically and theologically viable reading of al-Ghazālī's narrative and Muhammad's experience of divine commission.

The reflective Muslim may, however, note that their primary concern is whether the Jamesian account can offer a viable response to the question of entitlement which is consistent with the tradition of Islam. To recall, the question of entitlement can be stated as follows, i.e., would a person who believes that God exists be entitled to hold and act on their belief if they also concede that the evidence leaves open the question of God's existence? I have already argued that if we meet the constraints of the Jamesian account, then we are entitled to make a venture of faith while assuming the truth of religious ambiguity. A reflective Muslim, in principle, is also capable of satisfying the Jamesian constraints, thus: (a) belief in God is a live hypothesis (given that a person who is brought up with the tradition of Islam will likely believe in God); (b) the option is forced – the reflective Muslim faces a choice whether they want to continue to live in accordance with their belief in God or not; and (c) the option is also momentous, as it turns on whether they will fulfil a major requirement for living as a Muslim and being part of the Muslim *ummah* or community. The final requirement, which I believe can be fulfilled, is that the kind of God a Muslim believes in, and the passional cause which motivates belief in God can be morally worthy. If a reflective Muslim satisfies the Jamesian constraints, then they will be entitled to a venture of faith, thus resolving the question of entitlement that the reflective Muslim poses. The reflective Muslim may concede that they satisfy James's constraints, although they may harbour doubts about the assumption of religious ambiguity and the religious pluralism that is implicit in the account. I articulate and evaluate these concerns in the section to follow.

4.4 Pluralism and ambiguity

A Muslim, reflective or otherwise, can rightly question whether the ambiguity thesis and the pluralism that is associated with the Jamesian account are consistent with the tradition of Islamic theism. The thesis of religious ambiguity holds that the total relevant evidence shows belief in God to be neither true nor false. This assumption, as I have noted, is open to question, accordingly the reflective Muslim is likely to question whether the assumption is consistent with the ethos of Islamic theism. Similarly, there will be a concern with the pluralistic nature of the Jamesian account. The concern is that the constraints of James's account can, in principle, be satisfied by a reflective Christian, Jew or atheist. Thus, a reflective Muslim who endorses the Jamesian account must also be prepared to commit themselves to a form of religious pluralism; that is, they will have to acknowledge that the Jamesian account does not preclude entitlements that are aligned with Christianity, Judaism or atheism. The Jamesian account allows for a diverse range of entitlements, since its constraints are capable of being satisfied by reflective individuals from a variety of theistic and non-theistic traditions. Accordingly, the reflective Muslim is likely to question whether the pluralism associated with the Jamesian account is consistent with the tradition of Islamic theism. There will be a number of Muslims who will think that the pluralism implicit in James's account is inconsistent with the tradition of Islam, and they may, in the words of Tim Winter, observe that:

> Muslim theologians have almost invariably read their revelation as a frankly supersessionist event, proclaiming that abrogation (*naskh*) of prior religion by the Prophet's faith. Rooted in an original context of polemic against entrenched Arab idolatry, and later ... against local representatives of Judaism and Christianity, the Quran and the *hadith* seem not merely to *describe* all of these faiths, but to *argue* against them.[13]

The concerned Muslim may argue that the standard view of Islam seems to indicate a commitment to an exclusivist stance which denies entitlement to faith commitments other than Islam. This view, if true, would suggest that James's account is inconsistent with Islamic theism. There is, however, an alternative view to that offered by Winter. According to Abdulaziz Sachedina, 'Islamic revelation found expression in a world of religious pluralism, a world which it acknowledged and evaluated critically but never rejected as false'.[14] We note that the two views agree that the Islamic revelation did engage with other faith traditions, although the nature of this engagement is described very differently. If we accept Winter's construal, then Islamic revelation is seen to engage with other traditions so as to oppose them. On the other hand, if we accept Sachedina's construal, then Islamic revelation is seen merely to engage in critical dialogue, and if true, this view seems compatible with a spirit of collegiality and ecumenism. We are then confronted with two very different views of how Islamic revelation engages with other religious traditions. The challenge is to find a way to arbitrate between these two views of Islam.

One way in which we can arbitrate between the competing views is if we can identify a scholarly consensus in favour of one of the views in question. The appeal to scholarly consensus can be viewed as problematic, since it is viewed as an appeal to authority. There is a concern that not every appeal to authority is legitimate, and that an appeal to authority is legitimate only if the authority is a genuine authority in the area in question, and that there is an agreement among authorities.[15] If I am to appeal to scholarly consensus, then I will have to show that the individuals in question are authorities in the field of Islamic Studies and that there is an agreement among the authorities in question. I believe that both conditions of a legitimate appeal to authority can be met, and that there currently exists a scholarly consensus in favour of an ecumenical reading of the tradition of Islam. The consensus has come to light in a document entitled *A Common Word between Us and You*.[16] This document was originally signed by 138 individuals from across the Muslim world, and the majority of signatories are specialists in the field of Islamic studies.[17] The document is written as an open letter to leaders of Christian churches, although it message is also applicable to Jewish leaders as well. There are three aspects of this document which are relevant to my argument in this chapter.

The first aspect relates to the document's acknowledgment that Islam and Christianity have two principles in common, i.e., love of the One God, and love of the neighbour. Readers are then advised that 'justice and freedom of religion are a crucial part of love of the neighbour'.[18] This is further emphasised by the observations that the 'necessity for love of fellow human beings (and thus justice), underlie all true religion'.[19] If freedom of religion and love of fellow human beings are integral parts of Islam, then Islamic theism can be said to acknowledge and tolerate religious diversity. The tolerance that is expressed toward others would have to be in accordance with being prepared to love the other. The principles of freedom and love allow for a person to make their own choices about their religious commitments, and they oblige Muslims to respect and love a person, even though the person may choose not to be a Muslim.

The second relevant aspect of this document emerges from the declaration 'that Muslims, Christians and Jews should be free to each follow what God commanded them'.[20] Muslims, Christians and Jews are also urged not to use the differences between them in order to cause hatred and strife; rather, each community is advised to 'vie with each other only in righteousness and good works'.[21] This view of Christians and Jews serves to undercut the view that Islamic revelation wholly abrogates previous revelations and therefore supersedes Judaism and Christianity. A person may argue that Christians and Jews are unable to follow what God has commanded them, since what was revealed to them has been lost or corrupted. If a person chose to pursue this strategy then they would have the unenviable task of having to prove that the Christian and Jewish revelations have been lost or corrupted. Furthermore, they would also have to provide arguments that prove the Islamic revelation to be solely authentic and uncorrupted.

The third feature of the document which is relevant relates to the concept of faith. A person, according to the document, is described by the Quran as having three main faculties 'the mind or the intelligence, which is made for comprehending the truth; the will which is made for freedom of choice, and sentiment which is made for loving the good and the beautiful'.[22] And through these faculties a person 'knows through *understanding* the truth, through *willing* the good, and through virtuous emotions and *feeling* love for God'.[23] If a person engages these three faculties, 'the faculties of knowledge, will, and love', they 'may come to be purified and attain ultimate success'.[24] These three faculties, I believe, allow us to broadly connect Islamic theism with James's account of faith. The three faculties in question allow a person to understand, to will and to feel, and the Jamesian account presupposes the use of each of these faculties. A person who endorses James's account will need to be prepared to exercise their mind so as to decide whether the option in question can be decided on intellectual grounds; they also need to be prepared to exercise their will so as to make a choice, and they must also be prepared to respond to the promptings of their passional nature. Accordingly, the faculties which have been identified by the Common Word document as being intrinsic to faith are also the faculties which are central to the Jamesian account.[25]

There are two claims which emerge from the above discussion: (a) a significant number of contemporary scholars of Islam view the tradition of Islam as being consistent with a form of pluralism which accepts that Christianity and Judaism can be aligned with truth, and (b) the Jamesian account of faith is broadly consistent with an understanding of faith that is endorsed by contemporary scholars of Islam. We should note there are also two areas in which the Common Word document does not, as yet, fit comfortably with the Jamesian account. The first area relates to the degree of pluralism that is permitted by the Common Word document and the Jamesian account. The document can be interpreted as advocating a form of social pluralism which encourages Muslims to live in harmony with Christians and Jews. This form of social pluralism is distinct from the claim that Judaism and Christianity are on an epistemic par with the tradition of Islamic theism. The concern is that the Common Word is only a call for Christians, Jews and Muslims to live peacefully. Thus, the document can be seen only to endorse social pluralism and not to acknowledge that Christianity and Judaism are in fact aligned with truth. On the other hand, leaving open the question of whether religious beliefs are aligned with truth need not be viewed as problematic, since it is a concern which has been raised and continues to be thought about within the traditions of Christianity and Judaism.

There is also a concern that a person who endorses the Jamesian account is committed to a form of pluralism that allows for entitlements which are not only theistic but also atheistic in nature, but the form of pluralism endorsed by the Common Word document is open only to Judaism and Christianity. This concern, I believe, can be addressed with reference to the principle of 'the freedom of religion' which is endorsed by the Common Word document. The freedom of religion, in its broadest sense, would apply not only to Islam, Judaism and Christianity, but also to a person who chose to be an atheist. One can also argue that the Common Word document is representative of a sea-change among Muslim scholars toward a pluralist reading of Islam. The sea-change toward pluralism is not limited to the view of Muslim scholars but is also occurring among everyday Muslims, as Abdullah Saeed observes:

> It seems that, with the exception of a vocal group of militants, ultra-conservatives and some extremists, a large number of Muslims throughout the Muslim world are moving away from the notion of an enforced religion to one of the profession of a religion as a covenant between an individual and God. This is close to the Quranic idea of non-coercion in matters of faith and religion...Unlike the pre-modern period in which 'non-coercion in religion' was considered to have been 'abrogated', the modern view that is emerging now among Muslims is that non-coercion remains a fundamental principle of Islam and that Islam guarantees religious freedom to all.[26]

If the movement toward pluralism continues, and Muslims continue moving toward a view of Islam as guaranteeing religious freedom to all, then the door is very much open to the kind of pluralism that is associated with James's account.

The second area in which there is potential for disagreement between James's account and the Common Word document is in relation to the ambiguity thesis. There is room within the tradition of Islam, I believe, for the ambiguity thesis. This view can be defended with reference to the opening verses from the second chapter of the Quran: 'This divine writ – let there be no doubt about it – is [meant to be] a guidance for all the God-conscious who believe in [the existence of] that which is beyond the reach of human perception (*al-ghayb*)'.[27] The term *al-ghayb* is used in the Quran in order to refer to 'what is hidden, inaccessible to the senses and to reason – thus, at the same time absent from human knowledge and hidden in divine wisdom'.[28] In his commentary on the term *al-ghayb*, Ibn Kathir notes that faith in *al-ghayb* includes belief in God.[29] This is also confirmed by Asad, who writes that *al-ghayb* is used in the Quran to denote all those sectors or phases of reality which lie beyond the range of human perception, including belief in the existence of God.[30] When *al-ghayb* is taken to refer to matters which are inaccessible to sense perception and to human reason, we may then argue that believing in *al-ghayb* entails believing in something that is beyond the reach of human perception and/or human reason. Once we recognise that belief in the existence God is also an instance of belief in *al-ghayb* then, it can be argued, belief in God involves believing beyond what can be established by sense perception and reason. If the exegesis I have offered is accepted, then the ambiguity thesis is not inconsistent with Islamic theism, since the ambiguity thesis, much like the doctrine of *al-ghayb*, entails that the question of God's existence cannot be settled with reference to either sense perception or through the exercise of reason.[31]

So, it seems that concerns regarding the consistency of James's account with Islamic theism can be laid to rest (for the time being at least). Given my arguments in this section, I believe that, in principle, the ambiguity thesis and the pluralism that is associated with it are not incompatible with the tradition of Islamic theism.

4.5 Summary

The aim of this chapter was to offer a Jamesian interpretation of al-Ghazālī's enlightenment experience. I have argued that the Jamesian reading provides an interpretation that is philosophically and theologically more viable than al-Ghazālī's Sufi account. The Jamesian reading of al-Ghazālī also provides the reflective Muslim with good reasons to think that James's account can have a significant role to play within the tradition of Islamic theism. This view was further reinforced by a successful application of the Jamesian account to Muhammad's experience of divine commission. We also addressed the question of whether a reflective Muslim can be entitled to believe in God, given the assumption of religious ambiguity. This question, I argued, can be resolved with an appeal to the Jamesian account. Nevertheless, there were also concerns as to whether the Jamesian account is consistent with the ethos of Islamic theism, in particular, the concerns related to the religious pluralism and the ambiguity thesis that are associated with James's account. I argued that the concerns raised did not undermine the theological viability of James's account, and that religious pluralism and the ambiguity thesis are not inconsistent with the ethos of Islamic theism.

There are then three main claims that have been argued for in this chapter: (a) James's account provides an interpretation of al-Ghazālī that is philosophically and theologically more viable than al-Ghazālī's Sufi account; (b) that the account can be successfully applied to Muhammad's experience of divine commission; and (c) that it provides a resolution to the question of entitlement to believe in God that is consistent with ethos of Islamic theism. If these claims are endorsed by the reflective Muslim, then the Jamesian account can be seen to have a definitive role to play within the tradition of Islamic theism. Once the reflective Muslim endorses the Jamesian account, they also need to be aware that there remain a number of challenges which need to be considered. The chapters to follow will consider two specific challenges. First, I consider a contemporary defence of evidentialism which maintains that believing beyond the evidence cannot be justified, since it violates the very concept of belief. Second, I evaluate a form of religious exclusivism that commits its proponents to the view that those who hold faith commitments other than their own are cognitively impaired. These challenges need to be carefully considered, since a proponent of James's account is committed to the view that believing beyond the evidence can, in certain circumstances, be justified. Furthermore, a proponent of James's account is committed to the ambiguity thesis, and this assumption, if true, rules out an appeal to epistemic impairment as an adequate explanation of religious diversity. The chapters that follow aim to defend the Jamesian account by critically engaging the challenges outlined.

5
The Challenge of Contemporary Evidentialism

> I do not feel obligated to believe that the same God who has endowed us with sense, reason and intellect has intended us to forgo their use.
>
> – Galileo Galilei

The reflective Muslim, I maintain, is capable of satisfying the constraints associated with the Jamesian account of faith. That is, if the reflective Muslim has a passionally caused belief in the existence of God that decides a genuine option, and if the passional cause of the belief and its contents are morally acceptable, then believing beyond the evidence seems justified. There are also good reasons to think that the Jamesian account can be welcomed within the tradition of Islamic theism. Firstly, the Jamesian account allows us to interpret al-Ghazālī's resolution of his crisis in a way that is philosophically and theologically viable. To recall, al-Ghazālī's account of faith focuses on achieving certainty; however, the demand for certainty, we observed, ran counter to his acceptance of the limitations of human cognition and also ran the risk of cognitive idolatry. A Jamesian reading of al-Ghazālī's resolution involves shifting our focus away from the demand for certainty. The Jamesian reading interprets al-Ghazālī's illumination experience as involving a passional cause of belief, and it is the passionally caused belief which helps resolve the question of whether human reason is trustworthy. This interpretation can also be seen as providing a reading of al-Ghazālī's resolution of scepticism. The resolution is not predicated on the achievement of certainty, or the elimination of doubt; rather, it is a resolution at the level of practical commitment. That is, al-Ghazālī would be entitled to act on the belief that human reason is worthy of trust, but the entitlement is in no way contingent on the achievement of epistemic certainty. Thus a Jamesian reading of al-Ghazālī's resolution provides us with an interpretation that is philosophically and theologically viable. Accordingly, the reflective Muslim has good reason to think that the Jamesian account can have a role to play within the intellectual tradition of Islam. The second reason the reflective Muslim may welcome the Jamesian account relates to Muhammad's reported experience of divine commission. At face value, Muhammad's response to the encounter with the divine agent seems to satisfy the constraints of the Jamesian account. Muhammad has to decide whether he will obey God with confidence and trust. The choice not to obey is not a possibility that Muhammad takes seriously. Importantly, this choice, presented by the reported encounter with the divine agent, does not seem to be decidable on the basis of evidential considerations. This is reflected in Muhammad's dialogue with his wife soon after his encounter, i.e., his state of mind is one of doubt. Thus, Muhammad's reported experience of accepting the divine commission is interpretable within the framework of James's account of faith. The viability of the Jamesian reading of this commissioning event is the second reason why the reflective Muslim may think that James's account can have a significant role to play within the tradition of Islam. The third reason for welcoming the Jamesian account is due to the *prima facie* compatibility which the ambiguity thesis and the pluralist ethos have with the tradition of Islam.

There are, then, good reasons for the reflective Muslim to welcome and endorse the Jamesian account within the tradition of Islamic theism. I noted earlier that even if we concede the philosophical and theological viability of James's account, there remain a number of challenges that require ongoing consideration. The aim of this chapter is to consider one such challenge, and that is the challenge of contemporary evidentialism. If we recall, the case for the philosophical viability of James's account involved an engagement with Cliffordian evidentialism. Clifford maintained that it is always wrong to believe on insufficient evidence. In reply, James presented a number of arguments which aimed to show that Clifford's evidentialist maxim does not apply without exception. We do not, of course, have the benefit of any responses to James's criticisms from Clifford. Nevertheless, there are contemporary proponents of evidentialism who have argued against James's justification of believing beyond the evidence. The central aim of this chapter is to consider the work of Jonathan Adler, who argues that the very concept of belief requires that one believe only if one has adequate evidence for the belief.[1] Adler's case for evidentialism is conceptual in nature and thus poses a much stronger challenge to James's account than that posed by Clifford. Adler has also made a concerted effort to interpret and critique James's account of faith. Accordingly, this chapter will first consider Alder's evidentialist critique of James and then proceed to critically engage with his defence of evidentialism.

5.1 Adler's evidentialist critique

Adler describes his defence of evidentialism as based on an intrinsic approach to the ethics of belief. The intrinsic approach requires that we ask what the concept of belief itself demands.[2] The answer, according to Adler, is that the concept of belief requires the *subjective principle of sufficient reason*, which is the claim that 'when one attends to any of one's beliefs, one must regard it as believed for sufficient or adequate reasons'.[3] Given Adler's understanding of belief, a venture beyond the evidence is problematic, since it is open to the charge of contravening the very concept of belief. Faith as understood by James involves believing beyond the evidence, or believing while recognising that one lacks adequate evidential support for the truth of that belief. If, however, Adler is correct in his claim that the concept of belief presupposes the requirement that a belief be based on sufficient and adequate evidence, then the Jamesian account is guilty of violating the concept of belief. Adler is aware that James's case for believing beyond the evidence does pose a challenge to his evidentialist commitments, and he engages James's case directly, arguing that the Jamesian account is inadequate.

As part of his multi-pronged critique of James, Adler argues that James's account is guilty of a stark contradiction akin to Moore's paradox. In defence of this claim, Adler first draws a parallel between belief and assertion. He notes that we often assume that a person who makes an assertion also believes the assertion to be true. That is, we generally assume that the person making an assertion is sincere. Adler further construes belief as an 'inner assertion', and he notes that 'just as for a speaker to assert that *p* is for the speaker to claim the truth of what is asserted, so too believing that *p* is tacitly to assert to oneself, and so thereby to claim the truth of what is believed'.[4] Adler notes that on the basis of this parallel, 'claims about what it is permissible to believe or possible to believe can be tested against our everyday judgments of what is assertible'.[5]

Adler draws on the parallel between assertion and belief and contends that the Jamesian account is deeply problematic, since it involves an assertion that is akin to Moore's paradox. Moore's paradox involves the following assertion: *p, but I do not believe that p*. This is problematic since asserting *p* implies that you believe *p*, but the second part of the assertion denies that you believe *p*. The assertion is incoherent since it implies that you believe and do not believe *p*. Adler contends that James's account is guilty of a similar contradiction. That is, James's account is committed to the view that one can believe while recognising that one lacks adequate evidence for the truth of the belief. Given that Alder construes belief as an inner assertion, we can represent James's account as asserting the following: *p, but I lack adequate evidence that p*. Adler contends that this assertion is a paradox. The paradox involved with this assertion can be spelled out as follows: Asserting *p* is taken to imply that you believe *p* to be true, and we have to keep in mind that Adler defends the view that assertions and beliefs make a claim to truth, and that evidence or epistemic reasons are the only indicators of truth.[6] Consequently, to assert *p* is to imply that you believe *p* to be true on the basis of adequate evidence. The second part of the assertion, however, asserts that you *lack adequate evidence that p*. This means that you do not have adequate evidence which establishes the truth of *p*. The first half of the assertion thus contradicts the second half, much like Moore's paradox. If James's account is guilty of this contradiction, then the account would need to be reformulated or completely set aside.

Now, although Adler does recognise that James endorses believing beyond the evidence, he also finds in James commitments that seem to entail an endorsement of a strong form of evidentialism. And, interestingly, he finds that James's commitment to evidentialism is revealed in his critique of the view that beliefs can be acquired voluntarily. James states that it seems preposterous on the very face of it to talk of our beliefs as being acquired at will:

> ...can we, by just willing it, believe that Abraham Lincoln's existence is a myth, and that the portraits of him...are all of someone else?...We can say any of these things, but we are absolutely impotent to believe them; and of just such things is the whole fabric of the truths that we do believe in made up...[7]

The passage above is cited by Adler in support of the view that James is committed to a form of evidentialism that is stronger than Clifford's, since Clifford only holds that one ought not to believe beyond the evidence, not that one is impotent to believe.[8] Adler observes that we have empirical proof that Abraham Lincoln's existence is not a myth, and when we are asked to believe otherwise:

> ... it is impossible for us to believe, [given that we are operating] on the assumption that it is impossible to believe an overt contradiction (I believe that Lincoln's existence is a myth and that I fail to satisfy the conditions for believing [which involves having adequate evidence] that Lincoln's existence is a myth).[9]

We cannot will-to-believe that Lincoln's existence is a myth, since there is overwhelming evidence that Lincoln existed, and hence an overwhelming absence of good reasons to believe Lincoln's existence is a myth. And, in the absence of such good reasons for believing – Adler thinks – we simply cannot believe. Given that we are *unable* to believe that Lincoln's existence is a myth, Adler contends that this example justifies a broader generalisation than merely 'that to believe something you cannot believe that the balance of evidence is strongly against it'.[10] The broader generalisation, which Adler argues is justified by the example, is that 'you cannot believe that *p* if it is manifest to you that your grounds, evidence or reasons do not establish that *p* is true'.[11] In essence, James's caution against believing at will is open to being interpreted as an endorsement of the strong kind of evidentialism that Adler is defending. If Adler is correct that James is committed to an evidentialism which holds that one can believe only on the basis of the evidence, then the Jamesian account is rendered internally inconsistent. The inconsistency is between James's contention that, under the conditions of a genuine option, we are justified in believing beyond the evidence, and James's implicit commitment to a strong form of evidentialism that holds believing to be possible only on the basis of adequate evidence. If James's defence is internally inconsistent, then the Jamesian account as it stands is inadequate and would need to be significantly modified to overcome the inconsistency.

In addition to the charge of inconsistency, Adler alleges that the Jamesian account rests on an argument from ignorance. He interprets James as follows: 'James claimed that if the evidence for a proposition is indeterminate but there are deep personal reasons for believing it – and suspending judgement is effectively no different from disbelieving – then it is permissible (and rational) to come to believe that proposition'.[12] Adler notes that James's reasoning is identical to that found in arguments from ignorance. Arguments from ignorance, observes Adler, typically have the following structure:

(1) No one has disproved (refuted) that *p*.
So, (2) it is possible that *p* is true.
So, (3) there is good reason not to reject *p* as false (or, *p*'s truth is seriously possible).
(4) If there is reason not to reject *p* as false, then we should keep our minds open to the investigation of *p*'s truth.
So, (5) we should keep our minds open to the investigation of *p*'s truth.
(6) If we should keep our minds open to the investigation of *p*'s truth, then it is reasonable (permissible) to believe that *p*.
So, (7) it is reasonable (permissible) to believe that *p*.[13]

Adler argues that James's account of belief illustrates and defends the steps from (5) through (7). Steps (5) through (7) move from the possibility of *p* being true to the justifiability of believing that *p* – this move appears to rest on inferring that *p*, just from the fact that there is a possibility that *p* is true. The problem with this type of argument is that it overlooks the possibility of suspending judgement or belief, which involves neither believing nor disbelieving. Adler says that James overlooks this possibility because his focus is on practical reasoning:

> In general, when options press themselves on us and call for decision, action is effectively under a 'one must act' axiom, and so in the simplest case, the choice is doing A or doing nothing: *Not-doing A implies (effectively) doing not-A* (e.g., not applying to medical school implies [effectively] deciding not to apply to medical school). It is this axiom that James wants to import into belief.[14]

The axiom 'Not-doing A implies (effectively) doing not-A' arises in the course of practical reasoning when an option is forced. Adler acknowledges that forced options do arise within the context of practical reason, and in these cases suspending judgement on *p* is practically equivalent to judging that not-*p*. However, this axiom, suggests Adler, cannot be imported into belief, since the choice between believing and disbelieving is not an excluded middle.[15] There is the possibility of suspending belief, and it is a possibility distinct from that of not-believing. Accordingly, it is step (6) which is being challenged, namely, if we should keep our minds open to the investigation of *p*'s truth, then it is reasonable (permissible) to believe that *p*. The conditional assumes that the choice between belief and disbelief is an excluded middle, and overlooks the possibility of suspending belief. I agree with Adler that suspending belief is not equivalent to disbelieving, since disbelieving *p* means believing that *p* is false, while suspending belief means that we neither believe *p* to be true or false. Adler does concede, however, that in the context of practical reasoning, a forced option renders disbelieving and suspending belief *practically* equivalent. Nevertheless, the difference between disbelieving and suspending belief serves to undermine the conditional expressed in step (6) and according to Adler, this premise is endorsed by James, therefore the Jamesian account is also undermined.

Adler gestures at what he perceives as James's pragmatic justification for importing an axiom of practical reason into the concept of belief, and that is the risk of losing truth. The reason one would choose to believe, rather than suspend judgment, is the risk of losing truth. It may be the case that some proposition *q* is true, although the evidence available is indeterminate in relation to *q*'s truth. Given these circumstances, if we believed *q* to be false or suspended belief altogether, we would then be losing truth. On the other hand, if we did believe in *q*, by venturing beyond the evidence, then we would have grasped truth. Therefore, James could argue that disbelieving and suspending belief are equivalent, in that, if *q* is true then both run an equal risk of losing truth, and it is only in being prepared to venture beyond the evidence that we avoid this risk. This line of thought, however, does expose itself to an obvious reply, that is, Adler can agree that in choosing to suspend judgement when the evidence is indeterminate, we risk losing truth but emphasise that we also avoid the risk of error, if it turns out the belief is false. The advantage of suspending judgment is that we avoid the risk of error, although, we risk losing truth if the belief in question is true.

In addition to the risk of error, Adler argues that there is a more fundamental problem with the view that beliefs can be acquired at will. (This view has been referred to in the literature as doxastic voluntarism.) Adler reads James as endorsing doxastic voluntarism, and this endorsement, he believes, exposes James's account to the following criticism:

> Just think of all the facts that are buried in the past and that would greatly assist our understanding of history…it would surely not serve an interest in truth to 'will to believe' those unknown facts. It is a commonplace that we risk error in accepting hypotheses, which always apply beyond the evidence, but taking that risk is not the same as knowingly adopting an attitude (belief) under conditions false to it.[16]

The central point in the quote above relates to the involuntary nature of belief, which is a view that is accepted by perhaps the majority of contemporary philosophers.[17] The involuntary nature of belief can be understood to mean that 'we cannot believe a proposition at a moment's notice',[18] or as Richard Swinburne states, 'we cannot choose immediately what to believe about some matter'.[19] We cannot simply choose to believe at will; rather, beliefs arise from our interaction with the world at large. We have a choice as to the degree to which we interact with the world, and this introduces a voluntary component into belief formation, albeit in an indirect way. The significant insight, observes Swinburne, is that 'if we could choose what to believe and if our choices were immediately efficacious:

> ... we would realize that our 'beliefs' resulted from our choices and were not forced on us by the world. Hence we would realize that our 'beliefs' had no connection with how things were in the world, and so we would have no reason for supposing those 'beliefs' to be true and so we would not really believe them.[20]

We can paraphrase Swinburne's argument as follows: If we have no reason to think that our beliefs are true, then we would not really believe them. When we choose to acquire beliefs at will, we do so without having reasons to think that those beliefs are true. Therefore, we could not really believe in beliefs we choose to acquire at will. The inability to really believe undermines any pragmatic reason one thinks could justify acquiring a belief at will, i.e., making yourself believe a proposition to be true because you do not want to lose truth is counter-productive, as you would realise that you lack reasons to think that the belief is true, and it is this realisation that will undermine your ability to believe the proposition as being true. If acquiring beliefs at will is conceptually problematic and runs counter to the consensus in favour of the involuntary nature of belief, then Adler has good reason to view doxastic voluntarism as being problematic.

Now, the problematic nature of doxastic voluntarism may affect the Jamesian account in the following two ways: (a) if James is endorsing doxastic voluntarism, then the Jamesian account is vulnerable to Swinburne's criticism discussed above, and (b) given our earlier discussion of James's negative attitude toward doxastic voluntarism (i.e., in his discussion of the impossibility of believing that Abraham Lincoln did not exist), we may then charge James with inconsistency, since his own account of faith appears to endorse doxastic voluntarism.

We may now summarise Adler's critique of James into five distinct components:

First, the case for believing beyond the evidence incorrectly treats the options between believing and disbelieving as an excluded middle. James is said to overlook the possibility that one may suspend judgement or belief, i.e., neither viewing it to be true nor as false. One reason for this oversight, according to Adler, is that James imports an axiom of practical reason into the concept of belief.

Second, the Jamesian case also suggests that it is permissible to believe a proposition, so long as it is logically possible that the proposition is true and has not been shown to be false. This mode of reasoning is considered to be an argument from ignorance, i.e., even if a belief has not been shown to be false, it does not follow that it is true, or that it is reasonable to believe it to be true. In other words, a belief does not become true, or become reasonable, simply because it has not been shown to be false.

Third, James's account seems to assume an endorsement of the problematic doctrine of doxastic voluntarism. This endorsement runs counter to the consensus regarding the involuntary nature of belief.

Fourth, James's case for believing beyond the evidence is internally inconsistent as he seems to endorse a form of evidentialism which requires that we be able to believe only on the basis of sufficient and adequate evidence. Adler notes that the evidentialism which James endorses is stronger than that proposed by Clifford.

Fifth, the Jamesian account, which endorses believing beyond the evidence, conflicts with the very nature of belief which requires that belief be in proportion to sufficient and adequate evidence. James's view of belief is thus inconsistent with the concept of belief.

These five criticisms, if correct, would be reason enough to reject James's account. Given that Adler has posed a radical contemporary challenge to the philosophical viability of the Jamesian account, which is the very thing that we are seeking to defend, there is an urgent need to respond to these criticisms.

5.2   Evaluating Adler's critique of James

The evaluation of Adler's critique will be divided into two parts: first, I will consider his critique of James, then I will proceed to consider his broader justification of evidentialism. With regard to his case against James, I argue that Adler's critique applies only to a certain reading of James, and that there is a preferred reading, which I endorse, that is immune to his critique. Adler's reading of James's account is revealed through his formalisation of it, which is as follows:

(1) Assume that a hypothesis...is an option with which you can live in accordance and if so, it would make a momentous, rather than a trivial, difference to your life. Finally, the option is forced – you must either believe it or disbelieve it. (The logically further option of agnosticism is practically ruled out because it justifies only the same...practices as atheism).

(2) The evidence or intellectual grounds cannot favour either of these options.

(3) It is not irrational for you to take either option (and, by (1), one of these must hold).

(4) We have two goals as inquirers or believers: to obtain truth and to avoid error. Aiming to avoid error is a cautious policy offering small rewards; aiming to obtain truth is a risky policy offering large rewards. Both of these are legitimate...goals, and there is no a priori reason to prefer one to the other.

(5) Only by believing the religious hypothesis – neither atheism nor agnosticism – do you have the opportunity for the great benefits of discovering its truth, if the religious hypothesis is true (that is, only the option of believing [(1) and (4)] can satisfy the goal of seeking truth, as contrasted to merely avoiding error).

(6) When the potential (cognitive) reward (truth) of holding a belief is a live, momentous, and forced option (for you) [(1)], and neither option can be ruled out as irrational [(2) and (3)] and the only way to achieve the reward is by believing [(4) and (5)] then it would not be irrational for you to 'will to believe', and, in fact, under these conditions, it would be irrational for you not to believe (merely for the sake of avoiding error).

(7) So, you are entitled to believe the religious hypotheses, even in the absence of favourable grounds.

(8) So you ought to will-to-believe it.[21]

The problem with Adler's critique arises from his reading of James. A good example of what I have in mind can be found in the first premise, which characterises James's account as giving us the choice of whether to believe or disbelieve. Adler's characterisation is problematic, since James need not be interpreted as being concerned with the choice to believe or disbelieve; rather, James's 'justification of faith' can be read as a justification of *taking the action of committing oneself practically to a pre-existing belief under the condition of evidential ambiguity.* This reading interprets James as concerned with the justifiability of acting on a belief whose truth is evidentially indeterminate, i.e., of taking a pre-existing belief to be true in one's practical reasoning. This is the reading of James I endorse: one may thus understand a forced option as the choice between deciding to act on a belief (which means taking the belief to be true in our practical reasoning), or not acting on a belief (which means not taking the belief to be true in our practical reasoning). This contrasts with Adler's reading, under which a forced option involves a choice between believing and disbelieving.

The reading of James endorsed by Adler is supported, to a degree, by the text of James's 'Will-to-Believe' essay. At the beginning of his essay, James writes that he intends to defend 'our right to adopt a believing attitude in religious matters, in spite of the fact that our merely logical intellect may not have been coerced'. This one line suggests James is concerned with the right to acquire belief, or at least a believing attitude. Adler is not alone in interpreting James in this way, as there are a number of commentators who do read James as offering a justification for voluntarily acquiring a believing attitude. My response to Adler is a challenge to the way he has interpreted James. The alternative reading that I endorse is also a fair interpretation of James's essay: my exposition of the Jamesian account, at the beginning of this study, aimed to draw out from the text a justification for acting on a belief under the condition of evidential ambiguity. Perhaps we may speak of multiple Jamesian accounts which, one may argue, arise from ambiguities within James's essay.

There are also points of agreement between the reading I endorse, and that endorsed by Adler. This can be seen in the second premise, which expresses the condition that the evidence or intellectual grounds *cannot* favour either of the choices available. I agree with Adler's reading that the choice must be of such a nature that it cannot be resolved on the basis of the evidence. I also endorse Adler's clarification regarding the use of the word 'cannot', which he construes firstly, as an in-principle barrier to determination of truth either by evidence or proof, and secondly, as an in-practice barrier, as when further delay in decision will eliminate the availability of a significant choice.[22] In relation to the remaining seven premises of Adler's argument, there arise significant points of difference, some of which, I believe, are due to Adler's misreading of James.

The third premise states that it is not irrational for you to take either choice, and if the choice is forced, then you must either believe or disbelieve. Once, again, my response to this premise arises from a difference of interpretation. On the reading I endorse, the choice is not between believing and disbelieving, rather it relates to whether we will choose to act on a pre-existing belief. When the idea of a forced option is interpreted as relating only to the exercise of practical reason, we avoid Adler's charge that an axiom of practical reason has been imported into belief. A forced option, on this understanding, relates to whether or not we will take a belief to be true in our practical reasoning. The reading I have adopted is not committed to the view, which I agree is mistaken, that the choice between believing and disbelieving is an excluded middle.

Underlying the fourth premise is the view that the twin goals of obtaining truth and avoiding error are equally legitimate. The policy of avoiding error, so it is argued, leads to smaller rewards as it is risk averse; however, the policy of obtaining truth offers larger rewards as there is less fear of taking a risk. If we accept Adler's reading of the twin goals, then James is interpreted as maintaining that the best policy would be to obtain truth even at the risk of error. One problem with this interpretation is that it does not take into account James's assertion that each of the choices encountered in a forced option are attended with the same risk of losing truth. The central contention defended by James relates to the shared risk of losing truth. While it may be true that a policy which accepts risk may result in larger rewards, James argues that the twin goals are on an epistemic par.[23] James's intention is to undercut the view that the evidentialist prohibition on commitment beyond the evidence is favoured by a policy of avoiding error: under conditions of evidential ambiguity, choosing not to venture carries the same risk of failure in aligning one's commitments with the truth as venturing does. The Jamesian argument, I believe, is not motivated purely by a will to maximise the rewards of gaining truth; rather, it aims to defend the view that a venture beyond the evidence, under certain conditions, is epistemically on a par with a policy of avoiding error. There is a risk of error in a venture beyond the evidence, but choosing not to venture *also* risks error, e.g., a suitor who chooses to disclose his feelings is taking a risk, but if the suitor chooses not to disclose his feelings because he wants to avoid being rejected, then he risks missing out on the relationship that he is seeking to achieve. The suitor cannot avoid the risk of not gaining the wanted relationship, and on this basis one may argue by analogy that in the case of an evidentially ambiguous genuine option, there is no fail-safe method for avoiding the risk of error.[24]

The fifth premise also rests on a reading of James which treats believing and disbelieving as an excluded middle. The motivation to believe, given Adler's reading, is that if the proposition in question is true, then only by believing in it will truth be gained, whereas a policy which seeks to avoid error would refrain from believing, and therefore fail to gain truth. However, as I have already stated, my reading of James is not committed to the view that believing and disbelieving is an excluded middle. A careful reading of the fifth premise also reveals the following conditional: If the religious hypothesis is true, then only by believing the religious hypothesis do you have the opportunity for the great benefits of discovering its truth. (I comment further on this conditional shortly.)

The sixth premise affirms the view that under the condition of evidential ambiguity, it would be irrational for you, merely for the sake of avoiding error, not to acquire a belief that is a genuine option given the rewards at stake. This premise, I suggest, conflicts with the account of James I defend. The reading I adopt in no way legitimises acquiring beliefs at will.

Premise seven states that you can be entitled to believe even in the absence of favourable grounds. Once again, this premise rests on a reading of James that is significantly different to my own. The reading I endorse maintains that we may be justified in taking to be true in our practical reasoning what we already believe to be true on passional, rather than evidential, grounds. The conclusion of the Jamesian account, as presented by Adler, leaps from the entitlement to believe, to a prescription that one ought to believe. The reading I endorse does not demand that one ought to believe; rather, I take James's explicit concern as being one of justification. By explicit concern, I mean a concern that believing (or, rather, practical commitment to a belief's truth) should be justifiable in the sense of being permissible, not in the sense of being obligatory.

The reading I endorse is thus significantly different to Adler's, and, in the interest of clarity, we may summarise these points of difference as follows:

(1) Adler reads James as endorsing doxastic voluntarism, although he notes that at a certain point in his essay, James himself critiques doxastic voluntarism. The reading of James which I endorse does not commit James to doxastic voluntarism, and this reading may be defended in the light of the text, and has precedent in the literature

on James's will-to-believe doctrine. One may suggest, then, that Adler's reading and critique have not explored deeply enough the various interpretations of James.[25]

(2) The concept of a forced option is presented by Adler as the choice between believing and disbelieving. I agree with Adler that if a forced option is understood by James as the choice between belief and disbelief, then James is mistaken as taking it to be forced, as it is possible to suspend belief. The reading I endorse defines a forced option as the pressing choice of whether we should, or should not, act on a belief. A forced option, as I read James, relates to practical reasoning, and whether we do, or do not, take a pre-existing belief to be true as part of our practical reasoning (under the condition of evidential ambiguity).

(3) There is a strong emphasis by Adler on the function of reward as a motivating factor in James's account (see Premises Four and Five). Reading Adler's account of James, one gets the impression that James treats believing and the pursuit of truth as means to an end. The Jamesian account, on Adler's reading, comes across as a justification for the pursuit of reward rather than an account of how best to pursue truth. It is as though believing truth is valuable only insofar as it is linked to some further reward. I think this construal of James is not wholly accurate. As I interpret him, James is on the side of those who seek truth even at the risk of error, not those who are untroubled by the risk of error. In fact, my reading of James suggests he is deeply concerned with the risk of error, although, if the belief in question decides a genuine option, and its truth is evidentially indeterminate, then there is a risk of error no matter what choice we make. The focus, I believe, of the Jamesian account is not so much the potential for reward; rather, it is the opportunity to gain truth even if there is a risk of error.

(4) The final point of difference I want to emphasise concerns the conclusion which James's arguments aim to defend. According to Adler, the Jamesian account defends the view that one ought to believe, especially in the case of the religious hypothesis, only then can we gain the reward of believing in its truth. As stated above, my reading of James suggests that his concern relates to the question of permissibility, i.e., are there conditions which will justify venturing beyond the evidence? The conclusion I see as being central to the Jamesian account is that, under certain conditions, a venture beyond the evidence is justified.

With these differences in mind, we are now able to evaluate Adler's five-part critique of the Jamesian account. Given that my reading of James is significantly different to that of Adler's, we can refine our approach and evaluate Adler's critique in relation to the reading of James that I have endorsed. Working from the reading I offer, we can easily set aside three of the five criticisms. The first criticism relates to treating believing and disbelieving as an excluded middle. If my reading is a viable interpretation of James, then a forced option does not necessarily relate to a choice between believing and disbelieving, accordingly, the first criticism does not apply to my reading of James. A forced option, if we recall, results when two hypotheses occur in the form of a 'complete logical disjunction', e.g., 'either accept this truth or go without it'. The second criticism asserts that the Jamesian account is an argument from ignorance. This criticism is also inapplicable, since James, as I read him, is not defending the view that it is permissible to have and acquire a belief so long as the belief has not been proved to be false. There is also the suggestion that the Jamesian account is based on an argument from ignorance since it overlooks the possibility of suspending judgment. This criticism is successful only if we assume that James treats believing and disbelieving as an excluded middle (which he does not do, on my reading). The third criticism states that the Jamesian account endorses the controversial doctrine of doxastic voluntarism. Once again, my reading of James does not commit him to doxastic voluntarism; accordingly, this criticism is inapplicable to my interpretation of the Jamesian account.

The fourth and fifth criticisms cannot be so easily set aside, as they relate directly to Adler's defence of evidentialism. As part of the fourth criticism of James, Adler argues that James endorses a form of evidentialism which holds that: 'you cannot believe that p if it is manifest to you that your grounds, evidence or reasons do not establish that p is true'.[26] This form of evidentialism is in harmony with the view defended by Adler, but this is problematic for James, since, it is inconsistent with his defence of ventures beyond the evidence. The fifth criticism taps directly into Adler's defence of evidentialism, which states that the Jamesian account in permitting ventures beyond the evidence violates the concept of belief. Even though the version of the Jamesian account I endorse avoids commitment to a strong form of evidentialism, Adler's criticisms need further consideration, as Adler can argue that believing beyond the evidence violates the concept of belief. Given that my reading of James presupposes that one can believe on a passional, rather than an evidential, basis, it will be necessary to address Adler's arguments regarding the concept of belief.

5.3 Evaluating Adler's concept of belief

Adler states that when we ask what the concept of belief itself demands, we encounter the *subjective principle of sufficient reason*, i.e., when one attends to any of one's beliefs, one must regard it as believed for sufficient or adequate reasons. In defence of this principle, Adler presents us with four arguments which attempt to show that we impose the demands of the principle on ourselves because these correspond to the demands of belief.[27] Adler articulates his arguments as follows:

(1) The central reason to believe that the subjective principle is a fact is that we find ourselves compelled to follow it. The compulsion is due to our recognition, when attending to any particular belief, that we are entitled to the belief only if it is well founded.[28]

(2) We also attribute acceptance of the subjective principle to others, at least for what they *assert*, and in setting out the grounds for that attribution we capture in brief the intuitive argument for evidentialism. If Sally...asserts that *p*... to Harry...then, normally, Harry takes Sally to have good reasons to believe that *p*. For otherwise Harry will not accept that *p* as a result of Sally's asserting it.[29]

(3) We would not impose the subjective principle on ourselves by inclination. We would surely prefer to avoid the burden of sufficient reasons or evidence – this is true especially of those who hold wild or paranoid beliefs. ... But even they accept the burden, as shown by their own tortured defences of these beliefs.[30]

(4) In general, across a wide spectrum of related psychological studies, subjects are influenced to form beliefs whose causes they deny or cannot know. Yet, they offer reasons for their relevant beliefs, and, though from our point of view these are rationalisations, subjects feel compelled to offer them. The felt need to rationalise is plausibly explained as reflecting the demands of the subjective principle.[31]

These four arguments aim to prove that the demands of belief require a belief to be based on sufficient or adequate evidence. Accordingly, Adler proposes *the incoherence test,* which aims to expose not only what ought not to be believed, but also what cannot be believed.[32] The test says that:

It is incoherent for you in full-awareness (overtness) to believe both that *p* and that your belief that *p* is not based on reasons that establish that *p* is true.[33]

We can appreciate how this test works when it is applied to the following assertion: 'The number of stars is even, but I lack sufficient evidence that the number of stars is even'. This assertion fails *the incoherence test*. In detail, the incoherence arises as follows: 'I believe that the number of stars is even. All that can secure for me the belief's claim of truth is adequate evidence (reason) of its truth. I lack adequate evidence. So I am not in a position to judge that the number of stars is even. So I do not judge it true. So I do not believe that the number of stars is even'.[34] This incoherence is akin to Moore's paradox, which we mentioned earlier. Moore's paradox involves the following assertion: p, but I do not believe that p. Moore's paradox is that the assertion implies that one believes p and that one does not believe p, which is an explicit contradiction.[35] Similarly, the incoherence or contradiction, in the case just cited, arises from the conjunction of the following two claims: (a) that when I attend to any of my beliefs, I must regard it as believed for sufficient or adequate reasons, and (b) I have a belief for which there is insufficient or inadequate reasons to judge it to be true. The claim being made is that you have a belief which violates your own standards for properly believing. Accordingly, if you accept that believing p is proper if and only if one has truth-indicating grounds (reasons, evidence) sufficient to imply (or establish) that, p, then it would be inconsistent with this standard to believe on the basis of insufficient or inadequate evidence.

Adler then proceeds to articulate the following argument for evidentialism:

(1) Necessarily, if in full awareness one attends to one's believing that p, one regards it as believed for adequate reasons.

So, (2) One cannot recognise oneself as fully believing that p (rather than believing p to a high degree) and that one's reasons for belief are inadequate (yielding less than full support).

(3) The reason that one *cannot* so recognise oneself is that the thought would be a stark contradiction.

So, (4) The 'cannot' is conceptual, not merely an inability, and the concept that generates the contradiction is belief.

(5) The impossibility of believing implies that in first-person awareness we recognise the demands of belief, and that those demands are for adequate reasons of the truth of what is believed.

So, (6) One believes that p in accordance with the concept of belief only if one has adequate reasons that p.

So, (7) One ought to believe that p only if one has adequate reasons that p.[36]

The nub of Adler's disagreement with James arises in the first premise, since the debate will turn on the question whether it is necessarily true that when in full awareness one attends to one's believing that *p*, one regards it as believed for adequate reasons. I contend that Adler's four arguments (pp.131–132) do not establish the *subjective principle of sufficient reason* which underpins the first premise.

My initial concern is with the subjective element of Adler's argument. This is most evident in Adler's formulation of the *subjective principle of sufficient reason*; this principle states that when one attends to any of one's beliefs, one must regard it as believed for sufficient or adequate reasons. The subjective element of this principle lies in the judgment of whether our reasons for believing are sufficient or adequate. The four arguments which Adler invokes in defence of the *subjective principle of sufficient reason* successfully link believing with sufficient or adequate evidence, but the arguments do not yield an agreed-upon standard as to what qualifies evidence as being adequate or sufficient. This is problematic, since we can conceive of a situation where a person judges her reasons for believing to be sufficient and adequate, yet, this person may also concede that her reasons may not necessarily be perceived as sufficient or adequate by others. This is a problem for Adler, since believing correctly rests only on one's judgment that the reasons for which one holds the belief to be true are adequate, i.e., if you judge your reasons for believing to be adequate and sufficient, then you believe correctly. The problem is that a reason which is judged to be adequate and sufficient may have been judged incorrectly. My concern, then, with the first premise of Adler's overall argument for evidentialism is that he uses the concept of adequate and sufficient evidence as though it were a common agreed-upon standard. This, however, is not the case, since it is the individual believer, on Adler's account, who judges what is to qualify as adequate or sufficient reasons. These individual judgments will vary from person to person, and at times the variance will be radical in nature, as it is in the debate between theism and atheism.

We encounter a more significant problem with Adler's very strong claim made in the first premise of the overall argument for evidentialism. The problem arises as part of Adler's discussion of an apparent counter-example to his position. The counter-example involves the possibility of emotion-laden responses to the actions of others. Peter Strawson refers to these responses as reactive attitudes, such as resentment and gratitude.[37] Adler observes that reactive attitude judgements imply full beliefs, e.g., if Joe resents Marcia interrupting him when he is

speaking, then Joe believes that Marcia rudely (and so, wrongly) inter-
rupted him.[38]

The claim that Adler advances, in response to this counter-example,
is that 'our reactive attitude judgments are made under conditions of
limited inquiry'.[39] There are conceptual and social limitations that
commonly restrict the evidence available. Adler explains:

> Conceptually, the attitude toward seeking further evidence, even
> setting aside the implied full belief, is sometimes in conflict with
> the spontaneity that is a feature of many of our reactive attitudes.
> Socially, it is often inappropriate to attempt to settle the open ques-
> tions that one's judgment implies are foreclosed. The questions
> needed for judgment are heard as accusatory or presumptuous.
> Frequently, the policy that the reactor adopts toward the actor is
> avoidance...if instead one queries others, then that is often to be
> nosy, or risk appearing to be so.[40]

In light of these restrictions which apply to reactive attitude judgments,
Adler endorses the conclusion that we must often form full beliefs with
limited investigation.[41] He also defends this stance against a would-be
objector, who may argue that we are not entitled to hold or act on full
beliefs that are caused by reactive judgments, since such beliefs will
frequently be mistaken, as they are readily formed under conditions
which do not permit extensive inquiry, therefore the actions they guide
will fail. The lack of a critical stance toward these attitudes, argues the
objector, undercuts the justifiability of these judgments. Adler responds
to this objection by stating that:

> ...the objection falsely equates falling short of a high level of certainty
> with actual error. The claim I am advancing is that our reactive atti-
> tudes judgments are made under conditions of limited inquiry. The
> objection falsely equates that claim with the much stronger and
> dubious claim that these judgments are seriously prone to error.[42]

Adler's discussion of reactive attitude judgments seems to concede that
there are conditions which permit full beliefs under conditions where
evidential inquiry is constrained. If I have read him correctly, Adler's
concession is inconsistent with the first premise of his argument above.
The first premise states that it is necessarily true, that if in full awareness one attends to one's believing that *p*, one regards it as believed for
adequate reasons; however, reactive attitude judgments which involve

full beliefs are often formed in conditions which limit evidential inquiry. So, the case of reactive attitude judgments shows that there is a category of full beliefs which we do hold without the full support of the evidence. In accepting that such beliefs are justified, we also rebut the second and third premises, of Adler's argument (pp. 133–134), which state that we cannot have such beliefs because it would involve a stark contradiction. The fact that we do have such beliefs suggests not only the psychological possibility, but also the conceptual possibility that we can hold full beliefs without full evidential support.

If full beliefs can be held justifiably in conditions which limit evidential inquiry, then we can also challenge what the concept of belief itself demands. According to Adler, the concept of belief demands that when one attends to any of one's beliefs, one must regard it as believed for sufficient or adequate reasons and it is on the basis of this principle, that Adler holds to the following conditional – i.e., 'one's believing is correct only if one has (epistemic) reasons, evidence, or grounds to establish that the belief is true – effectively, to know it'. In light of reactive attitude judgments, however, Adler's conditional is undermined, assuming that the process of believing correctly includes forming beliefs through reactive judgments. If Adler does concede the justifiability of reactive attitude judgments, which he seems to do, then he cannot consistently endorse the first premise, or subsequent premises, of his overall argument for evidentialism.

Another important aspect of Adler's endorsement of reactive attitude judgments is that it complements the reading of James that I have endorsed. To recall, we defined a passional cause as a catch-all category capturing the various non-evidential causes of belief (e.g., emotions, desires, affection and affiliations – including cultural and religious traditions). Now, Adler's acceptance of reactive attitude judgments also amounts to an acceptance that there are non-evidential causes of full beliefs, and that we can be justified in holding and acting on these beliefs under conditions which constrain evidential inquiry – and this is in perfect harmony with the Jamesian account I am defending. Adler himself acknowledges that James's account 'looks better' given the justifiability of reactive attitudes.[43] However, the problem with James, according to Adler, is that 'he is claiming the right to believe in the wholesale absence of evidential support'.[44] This criticism encapsulates Adler's critique of James as discussed above, i.e., that James is committed to doxastic voluntarism and treats believing and disbelieving as an excluded middle. My discussion of Adler's reading and subsequent critique of James, however, argues that there is an alternative reading of

James; namely, as holding that we can be entitled under certain conditions to act on a belief that we already hold to be true. This reading avoids committing James neither to doxastic voluntarism nor to importing an axiom of practical reason into belief. On my reading, James insists that, in acting on our beliefs, we must aim to grasp truth and avoid error – and imposes strict constraints on venturing beyond evidential support to reflect these epistemic concerns.

A final, minor concern I have relates to Adler's understanding of what the concept of belief demands. As discussed earlier, Adler argues that it follows from the concept of belief that 'one's believing is correct only if one has (epistemic) reasons, evidence, or grounds to establish that the belief is true – effectively, to know it.'[45] Adler defends this stance by observing that:

> ...the standard form of challenge (or query) to a speaker's assertions that p (e.g., the cat is in the yard) is for the hearer to ask 'how do you know that p?' There is a tight connection between the requirement of knowledge and the mutual expectation (of speaker and hearer) that what is asserted is backed by adequate reasons.[46]

Adler's defence hinges on the mutual expectation between the speaker and hearer, however, this approach it is not without problems. Consider the example of Sally, who asserts that the cat is in the backyard; now Harry asks Sally how she knows that the cat is in the backyard. In response to Harry, Sally may say that she does not really know that the cat is in the backyard, but that is where she believes the cat is at the moment. The exchange between Sally and Harry suggests that believing on the basis of adequate reasons is not always treated as being the same as knowledge, i.e., having adequate reasons for believing is not always perceived as equivalent to knowing, and that it is accepted that one may assert *p* without being taken to claim to know *p*. This objection is directed at Adler's understanding of what the concept of belief itself demands, since it is Adler's, contention that believing correctly also entails knowing, and that one should assert *p* only if one knows *p*.[47] My contention is that one can assert *p* (i.e., believe *p* to be true) without having to claim that one knows *p*. For example, one can say that they have good reasons to believe the cat is in the backyard, but that they do not know if the cat is actually in the backyard. The problem with Adler's characterisation of the concept of belief and its demands is that it overlooks cases where belief and knowledge seem to come apart.[48] There seems to be good reason to think that believing properly does not entail knowing. If this view is correct, then Adler will have to withdraw the claim that one's believing is correct only if one has (epistemic) reasons, evidence or grounds to establish that the belief is true – effectively, to know it.[49]

Adler, to recall, contends that when one is attending to any of one's beliefs, one must regard it as believed for sufficient or adequate reasons. Given our discussions thus far, there are three overarching considerations which undermine Adler's concept of belief: (a) Adler appears to employ the concept of 'adequate and sufficient evidence' as an agreed-upon standard, whereas it is open to varying interpretations; (b) Adler acknowledges the justifiability of reactive attitude judgments which can involve the formation of full beliefs under conditions which restrict evidential inquiry; this view suggests that we can be entitled to a belief even though we cannot determine whether the belief is supported by sufficient or adequate reasons; and (c) we also defended the view that believing on the basis of adequate reasons, is not always perceived as being the same as knowledge; this view undermines Adler's contention that believing on the basis of adequate reasons entails having knowledge. These considerations provide us with good reasons to set aside Adler's concept of belief, and once this is done, we can also dismiss Adler's critique of the Jamesian account of faith.

5.4 Summary

The discussion of Adler's critique of James brought to light five distinct arguments. I have argued that none of the five arguments is successful, and the primary reason for this is due the reading of James that I have endorsed. The interpretation that I endorse is not committed to the problematic doctrine of doxastic voluntarism, and neither is it committed to importing an axiom of practical reasoning into the domain of belief. Adler's reading, however, does commit James to doxastic voluntarism and also commits James to the incorrect view that believing and disbelieving constitutes a logical disjunction. Accordingly, the reading I endorse is immune to much of the criticism which Adler directs at James. In addition, I also argued that there were major concerns with Adler's defence of evidentialism. The first related to the subjective element that characterised the *subjective principle of sufficient reason*, i.e., when one attends to any of one's beliefs, one must regard it as believed for sufficient or adequate reasons. Alder's arguments do not address what should be taken to be sufficient or adequate evidence. The requirement of sufficient or adequate evidence is open to a wide variety of interpretations, of which some may be mutually exclusive. I also argued that reactive attitude judgements, which establishe that full belief can properly form under conditions of limited evidential inquiry, undermine Adler's claim that we are able to believe only if we have adequate evidence for the belief. Adler's concession that reactive attitude judgments are justified also aligns with James's view on passionally caused beliefs. Moreover, we were also able to undermine Alder's claim that the concept of belief requires that we equate believing with knowing. There are then good reasons for the reflective Muslim to set aside Adler's contemporary evidentialist critique of James. I should note that there are further contemporary defences of evidentialism, and each would need to be considered for a full vindication of the Jamesian account that I am defending, but such a task is beyond the scope of this study. Thus, we may not conclude that once we set aside Adler's critique, all evidentialist-inspired criticism of James is rebutted. I suggest, however, that our evaluation of Adler is sufficient to further support the *prima facie* case in favour of the philosophically viability of the Jamesian account of faith.

This chapter was motivated by the recognition that the reflective Muslim will face further challenges even after they endorse the Jamesian account of faith as compatible with their religious perspective. Adler's evidentialism is an example of such a challenge. The chapter to follow will consider a second challenge, namely the claim that religious pluralism is philosophically, psychologically and theologically misguided.

6
Challenges to Religious Pluralism

> It was pride that changed angels into devils; it is humility that makes men as angels.
>
> – St Augustine

My aim in this chapter is to evaluate three distinct challenges to the pluralism that is associated with the Jamesian account of faith. I have previously noted that the Jamesian account can be employed by a reflective atheist, Christian or Jew. The reason why the account is broadly applicable is that the question of entitlement to believe in God can arise for the atheist, Jew or Christian, in much the same way as it arises for the reflective Muslim. If reflective individuals, on considering the question of whether God exists conclude that the question cannot be decided on intellectual grounds, and they also find that they have a passionally caused belief which decides a genuine option, then they are entitled to a venture beyond the evidence. The constraints associated with the Jamesian account thus allow for a plurality of entitlements, some of which are mutually exclusive of each other. For example, if the reflective Muslim satisfies the constraints of the Jamesian account, then they are entitled to act on their belief. Similarly, the reflective atheist can also be entitled to venture if they also satisfy the Jamesian constraints. If a person, such as the reflective Muslim, were to endorse the Jamesian account, they would also have to concede that the account permits ventures that are incompatible with their own.

The reflective Muslim, in endorsing James's account, would then be committed to a form of pluralism, whereby they acknowledge that a person can be entitled to a venture that is incompatible with their own. The pluralism associated with the Jamesian account is discomforting for many, and for the purposes of this chapter, I will consider three challenges to the pluralism that is associated with James's account. The first, 'philosophical', challenge emerges from the work of Alvin Plantinga: I consider his argument in support of religious exclusivism (which I will define shortly) and evaluate his claim that religious pluralism is self-referentially incoherent. The second, 'psychological', challenge is motivated by the belief that pluralism has the effect of undermining hope, and since hope is an important component of faith, pluralism, it is argued, undermines faith. The third, 'theological', challenge I consider, is the exclusivist reading of Islam – this is the view that non-belief in the truth of Islam is always culpable and thus deserving of censure. I engage with an exclusivist reading of Islam, articulated by Imran Aijaz, which draws on the Quran and the prophetic traditions in order to justify its stance.

The reading provided by Aijaz is guided by two distinct principles.[1] The first principle concerns what we take to be the meaning of the Quran. Aijaz notes that, 'the locus of meaning is *between* the reader who interprets a text and the text itself, and this means ... that meaning is inseparable from the interpreter'.[2] If we accept this principle, then it would be arbitrary to separate the meaning of the Quran from how people read and understand the Quran. The second principle involves adopting a 'traditional' approach whereby we take 'the apparent meaning of the text, making reference to what other people have said about the meaning of the word or phrase in question when appropriate'.[3] These two principles serve as broad guidelines as to how the Quran, and the traditions attributed to Muhammad, can be interpreted. I will work within this framework to engage with the exclusivist stance. Accordingly, this chapter has three distinct components which critically engage with philosophical, psychological and theological critiques of religious pluralism. The first section of this chapter has Plantinga's defence of religious exclusivism as its focus.

6.1 Plantinga's religious exclusivism

Plantinga's discussion of exclusivism and pluralism is not motivated by an interest in the Jamesian account, although, his work, I believe, does pose a challenge. The first challenge arises from his defence of exclusivism, which is the view that 'the tenets or some of the tenets of one religion [Christianity, in the case of Plantinga] are in fact true and that any propositions, including other religious beliefs, that are incompatible with those tenets are false'.[4] There are three further elements to the exclusivist stance, and I will discuss these in the sections to follow. For the purposes of this section, we will focus on Plantinga's defence of

Christian exclusivism – which is intended to respond to the following charge: that a person is being arbitrary in holding that only Christianity is true, and thus believing that other religious beliefs that are incompatible with Christianity are false. In response to the charge that an exclusivist commitment to Christianity is arbitrary, Plantinga argues that:

> ...the exclusivist is not in fact being merely arbitrary, because she doesn't believe that views incompatible with hers are 'as epistemologically well based' as her Christian belief. She may agree that the views of others seem just as true to them as hers do to her; they have all the same internal markers as her own. She may agree further that these others are justified, flouting no epistemic duty, in believing as they do. She may agree still further that she doesn't know of any arguments that would convince them that they are wrong and she is right. Nevertheless she thinks her own position is not only true, and thus alethically superior to views incompatible with her, but superior from an [overall] epistemic point of view as well: how then does she fall into arbitrariness?[5]

The claim being made by Plantinga is that exclusivism is not arbitrary, since the exclusivist belief is overall epistemically superior. Plantinga's response, however, raises the following concern, namely, the claim of epistemic superiority itself seems to be arbitrary. If a person concedes that beliefs incompatible with theirs are as justified as their own beliefs, then how can they also claim that their beliefs are epistemically superior? Plantinga responds to this concern with an analogy involving moral beliefs, and it is through this analogy that he attempts to reconcile the acknowledgement of internal epistemic parity with the claim of overall epistemic superiority. He writes:

> I believe it is dead wrong to discriminate against people on the basis of their race ... I realize that there are those who disagree with me; and I am prepared to concede that their views have for them the same internal marks mine have for me (they have the quality of seeming to be true); I am also prepared to concede that they are justified in holding these beliefs, in the sense that in holding them they are not flouting any epistemic duties. Do I therefore think their moral views are epistemologically as well based as my own? ... Certainly not. Even though I grant that those beliefs are on an *epistemic par* with mine [so far as internal markers are concerned] ... I don't believe they are with respect to other epistemic properties. I think the racist is the

victim of a bad upbringing, that in some way blinds him to what he should otherwise see; or perhaps he suffers from a certain cognitive glitch which prevents him from seeing the truth here ... And because I think these things, I am not arbitrarily holding on to views I see are no better based, epistemically speaking than others inconsistent with them. I am perhaps *mistaken*, but not arbitrary ... The same goes with respect to religious positions incompatible with my own.[6] (emphasis added)

The reconciliation between the acknowledgement of internal epistemic parity, with respect to internal markers, and the claim of overall epistemic superiority rests on an appeal to 'other epistemic properties'. A racist may wholeheartedly believe that their view is true, they may even believe that there are no good arguments against racism and that there are in fact reasons in favour of being a racist. The racist may then be on an epistemological par so far as internal markers are concerned with those who reject racism, but one may still regard the views of the racist as being overall epistemically deficient. Plantinga offers two possible reasons why the racist may be considered to be epistemically inferior: (a) the racist may be blinded by their upbringing, or (b) the racist has a cognitive glitch – both of these possibilities suggest that the racist's cognitive capacities are significantly impaired. If it is true that the racist is cognitively impaired, in the way described by Plantinga, then it would be reasonable to maintain that the racist's position is overall epistemically deficient. The internal epistemic parity between the racist and their critic relates to the fact that both parties may very well be exercising their cognitive capacities to the best of their ability, and genuinely feel their beliefs to be true. There is, however, overall disparity, since the racist is hindered in their ability to properly exercise their cognitive capacities. If the distinction I have drawn – internal epistemic parity vs. overall epistemic parity – is the distinction Plantinga had mind, then I think we can agree with him that there need not be an inconsistency between acknowledging internal epistemic parity and the claim of overall epistemic superiority. Given these distinctions, we now need to ask whether a particular religious belief can be viewed as being overall epistemically superior to other incompatible beliefs.

6.1.1   Evaluating Plantinga's exclusivism

Plantinga maintains that Christians can claim overall epistemic superiority, since a person who has a belief that is incompatible with Christian theism can be said to suffer from epistemic, or cognitive impairment. The case of the racist is an example where we seem to be entitled to appeal to epistemic impairment as a reasonable explanation of why a person would endorse racist views. Similarly, it is being argued, the Christian is also being reasonable when they regard non-Christians as being impaired. If the non-Christian is impaired, then there will be grounds to deny cognitive parity. The caveat relevant to Plantinga's stance is that exclusivism is true only if non-Christians are in some way cognitively impaired. If it is reasonable to believe that non-Christians do suffer from cognitive impairment, then Christian exclusivism would be justified, and the pluralism associated with James's account will be significantly impaired. That is, the Jamesian account allows for mutually exclusive ventures, whereby the individuals who are making the ventures are regarded as being on a complete epistemological par, thus blocking any claim to epistemic superiority. I grant that Plantinga's exclusivism does challenge James's account, although, I believe, the challenge is unsuccessful and the reasons for this view are as follows:

(1) The first reason why I think Plantinga's challenge is unsuccessful is that there seems to be a significant difference between debates relating to the truth of religious belief and the debate on racism. The main point of difference is that there is a growing consensus that racism is immoral, but there is no consensus as to whether a particular religion is true. This difference, I believe, is significant, as it provides us with a basis to argue that there is in fact a disanalogy between debates relating to the truth of religious belief and the debate on racism. The disanalogy, I feel, provides a basis on which we can question whether the charge of cognitive impairment has a place in the debate on the truth of religious belief. Accordingly, the burden is very much on the exclusivist to show why they are entitled to regard those who disagree with them as being cognitively impaired; as it seems that the debate on racism and religious belief are two very different types of debate.

(2) The charge of cognitive impairment also appears to beg the question against other possible explanations of religious diversity. I acknowledge that it is possible to appeal to cognitive impairment as an explanation of disagreements between people, however, it does not follow from this that every disagreement can be explained by an appeal to cognitive impairment. The reason why we cannot appeal to cognitive impairment as the explanation for all disagreements is that there can be alternative explanations which better explain disagreement. For example, we would not appeal to cognitive

impairment to explain disagreements about the merits of a work of art, or a piece of music. There are contexts where there is room for differences of attitude and beliefs, and one can also envision contexts where differences and disagreements are of value, e.g., a democratic country where individuals are free to vote for one of a number of political parties. The problem with the exclusivist position is that cognitive impairment is invoked not only as a possible explanation for religious diversity, but it is offered as being 'the' explanation. This view begs the question against other possible explanation of religious diversity. For example, one may contend that God has created this world as one which elicits and sustains religious diversity. If true, this view would explain the diversity of religious beliefs without having to resort to the charge of cognitive impairment. While it is possible that cognitive impairment may be responsible for the religious diversity, there are other possibilities which need to be considered.

(3) The charge of cognitive impairment can also be seen as an example of a discrediting mechanism. A discrediting mechanism, according to McKim, is used 'to render other views unconvincing, and hence unthreatening'.[7] He also notes that the 'existence of such mechanisms is one case of a general tendency to insulate systems of belief from attack, to resist challenge or even inspection'.[8] The problem with accusing someone of cognitive impairment is that the accusation may be intended solely to discredit the person with whom you disagree. Once you have discredited the person, you may also feel that you are entitled to disregard those beliefs which are incompatible with yours. The problem, however, is that the accusation of impairment may very well be motivated by a sub-conscious desire to protect your beliefs from attack, to resist a perceived challenge, or even to resist having to critically reflect on your own beliefs. If the accusation of impairment is motivated in this way, then it would be the accuser who is guilty of suffering from cognitive impairment, while the accused may, in fact, be innocent of this charge.

(4) Plantinga's defence of exclusivism appears to be overly charitable toward Christian theism, especially when he reflects on the impact religious diversity might have on religious belief. He states that an awareness of diversity 'could bring about an appraisal of one's religious life, a reawakening, a new or renewed and deepened grasp' that it 'could serve as an occasion for a renewed and more powerful working of the belief-producing process by which we come to apprehend'.[9] The overall effect of being aware of diversity may initially

serve as a defeater, although, Plantinga suggests it may have the opposite effect in the long term. Plantinga's comments indicate that belief in Christian theism may turn out to be strengthened through reflections on the plurality of religious beliefs. I agree with his sentiments that faith may indeed be strengthened, but I do not think that it is only the Christian who will benefit from reflecting on diversity. A Muslim who reflects on the diversity of belief may also find their faith reawakened, deepened and strengthened. There is a real possibility for diversity to strengthen the belief of the Christian, though the same could also apply to the Muslim, Jew or atheist. Unfortunately, Plantinga does not mention the possibility that reflections on the plurality of religious belief may strengthen beliefs incompatible with his own.

I acknowledge that if the non-Christian is cognitively impaired, and therefore blind to the truth of Christianity, then there will be grounds to deny overall epistemic parity. If Plantinga is successful in defending the charge of cognitive impairment, then he will also be entitled to adopt the stance of a Christian exclusivist. The four arguments discussed above, however, largely undermine the charge of epistemic impairment. We can summarise the four arguments as follows: (a) Plantinga's argument by analogy aimed to justify the charge of cognitive impairment, I argue is unsuccessful – as it incorrectly equates the debate on the truth of religious belief, with the debate on racism; (b) the charge of cognitive impairment seems to beg the question against competing explanations of religious diversity; (c) the exclusivist who raises the charge of cognitive impairment also runs the risk of being guilty of the same charge; and (d) Plantinga's overly charitable attitude toward Christian theism suggests that he is yet to fully come to terms with the intellectual depth, piety, devoutness and spirituality of religious traditions which are incompatible with his commitments. In addition to these arguments there are, I believe, two major weaknesses in Plantinga's overall approach which further undermine his attempt to defend exclusivism.

The first major weakness relates to Plantinga's definition and description of the exclusivist position he is defending. As noted above, the exclusivist holds that the tenets, or some of the tenets, of one religion are in fact true and that any propositions, including other religious beliefs that are incompatible with those tenets, are false. Plantinga also notes that the exclusivists he is defending must also satisfy the following three conditions, collectively referred to as 'Condition C'. The conditions are: (a) being rather fully aware of other religions; (b) knowing that there is much that at least *looks like* genuine piety and devout-ness in them; and (c) believing that they know of no arguments that would necessarily convince all or most honest and intelligent dissenters of your own religious allegiances.[10] My concern relates to the second of the three conditions, and the reason for being concerned with this second condition is that it seems to shy away from an acknowledg-ment that there is genuine piety and devoutness in religious traditions other than Christianity. Plantinga only allows for the possibility that it 'looks like' genuine piety and devoutness exists, this phrasing, seems to allow for the possibility that non-Christian piety and devoutness may not be genuine, but only 'look' genuine. If my construal of the second condition is correct, then we need to ask whether Plantinga is being uncharitable to non-Christian religious traditions. If there is internal epistemic parity among the Christian, Muslim and atheist, then all three are, in a sense, genuine with respect to their internal states, i.e., all three sincerely hold their beliefs to be true. If we concede that there is internal epistemic parity among those who have incompatible beliefs, and Plantinga seems happy to do this, then we should also be prepared to acknowledge that those with whom we disagree, also exhibit genuine piety and devoutness.

Perhaps I have read too much into the second condition, and Plantinga may very well be regarded as being charitable toward non-Christian traditions, since he does acknowledge that non-Christian piety and devoutness can be genuine. Given this consideration, I think we can interpret Plantinga a little more sympathetically, i.e., Plantinga is an exclusivist who recognises that non-Christians appear to be genuine in their commitments. However, given Plantinga's definition of exclu-sivism, he will regard all beliefs incompatible with his own Christian commitments as being false. The difficulty with this position is that it is once again overly charitable to Christian theism, as one can imagine a Muslim, or Jewish exclusivist who also holds their belief to be true, and regards all beliefs incompatible with theirs to be false.[11] A Muslim or Jewish exclusivist, much like the Christian exclusivist Plantinga has in mind, may also hold their belief with an absolute sense of certainty, and they may also regard those who choose not to embrace their particular view as suffering from cognitive impairment. The defence of exclusivism, as sketched out by Plantinga, can also be employed by the exclusivist Muslim or Jew, and this inevitably leads to a plurality of incompatible exclusivist stances. If Plantinga's framework can be employed in defence of a plurality of exclusivisms which are incompatible with each other, then, the question arises as to why one would choose to endorse and defend one particular exclusivist stance over another.

The question which Plantinga had initially set out to answer was whether it was arbitrary, given the plurality of religious views, to endorse only one as being true, and consign all the others to falsehood. His answer was to propose a framework within which it would not be arbitrary to endorse Christian exclusivism; however, his answer, as I have argued, is overly charitable toward the Christian exclusivist. I have noted that Plantinga's framework is, in principle, compatible with Islamic and Jewish exclusivism, therefore, the question he set out to answer remains, although in a slightly altered form, i.e., is it arbitrary, given the plurality of exclusivist views, to only endorse one as being true? Plantinga's defence of exclusivism has not really answered the question he had in mind, at best, his work has only helped to reformulate the question. The major weakness, I believe, in Plantinga's defence is that he is overly charitable toward the Christian exclusivist, and this has hampered his understanding of the intellectual and spiritual depth of other religious traditions.

The second major weakness with Plantinga's overall case for exclusivism emerges from his definition and understanding of pluralism. Plantinga defines the pluralist as someone who 'thinks the thing to do when there is internal epistemic parity is to withhold judgment'.[12] The definition, just given, is problematic, and Plantinga rightly observes that if the pluralist claims that in the case of internal epistemic parity the right course of action is to withhold judgments, then the pluralist position is open to the charge of being self-referentially incoherent. That is, if the pluralist acknowledges internal epistemic parity between them and the exclusivist, then, given Plantinga's definition, the pluralist would have to act on their own maxim and suspend their pluralist commitments. Once the pluralist suspends judgment, they can no longer hold pluralism to be true. In order to avoid the charge of incoherence, the pluralist can either present arguments to disambiguate in favour of their stance, or they may charge the exclusivist with being cognitively impaired.

There is a further problem with the pluralist stance, and this emerges from Plantinga's discussion of racism. To recall, Plantinga concedes that there exists a degree of internal epistemic parity between the racist and their critic, although, it is generally accepted that even so, the racist is deeply mistaken. If, however, we were to accept the pluralist's advice to withhold judgment when there is internal epistemic parity, then we would not be entitled to reject or criticise the racists' stance. There are then two good reasons, a proponent of Plantinga may argue, to reject pluralism: the first is that pluralism is open to the charge of being self-referentially incoherent, and secondly, pluralism would undermine significant moral precepts.

Plantinga's arguments against pluralism appear robust; nevertheless, I do not believe his arguments are successful. My response to Plantinga is motivated by his definition and understanding of pluralism. Plantinga presents us with only one definition of pluralism, and I suggest there can be other definitions which, if employed, would be immune to Plantinga's arguments. For example, a pluralist might say that *when there is internal epistemic parity, with respect to internal markers, we should hold off with charges of cognitive impairment and first explore possible explanations of why there is parity, and given this parity we should also be open to the possibility that our views are perhaps mistaken – unless of course there is good reason to doubt that there is overall epistemic parity (e.g., bad upbringing, cognitive impairment).*[13] This definition does not seem to be self-referentially incoherent, since, it allows a proponent of pluralism to retain their commitments to pluralism while also acknowledging internal epistemic parity.[14] If the pluralist suspects cognitive impairment, then the onus will be on them to provide good reasons in support of their case. The definition does not threaten significant moral precepts either, since it would allow a critic of racism, who might acknowledge internal parity, to retain their commitments. The definition I have offered also has two distinct advantages over Plantinga's exclusivist stance: (a) the pluralist, in withholding the charge of cognitive impairment, can genuinely be charitable toward those with whom they disagree – if at the outset you assume that those who disagree with you are epistemically inferior, then it is unlikely that you will be as charitable toward them; and (b) in acknowledging that one could be mistaken, the pluralist is also open to critical self-reflection, whereby they are open to evaluating whether they themselves are entitled to their beliefs – if at the outset you assume that you are in an epistemically superior position, then the impetus for critical self-reflection may be diminished Importantly, the pluralism associated with the Jamesian account is not committed to the type of pluralism that Plantinga has as his target. Rather, James's pluralism endorses the right to make a commitment when there is internal and perhaps overall epistemic parity. Thus, Jamesian pluralism entitles a range of commitments, including commitments which are exclusive of each other, e.g., Islamic theism and atheism. This form of pluralism is in fact a denial of the pluralism that Plantinga has in mind.

There are then three significant weaknesses which, I suggest, under-mine Plantinga's overall defence of religious exclusivism: (a) the defini-tion of exclusivism is open to the charge that it is does not adequately acknowledge the genuine piety and devoutness in religious traditions other than Christianity; (b) Plantinga's exclusivist framework can be employed to defend Muslim and Jewish exclusivism; and (c) the critique of pluralism is successful only if you accept the definition discussed by Plantinga; there are, however, other possible definitions of pluralism which are immune to his arguments. In light of these weaknesses, I maintain that we have good reason to reject Plantinga's case for religious exclusivism. If my arguments are correct then we can also conclude that Plantinga's exclusivism does not pose a philosophical challenge to the pluralism associated with the Jamesian account of faith (which allows for a plurality of entitlements, some of which are mutually exclusive of each other). There, are, however, two further challenges which remain to be considered. The section to follow will consider the psychological challenge of pluralism. Proponents of this challenge maintain that pluralism undermines wholehearted faith.

6.2 The psychological challenge

The psychological challenge directed toward proponents of pluralism turns on the view that religious faith requires a believer to have hope that their moral and spiritual efforts are not in vain. If it is the case that pluralism undermines hope with regard to one's moral and spiritual efforts, then accepting and endorsing pluralism can be said to under-mine religious faith. Proponents of the psychological challenge can then argue for the following claims: the first, quite strong, claim would be that accepting pluralism is inconsistent with religious faith, or they may claim that accepting pluralism has a demoralising effect on faith commitments. Kelly James Clark, in discussing the perils of pluralism, suggests the best course of action is for the pluralist to keep their views to themselves. Clark's pejorative attitude toward pluralism is motivated by the perceived demoralising effects of being a pluralist. His concerns are revealed as he muses on what would likely happen if his own son were to accept pluralism:

> If he [Clark's son] is not persuaded that reality is ultimately just and loving, he may lose incentive to pursue love and justice himself. Indeed, if he does not perceive that reality as just, he may reasonably affirm that he needs to protect his own interests at all costs... Human

beings, so it seems to me, are so constructed that they need hope that their moral and spiritual efforts are not in vain. To have that hope we must believe that reality is such that it enables or even empowers us to move from self-centeredness to reality centeredness. To believe that ultimate reality may be, for all we know, indifferent or hostile to human purposes, is demoralizing – one's best moral and spiritual efforts might in the end come to nothing. If so, it is likely that one will falter on the steps toward transformation.[15]

The pluralist allows for the possibility that those who hold a belief that is incompatible with theirs may be correct, and that their own view may perhaps be mistaken. Accordingly, if you believe in a perfectly loving and all-powerful God and also endorse pluralism, then you have to concede that it is possible that your belief may be mistaken, i.e., you have to allow for the possibility that a perfectly loving and all-powerful God may not in fact exist. The problem with pluralism is that it requires a person with religious faith to acknowledge the possibility that their moral and spiritual efforts may ultimately result in naught. Clark is correct to note that the realisation that your moral and spiritual efforts may be in vain can be demoralising. A person who concedes that the universe may ultimately be cold, pitiless and indifferent can easily lose hope, since there is no guarantee that their moral and spiritual efforts will untimely make any difference. If there is no God, or ultimate reality beyond this world, then would it really matter whether you lived a life filled with virtue or vice? Surely, if all ends at the grave, then the best thing to do would be to maximise one's own happiness. Such thoughts seem contrary to the selflessness that is intrinsic to many religious traditions, although, such thoughts, according to Clark, will inevitably arise once you concede that your faith commitments may perhaps be mistaken. The anxiety which underpins Clark's musings arise from the realisation that a person could embrace self-centeredness over selflessness, and this is especially troubling once you realise that it may be your loved ones who are making this choice.

I have acknowledged that a proponent of the Jamesian account of faith is committed to a form of pluralism, although I do not accept Clark's contention that pluralism necessarily undermines hope and thus demoralises religious faith. My disagreement with Clark is motivated by the following four considerations:

(1) Clark's concern with pluralism is motivated by a 'principle of protection' which seems self-defeating. If my reading of Clark is correct,

then the principle which underpins his concern with pluralism can be expressed as follows: 'A believer should not be exposed to anything which could demoralise their faith', or alternatively, 'anything which could demoralise faith should be kept hidden from the believer'. Whichever way the principle is formulated, the implication is that a believer is to be protected from anything which would threaten their faith, and this view, I suggest, undermines itself. Think again of Clark's son, who could very well reply to his father in the following terms: *Religious faith is a very important part of who I am, and I believe that I am mature enough spiritually and intellectually to make my own decisions about my own faith commitments – there is no use in trying to hide from me, or protect me from things which you think could undermine my faith. I respect your concern that my faith should be protected, but, I'm capable of making my own decisions – and you should trust me to be able to do so.* There is a danger that in acting on the principle of protection, outlined above, we may alienate ourselves from our loved ones. For example, a parent may become highly obsessive in trying to protect the faith commitments of their children, to the point where they become overbearing – the concern is that as children mature, they may react negatively to their over-protected upbringing and thereby distance themselves from their faith commitments.[16] In certain contexts, Clark's principle can itself have a demoralising effect on faith, therefore: if a believer should be protected from anything which could demoralise their faith, then they should also be protected from Clark's principle of protection.

(2) The concern with pluralism is also motivated by fear that it may cause a believer, who acknowledges that their position may in fact be mistaken, to become self-centred. Clark reasons that a believer will lose hope, along with their faith, once they acknowledge the possibility that God may not exist. Once a person concedes this possibility, then Clark maintains they will also realise that the universe may ultimately be indifferent to their moral and spiritual efforts. I believe that Clark's 'loss-of-faith' argument is problematic for the following reasons: the first reason is that one can accept something as possible without believing it to be true. There is no inconsistency between holding a proposition p to be true, while also acknowledging that you may be mistaken about the truth of p. As a result, it is possible to continue believing in God, while acknowledging the possibility that your belief may be mistaken. Therefore, I disagree with Clark that believers will lose their faith once they acknowledge the possibility that an incompatible belief has the possibility

of being true. The second reason I disagree with the loss-of-faith argument is that an acknowledgement of pluralism may in fact strengthen religious faith. A believer in accepting pluralism may experience an awakening of faith, or a renewed interest in their faith commitments. It is possible that people who realise that there are multiple faith ventures in addition to their own may adopt a more reflective attitude toward their commitments. The reflective believer could experience a deepening awareness and perhaps a strengthening of their faith. Accordingly, I do not think that an acceptance of pluralism will necessarily result in the loss of faith. The argument is also problematic since it is 'assumed' that an undesirable consequence follows from the position in question, i.e., no reason or evidence is given to think that the undesirable consequence is actually an outcome of the position. Clark's argument does not give us reason to think that accepting pluralism will actually result in the loss of hope and faith, and ultimately lead to a self-centred attitude. All that he has done is muse on the possibility that such a series of consequences could transpire, but such musings do not constitute a good reason to think that it will actually happen.

(3)   There is a second way in which Clark's stance falsely assumes that once religious faith is lost, a person will become self-centred. I have already argued against the view that pluralism necessarily leads to a loss of faith, and I think we should also reject Clark's contention that the loss of faith will also result in the loss of moral values. There is the possibility that a person retains moral values even though they have an atheistic view of the world. One good example is Arthur Schopenhauer, who believed that at 'the foundational being of everything was the Will – a mindless, aimless and non-rational urge', however, he also 'acknowledges traditional moral values', although he does this, 'without the need to postulate the existence of God'.[17] We could question the coherence of Schopenhauer's philosophical outlook, nevertheless, his outlook suggests that it is at least psychologically possible to affirm moral values without believing in God. Conversely, one could argue that believing in God also carries with it the risk of becoming self-centred. We can imagine a person who uses their religious affiliations only to further their own financial interest, or to further their own political ambitions. With this in mind, I think we can reject the view that religious belief necessarily leads to selflessness, and that a rejection of religious faith will lead to self-centredness.

(4) A final concern I have with Clark's musings on pluralism is that his concerns can equally apply to exclusivism. Clark claims that pluralism can be demoralising, however, one could claim that exclusivism can also be demoralising. For example, there could be a form of exclusivism which maintains that only those who believe in God and go to church every Sunday will go to heaven, while those who believe in God but do not go to church will be condemned to hell. A person who is brought up with this belief may, in the course of time, come to regard it as being unfair, as a person can believe in God and be good without going to church. The believer may think it is unfair on the part of God to overlook the good within the person and punish them, only because they did not go to church. These thoughts can, over time, have a demoralising effect on faith, whereby the believer may no longer think that a God who treats people in such an unjust manner is worthy of worship. On the other hand, it can be argued that pluralism may, in fact, be morally uplifting. Think again of the believer who has rejected belief in the exclusivist view of God just described. They may very well be open to a pluralist's view of God. A pluralist might believe in a God who judges people on the basis of who they are and the life they have lived. The pluralist understanding of God would reject the view that a person would be punished for not attending church every Sunday, or the Mosque every Friday. A person, who has rejected the exclusivist understanding of God, may find this view of God morally uplifting, and thereby have their faith rekindled. I think Clark is mistaken in thinking that pluralism is demoralising, when there clearly are contexts where pluralism can rekindle an interest in faith commitments.

Given my discussion thus far, there are a number of reasons why I think Clark's anxiety toward pluralism is unjustified: the first relates to Clark's principle of protection, which seems to undermine itself; second, Clark's assertions that pluralism will lead to a loss of faith, and that a loss of faith will lead to self-centredness is unsupported; and third, there are contexts in which it is exclusivism, and not pluralism, that has the effect of demoralising faith. The reason just outlined, if correct, also suggests that the pluralism associated with the Jamesian account is coherent and viable, and is unaffected by Clark's psychological concerns with pluralism. In light of the above discussion, we can set aside Plantinga's philosophical challenge and Clark's psychological challenge. The section to follow will consider a theological challenge to pluralism. The theological challenge is motivated by claim that Islamic theism is exclusivist in nature, and therefore incompatible with the view that there can be a plurality of entitlements.

6.3   The challenge of muslim exclusivism

A reflective Muslim, who is considering the Jamesian account of faith, will likely question the compatibility of the Jamesian account with Islamic theism. There are a number of Muslims who will reject the compatibility of Islam with James's account. The concerned Muslim may argue that the ethos of the Islamic tradition is exclusivist in nature, i.e., that Islamic theism is overall epistemically superior and that all other incompatible beliefs are false. If Islamic theism is exclusivist, then in order for a Muslim to endorse the Jamesian account, along with the pluralism associated with it, they would have to acknowledge that they are acting against the ethos of Islam. The exclusivist nature of Islam will also have implications for those who think there are good reasons for endorsing the Jamesian account. If Islam is exclusivist in nature, and the reflective Muslim believes that the Jamesian account is philosophically viable, then the reflective Muslim is confronted with the following choices: (a) withdraw their endorsement of the Jamesian account; (b) decide that the tradition of Islam is itself misguided; or (c) suggest that the tradition of Islam is in need of reinterpretation. My preferred choice is to challenge the view that Islamic theism is exclusivist in nature. First, however, I will need to consider how an exclusivist reading of Islam might be articulated and defended.

6.3.1   Muslim exclusivism

For the purposes of this chapter, I will consider one example of how an exclusivist reading of Islam can be articulated and defended. The example I have in mind is drawn from a recent paper by Imran Aijaz, which presents a detailed account of how one could argue for exclusivism within the tradition of Islam.[18] We should note that Aijaz does not himself endorse the exclusivist reading; thus, my aim is to utilise Aijaz's account of the exclusivist reading, after which I will offer a response. Aijaz's work suggests that the Muslim exclusivist can argue that every person who chooses not to live in accordance with the principles of Islam does so in a way that is culpable and thus deserving of divine censure. In order to defend their stance, the exclusivist can argue that according to the tradition of Islam, every person knows that *tawhīd*

(Islamic monotheism) is true, and those who do not live as Muslims do so knowing that they are rejecting the truth. [19] We can formalise the exclusivist's argument as follows:

> Premise One: If a person knows *tawhīd* to be true but does not act in accordance with this knowledge, then that person is culpable.
>
> Premise Two: All persons in our world know *tawhīd* to be true.
>
> Conclusion: All persons in our world who do not live in accordance with *tawhīd* are culpable.[20]

If the above argument is sound then it would follow that all persons who do not live as Muslims – do not live in accordance with *tawhīd* – are culpable. This conclusion proves to be problematic for a defender of James's account since it would be inconsistent with the pluralist ethos that is associated with it. In order for the argument to succeed, the exclusivist will have to show that the two premises, of the above argument, are well supported within the tradition of Islam. If the exclusivist is successful in showing that both premises are well supported, then they would have shown that Islam is exclusivist in nature, and therefore inconsistent with the pluralism associated with the Jamesian account. The question a Muslim proponent of James will need to consider is whether there is adequate support within Islam for the two premises of the exclusivist argument.

I do not have any immediate objections to the first premise, and I think it is reasonable to maintain that if a person did know that *tawhīd* to be true, i.e., they knew it to be true that God exists, but did not live in accordance with their knowledge, then they would be culpable. The significant question, for me, is whether the second premise can be supported within the framework of Islam. Aijaz suggests that the exclusivist can defend the view that everyone does know *tawhīd* to be true, and this can be done on the basis of the following tradition-based arguments:

(1) The exclusivist can appeal to the concept of *fitrah*, which describes the natural disposition that inclines one towards the truth of *tawhīd*. The concept of *fitrah* can be traced back to the prophet Muhammad, who is reported to have said: 'Every child is born in a state of *fitrah*, and then his parents make him into a Jew or a Christian or a Magian'. There are also Quranic allusions to mankind's inborn disposition to believe and acknowledge the truth of *tawhīd*. For example, in the seventh chapter of the Quran, we encounter the following verse: '*When thy Lord drew forth from the Children of Adam – from*

their loins – their descendants, and made them testify concerning them-selves, (saying): 'Am I not your Lord (who cherishes and sustains you)?'- They said: 'Yea! We do testify!' (This), lest ye should say on the Day of Judgment: 'Of this we were never mindful'.[21] The exclusivist can appeal to this verse along with the tradition attributed to Muhammad, in support of the view that within the tradition of Islam, every person has an inborn disposition which informs them that *tawhīd* is true.

(2)   The second line of argument available to the exclusivist is linked with the concept of *ayah*, which is understood to mean 'sign', or more specifically 'signs of God'. According to the Quran, the signs of God include the 'the creation of heaven and the earth', the 'alteration of night and day' and 'the rain which brings the earth to life'. The signs mentioned in the Quran, the exclusivist can argue, are 'universal and unambiguously present'.[22] If, according to the Quran, the signs which testify to the existence of God are universal and unambiguous, then the evidence which justifies belief in *tawhīd* is available to everyone. Therefore, no person can claim that there is not enough evidence or that the truth of *tawhīd* is ambiguous.

(3)   A defender of the exclusivist argument can also appeal to the Quranic distinction between the *mu'min* and the *kāfir*. The word *mu'min* describes someone who lives wholeheartedly in accordance with *tawhīd*, while the *kāfir* is someone who knows *tawhīd* to be true but does not live in accordance with *tawhīd*. [23] According to a number of commentators, the Quran distinguishes a person as being either a *mu'min* or *kāfir*. In support of this view, Aijaz cites Toshihiko Izutsu, who comments that:

The Koranic system reveals a very simple structure based on a clearcut distinction between Muslims and Kāfirs. All Muslims are members of the community... And they stand in sharp opposition to those who... refuse to listen seriously to Muhammad's teaching and to believe in God. In this simple structure there is no place for confusion or ambiguity. The *ummah* or (*Muslim*) community... divides men neatly into two opposing sections. Man is either Muslim or Kāfir.[24]

Aijaz argues that if the above reading is correct, then it follows that everyone believes that *tawhīd* is true, since according to the Quran, a person is either a *mu'min* (Muslim) or *kāfir*, and there is no other alternative given in the Quran. If there is no alternative to being a *mu'min* (Muslim) or a *kāfir*, then it follows that according to the Quranic worldview everyone knows and believes that *tawhīd* is true.

The *kāfir* is regarded as being culpable, since they live a life that runs counter to what they know to be true. A person who does not live in accordance with *tawhīd* is also described in the Quran as someone who will be excluded from salvation (Quran 3.85). The Quranic distinction between *mu'min* and *kāfir*, according to Aijaz, 'gives us a picture where anyone who is not a Muslim, e.g. a Jew or a Christian, is a rejecter of faith', and that 'non-Muslims are therefore culpable and excluded from God's plan of salvation'.[25] Aijaz's characterisation of the Quranic *weltan-shaung*, if true, provides very strong support for second premise, namely, the tradition of Islam endorses the view that all persons in our world know *tawhīd* to be true.

The arguments discussed above allow the exclusivist to defend the second premise with the following three arguments: (a) the concept of *fitrah* suggests that there is an inborn disposition in every person to accept *tawhīd* as true; (b) the concept of *ayah* suggests that there exist universal and unambiguous signs which point toward the truth of *tawhīd*; and (c) the Quranic distinction between *mu'min* and *kāfir* presupposes that every person does know *tawhīd* to be true. If these three arguments are correct, then the exclusivist argument is successful and we would have to concede that the tradition of Islamic theism is exclusivist in nature. The exclusivist argument, if successful, would also suggest that the pluralist ethos of the Jamesian account would be inconsistent with Islamic theism. There are then a number of choices, mentioned at the outset, which the reflective Muslim could choose to pursue; the reflective Muslim may discard the Jamesian account of faith, or conclude that the tradition of Islam is itself misguided or in need of reinterpretation, otherwise they may challenge the exclusivist reading of Islamic theism. My preferred choice is to challenge the exclusivist reading, and in the section to follow I will explore ways in which this can be done.

6.3.2 Responding to the exclusivist reading

The first line of argument, available to the exclusivist, appeals to the concept of *fitrah* to argue that every human has an inborn disposition to believe in the truth of *tawhīd*. This view of *fitrah* is defended on the basis of a prophetic tradition which says that every person is born in a state of *fitrah*, and that it is their upbringing which causes them to become a Jew, Christian or Magian. My response to this line of argument rests on three considerations, two of which relate to the prophetic tradition just mentioned. The first consideration challenges the credence of the prophetic tradition in question. There have been schools of thought, within the tradition of Islamic theism, that have argued that the tradition in question cannot be given much credence as it runs counter to what is perceived to be orthodox Islam. Critics of this tradition maintain that a person's parents could only 'be secondary causes and that the guiding aright and leading astray must come from God'.[26] Accordingly, critics of this tradition maintain that it 'cannot be interpreted as saying that it is ultimately one's upbringing which decides their beliefs – [since] any change will have God as its primary cause'.[27] If the exclusivist is to appeal to the tradition in question, then they will first need to defend its credibility in light of what is perceived to be orthodox Islam. The second consideration also relates to how we interpret the prophetic tradition in question. The tradition states that a person's condition changes from being in harmony with *fitrah* to another whereby they become a Jew or Christian. When the tradition is read carefully, we notice an acknowledgment that a person's disposition to believe *tawḥīd* to be true is not permanent and is subject to change. If my reading is correct, then the tradition in question weighs against the exclusivist view that every person knows *tawḥīd* to be true. At best, the prophetic tradition supports the view that every person at birth knew *tawḥīd* to be true, although, it would not follow from this that all persons in our world continue to know *tawḥīd* to be true (as there can be changes in disposition). In addition to the prophetic tradition, we noted a verse from the Quran which declares that every person at some point in time testified to the truth of *tawḥīd*. As with the prophetic tradition, the verses only suggest that at some point in the past all persons knew *tawḥīd* to be true, but it would not follow from this verse that all persons in this world continue to know *tawḥīd* to be true. The third consideration relates to how the term *fitrah* is defined. There are schools of thought who maintain that *fitrah* refers only to a person 'being created in a healthy condition, like a sound animal, with a capacity for either belief or unbelief when the time should come'.[28] There is another school which maintains that *fitrah* refers 'to Allah's creating man with a capacity of either belief or unbelief'.[29] We should also note that there exist broader definitions, which view the term *fitrah* as describing a 'human beings essential nature, moral constitution, and original disposition...the primordial nature of the individual'.[30] The plurality of definitions suggests the term *fitrah* does not necessarily mean that every person believes in the truth of *tawḥīd*. Given the definitions just mentioned, the term *fitrah* can refer to a disposition to believe or not believe in the truth of *tawḥīd*, or it can refer to the moral dimension of human nature. The term *fitrah* allows for a plurality of meanings, some of which are significantly different to the exclusivist interpretation. A proponent of exclusivism therefore cannot claim that the concept of *fitrah* necessarily entails that every person knows *tawḥīd* to be true.

The second line of argument available to the exclusivist appeals to the concept of *ayah*. According to the exclusivist stance, *ayah* are universal and unambiguously point to the truth of *tawḥīd*. We can challenge this interpretation of *ayah* on the grounds that when the Quran refers to a phenomena as being an *ayah*, it does so by saying that the phenomena is an *ayah* for those who believe. For example, chapter forty-five of the Quran contains the following verses: *Verily in the heavens and the earth, are signs (ayah) for those who believe. And in the creation of yourselves ... are signs for those of assured faith.*[31] If we take these verses at face value, then they suggest that the *ayah* are signs only for those who already believe in God. This reading, if correct, suggests that there is an intimate link between believing in God and seeing the *ayah* as being signs of God. This reading suggests that those who 'believe' will see the *ayah* as being a sign of the divine. The verse seems compatible with the view that a person who does not believe in God or lacks assured faith may not view *ayah* as being signs of God. If this reading is correct, then the *ayah* mentioned in the Quran may not be unambiguous.

The third line of argument available to the exclusivist appeals to the distinction between the *mu'min* and the *kāfir*. A proponent of exclusivism can argue that a person according to the Quran can only fall in one of two categories, i.e., a person is either a *mu'min* or *kāfir*. The exclusivist may also argue that according to the Quran, both the *mu'min* and *kāfir* know *tawḥīd* to be true; thus, it may be argued that all people know *tawḥīd* to be true. One way to contest the exclusivist argument is to reflect on how the terms *mu'min* and the *kāfir* have been defined. For example, the term *mu'min* is used in the Quran as an attribute of God, 'God himself is called *mu'min*; logic compels one to conclude that the original Arabic meaning of someone who protects, gives safety is to be preferred in this context'.[32] There is also a suggestion that in other Quranic contexts, 'it is not easy to decide whether *mu'min* refers exclusively to those ... who recognise Muhammad as the messenger of God or whether other monotheists, e.g., the Jews ... are also included'.[33] If this reading is true then a non-Muslim can also be seen as a *mu'min*. The term *kāfir*, on the other hand, refers to 'unbelievers in general who are threatened with God's punishment'.[34] There also exists a prophetic tradition which says that a Muslim can also be *kāfir*, that tradition states that if a Muslim charges a fellow Muslim with being a *kāfir* then he himself is a *kāfir*, if the accusation should prove untrue'.[35] Some schools of thought within the tradition of Islamic theism have also held the view that 'every Muslim who dies with a mortal sin...which has not been repented of...is to be considered just a *kāfir*'.³⁶ Other schools, however, maintained that a Muslim who commits a mortal sin, which has not been repented of, is neither a Muslim nor a *kāfir*; rather, they occupy an 'intermediate position between believer and unbeliever, the so called "rejected" *fasik*'.³⁷ The terms *mu'min* and *kāfir*, if my discussion of them is correct, suggest that it may be possible for a non-Muslim to be a *mu'min* and a Muslim to be a *kāfir*, and that it is possible that a person can be neither a Muslim nor *kāfir*. These possibilities, if true, would undercut the exclusivist reading, which maintains that (a) from the perspective of the tradition of Islam, a person is either a *mu'min* or *kāfir*, and (b) there is no other category apart from *mu'min* or *kāfir*.

The proponent of exclusivism may contend that even if my observations are correct, they do not weaken the view that the *mu'min*, *kāfir* and the *fasik* all know *tawhīd* to be true. This contention can be challenged. Consider, for example, Asad's reflection on the term *kāfir*. He notes that 'a *kāfir* is "one who denies [or 'refuses to acknowledge'] the truth" in the widest, spiritual sense of this...term: that is irrespective of whether it relates to a cognition of the supreme truth – namely, the existence of God...'³⁸ Asad's reading of the term can yield the following distinction: (a) the *kāfir* as someone who knows *tawhīd* to be true, but denies this truth, and (b) the *kāfir* as someone who does not believe *tawhīd* to be true, and denies that it is true.

Our evaluation and critique of the exclusivist view of Islam suggests that the exclusivist position is based on a narrow reading of the sources in question. If we broaden our reading of the sources, we encounter interpretations which undercut the exclusivists' reading. The exclusivist stance can, however, be reformulated so as to be immune to my critique. A proponent of the exclusivist stance can argue that nothing I have said undercuts the view that according to the tradition of Islamic theism, all who do not live in accordance with *tawhīd* are culpable and deserving of divine censure. At best, my critique shows that the terms *mu'min* and *kāfir* are more malleable than originally thought, and that it is possible that a person may not know *tawhīd* to be true. The exclusivist may, however, argue that any person who does not live in accordance with *tawhīd*, irrespective of whether they know *tawhīd* to be true, is culpable and deserving of divine censure. The reformulation of the exclusivist stance, I believe, is no more successful than the original stance. The reformulated exclusivist stance, I maintain, is undermined by the Quran, the prophetic tradition and classical and contemporary Muslim scholarship.

6.3.3   A question of culpability

The exclusivist now maintains that all who do not live in accordance with *tawhīd*, irrespective of whether they believe it to be true, are culpable and deserving of divine censure. One way to challenge the exclusivist stance will be to show that within the tradition of Islamic theism, there is an acknowledgement that there are people who are inculpable in their non-belief. There is no verse in the Quran, as far as I am aware, which explicitly names such a category. We do, however, encounter verses which implicitly acknowledge the possibility of people who are not held to be culpable even though they do not live in accordance with *tawhīd*. A good example of this implicit acknowledgement can be seen in the following verses:

> Behold, those whom the angels gather in death while they are still sinning against themselves, [the angels] will ask. 'What was wrong with you' They will answer: 'we were too weak on earth'. [The angels] will say: 'was, then, God's earth not wide enough for you to forsake the domain of evil?' For such, then, the goal is hell – and how evil a journey's end! But excepted shall be the truly helpless – be they men or women or children – who cannot bring forth any strength and have *not been shown the right way*: as for them, God may well efface their sin – for God is indeed an absolver of sins, much-forgiving.[39]

Asad notes that the phrase '... not been shown the right way' can also be translated as 'cannot find the right way'.[40] According to Asad, the phrase has in mind those people who are 'helplessly confused and cannot, therefore grasp this basic demand of Islam; or, alternatively, that the message relating to this demand has not been adequately conveyed and explained to them'.[41] The basic demand of Islam, as understood by Asad, requires a 'spiritual exodus from the domain of evil to that of righteousness', and he adds that 'a person who does not 'migrate from evil unto God' cannot be considered a believer'.[42] In light of Asad's commentary, there does, then appear to be a category of people who do not recognise the basic demand of Islam, but their failure to recognise the demand is inculpable. If Asad's reading is correct, then a person is inculpable if they are helplessly confused, or if the basic demand of Islam has not been adequately conveyed and explained to them. This interpretation, if true, serves to undermine the exclusivist contention that all who do not live in accordance with *tawhīd* are culpable and deserving of divine censure. We can support Asad's commentary with the following prophetic tradition which also acknowledges that a person can be inculpable, if they do not live their life in accordance with *tawhīd*.

> al-Aswad ibn Saree', who reported that the Prophet said: 'There are four (who will protest) to God on the Day of Resurrection: the deaf man who never heard anything, the insane man, the very old man, and the man who died during the *fatrah* – the interval between the time of Jesus and the time of Muhammad. The deaf man will say, 'O Lord, Islam came but I never heard anything'. The insane man will say, 'O Lord, Islam came but the children ran after me and threw stones at me'. The very old man will say, 'O Lord, Islam came but I did not understand anything'. The man who died during the *fatrah* will say, 'O Lord, no Messenger from You came to me'. He will accept their promises of obedience, then word will be sent to them to enter the Fire. By the One in whose hand is the soul of Muhammad, if they enter it, it will be cool and safe for them'.[43]

The above tradition is quite clear in acknowledging that there are people who are held to be inculpable despite living a life that is not in accordance with *tawhīd*. If the prophetic tradition is accepted, then the exclusivist cannot claim that all who do not live in accordance with *tawhīd* are culpable. Defenders of the exclusivist stance can, once again, reformulate their argument in virtue of the tradition cited. They may argue that all persons who are sound of mind, educated and aware of the teachings of Islam are culpable if they do not live in accordance with *tawhīd*. This formulation of exclusivism is consistent with the view that, in principle, there are people who are inculpable for living a life that is not in accordance with *tawhīd*. The exclusivist can also limit those who are inculpable to those who are explicitly mentioned within the sources in question, e.g., the old, the deaf, the insane or those of the *fatrah*. If true, this version of exclusivism will again challenge the Jamesian account. The defender of exclusivism may note that the pluralism associated with James's account allows a person to be an atheist, a Jew or a Christian even if they are familiar with Islam. If exclusivists are correct in their reading of Islam then Islamic theism would be inconsistent with the Jamesian account. The exclusivist can also argue that a critique of exclusivism, even if successful, does not show that pluralism is correct. At best, a successful critique of the exclusivist stance would only suggest that the exclusivist is in need of better arguments, and nothing I have said thus far would serve as a basis to rule out exclusivism *a priori*. It also would be a mistake to think that since I have offered a critique of exclusivism, I have therefore shown pluralism to be consistent with Islamic theism. There is the possibility, even if we can set aside the claims of the Muslim exclusivist, that the pluralism that is associated with the Jamesian account is inconsistent with Islam. Given that I'm seeking to welcome James's model within the tradition of Islamic theism, the burden is on me to show that a person who is sound of mind, educated and aware of Islam can be inculpable if they decide not to live in accordance with *tawhīd*.

6.4   A Framework for culpability

The Quranic verses and the prophetic tradition that I have quoted above indicate that a person who does not live in accordance with *tawhīd* can be inculpable only if they are prevented from knowing the basic demand of Islam by circumstances beyond their control. This understanding of inculpability is also supported by al-Ghazālī's understanding of God's mercy. He argues that there are certain groups of non-Muslims who will be encompassed as part of God's mercy, and he defines the groups as follows:

(1) A party who never heard so much as the name Muhammad. These people are excused.
(2) A party among those who lived in lands adjacent to the lands of Islam and had contact, therefore with Muslims, who knew his name, his character, and the miracles he wrought. These are the blasphemous Unbelievers.
(3) A third party whose case falls between the two poles. These people knew the name Muhammad, but nothing of his character and attributes. Instead all they heard since childhood was that some arch-liar...named Muhammad claimed to be a prophet...this group,...is like the first group. Even though they heard his name, they heard the opposite of what his true attributes were. And this does not provide enough incentive to compel them to investigate (his true status).[44]

The first and third categories of non-Muslim are held to be inculpable and thus are encompassed by the mercy of God, while those in the second category are held to be culpable. Al-Ghazālī also notes that a person who has heard about Muhammad and takes 'it upon themselves to investigate (this matter) and seek (the truth thereof) and then be overcome by death before being able to confirm this, they too shall be forgiven...'.[45] There are two significant aspects to al-Ghazālī's discussion: the first is the distinction between knowing the true teachings of Islam, as opposed to a mischaracterisation of Islam, and the second important aspect is the process of investigation whereby a person seeks to confirm what they have heard about Islam. These two aspects suggest that the question of culpability will need to take into account a person's exposure to information about the true teachings of Islam, and their ability to verify whether the information is true.

Given al-Ghazālī's framework, we can maintain that, if a person is able to disambiguate in favour of Islam, and they come to know that the evidence does support the view that Muhammad was a recipient of divine revelation, then the person would be culpable if they were to choose not to live as a Muslim. On the other hand, al-Ghazālī's framework would also allow for the possibility that if a person were unable to disambiguate in favour of Muhammad's claim due to circumstances beyond their control, then they would be inculpable for not living as a Muslim. We can, with this framework in mind, distil the following two conditionals from al-Ghazālī's discussion:

(1) If a person is able to disambiguate in favour of Islam, then the person is culpable for not living in accordance with the teachings of Islam.
(2) If a person is restricted by factors beyond their control from disambiguating in favour of Islam, then they are inculpable for not living in accordance with the teachings of Islam.

If the characterisation of al-Ghazālī's discussion is correct, then we seem to have a basis to reject the exclusivist stance. The exclusivist maintains that all persons who are sound of mind, educated and aware of the teachings of Islam are culpable if they do not live in accordance with *tawhīd*. There would need to be a correction, in light of al-Ghazālī's framework, namely, the exclusivist would be entitled to maintain that a person can be held to be culpable for not living in accordance with *tawhīd*, only if it is established that the person in question was sound of mind, had access to information about the true teachings of Islam and had the opportunity to disambiguate in favour of its truth. The exclusivist may, at this point, reject my reading of al-Ghazālī, or even if they acknowledge that the reading is correct they may reject al-Ghazālī altogether. My reading, irrespective of how the exclusivist responds, does show that the question of culpability need not be restricted to the soundness of a person's mind, their level of education or their awareness of the teachings of Islam. The tradition of Islam, as reflected in the work of al-Ghazālī, can also take into account the kind of information a person has access to, and their ability to evaluate the information they have before them. A proponent of exclusivism may very well reject my reading, but they cannot deny that the reading I offer is motivated within the tradition of Islamic theism.[46]

The conditional we can derive from al-Ghazālī's discussion is that a person can be held to be culpable for not living in accordance with *tawhīd*, only if it can be established that the person in question is sound of mind, has access to information about the true teachings of Islam and has the opportunity to disambiguate in favour of its truth. There will be a debate on whether we can satisfy the conditional. A proponent of exclusivism may argue that we do have access to information about the true teachings of Islam and that we can disambiguate in favour of its truth. I concede that we can know about the true teachings of Islam, although, I maintain that at this point in time we are unable able to disambiguate in favour of its truth. My position is reflected in the ambiguity thesis, and while I have not articulated a defence of this assumption, I believe it is a reasonable assumption to make. If the assumption is justified, then we do have a basis to claim that we cannot disambiguate in favour of Islam. The evidence, I believe, leaves open the question of God's existence, and thereby it also leaves open the question of whether Muhammad was a messenger of God. The ambiguity thesis, if true, would mean that we cannot disambiguate in favour of Islamic theism, and therefore we cannot hold every person who is sound of mind, educated and aware of the true teachings of Islam to be culpable if they do not live in accordance with *tawhīd*.

The view of culpability I have just articulated also requires two further clarifications. The first clarification relates to what it means to live in accordance with *tawhīd*. I have suggested that to live in accordance with *tawhīd* implies that one lives as a Muslim, i.e., a person who embraces the five pillars of Islam. There is the possibility of alternative conceptions of what it means to live as a Muslim. Consider the following prophetic tradition:

> The Prophet said, 'Truthfulness leads to righteousness, and right-eousness leads to Paradise. And a man keeps on telling the truth until he becomes a truthful person. Falsehood leads to *Al-Fajur* (i.e., wickedness, evil-doing), and *Al-Fajur* (wickedness) leads to the (Hell) Fire...'[47]

The above tradition can be taken to support the idea that a Muslim is someone who pursues truth and righteousness, and eschews wickedness and evil-doing. If we accept this construal of what it means to live as a Muslim, we would then need to rethink the question of culpability. That is, a Muslim, who lives in accordance with *tawhīd* is someone who believes in God and strives to be virtuous. One may thus argue that a person is culpable if they eschew virtue and pursue vice. Accordingly, our stance on whether a person is culpable will turn on how we interpret the term *tawhīd*.

The second clarification relates to the possibility of disambiguation. I maintain that at this point in time, we are unable to disambiguate in favour of Islamic theism. My stance allows for the possibility that if God does exist, then there could have been moments in history when evidence was provided to a person or a community, or that there may be some point in the future when further evidence will emerge which will allow us to disambiguate. The important point to note is that I do not reject the possibility that disambiguation is possible, I only hold that at this point in time, we are unable to disambiguate in favour of Islamic theism.

Given these clarifications, we are now in a good position to reply to the Muslim exclusivist who claims that all who do not live in accordance with *tawhīd* are culpable and deserving of divine censure. We can reply to the exclusivist by noting that within the tradition of Islam, there are contexts where a person cannot be held to be to culpable if they do not live in accordance with *tawhīd*. The Ghazālīan-inspired framework for deciding culpability takes into account a person's state of mind, their access to information about the true teachings of Islam, and whether the person had the opportunity to disambiguate in favour of Islam. At this point, the reflective Muslim may agree that commitment to a tradition other than Islam need not be culpable and thus deserving of divine censure.

6.5   Summary

The reflective Muslim who endorses the Jamesian account of faith will need to be aware of the continued challenges which the account faces. This chapter has considered three distinct challenges to the pluralist ethos of the Jamesian account. I have argued that none of the three challenges is able to successfully undermine commitment to a Jamesian form of religious pluralism. The responses I have offered suggest that the exclusivist stance, as articulated by Plantinga, is deeply problematic, and this is especially due to the charge that 'non-believers' suffer from cognitive impairment. This charge against the 'non-believer' begs the question against other explanations of religious diversity. Furthermore, there is a genuine concern that those who deploy the charge of cognitive impairment may in fact be guilty of the very same charge. We also took issue with the mistaken claim that pluralism requires suspending belief when there is disagreement or internal epistemic parity. In addition, we argued that accepting pluralism need not be demoralising, or result in the loss of moral values. The final section of this chapter critically engaged with a form of Muslim exclusivism. Our reply to the exclusivist interpretation of Islam was to note that its viability was predicated on a narrow range of meanings that were associated with key terms. Once we take into account the diverse ways in which key terms such as *mu'min*, *kāfir* and *fitra* have been understood, then the exclusivist's stance is easily undermined. Importantly, I argued that there are resources within the tradition of Islam which can be drawn upon to defend a form of pluralism. That is, under the condition of religious ambiguity, where one is unable to disambiguate in favour of Islam, the reflective atheist, Christian or Jew need not be seen to be culpable or deserving of censure. This view, if accepted, aligns well with the Jamesian account which, in principle, allows for a diverse range of entitlements.

Conclusion

We have covered much ground, and now it is important to gain an overview of what this study has achieved. This study has aimed to establish that the Jamesian account provides us with a philosophically viable response to the question of entitlement to believe in God. The Jamesian account permits a venture beyond the evidence if and only if the following conditions are fulfilled:

(1) The option cannot be resolved on evidential grounds.
(2) The content of the option, and the passional commitment to the option is itself morally admirable or at least not morally flawed.
(3) The option is genuine, i.e., living, forced and momentous

The arguments detailed in Chapter 1 provide us with reasons to think that there is a good *prima facie* case for the philosophical viability of the Jamesian account.

Our *prima facie* case took into account the challenge posed by Clifford's absolutist evidentialist maxim. We observed that the debate with proponents of evidentialism often turns on interpreting each other's point of view. For example, our engagement with Adler's critique of James highlighted the ways in which James's 'Will-to-Believe' essay can be interpreted. That is, Adler reads James's essay as endorsing the problematic doctrine of doxastic voluntarism. However, the reading we have adopted for the purposes of this study is not committed to the doctrine of voluntarism. Accordingly, those involved in the debate on the viability of the Jamesian account of faith need to be aware of how James is being read. Once we resolve questions of interpretation, the findings of Chapter 1 and 5 strongly suggest that evidentialism does not undermine the Jamesian account of faith. This conclusion should not be taken to mean that the Jamesian account is wholly immune to all possible evidentialist critiques; rather, the claim is that the *prima facie* case outlined in Chapter 1 is not undermined by the forms of evidentialism that are articulated by Adler and Clifford.

This study has also aimed to establish that the reflective Muslim can endorse the Jamesian account while also being aligned with the tradition of Islam. There was a concern that even though the reflective Muslim could satisfy the constraints of the Jamesian account, there would be considerations from within the tradition of Islam that would prevent the reflective Muslim from embracing James's account of faith. This concern motivated our exploration of three major considerations which the reflective Muslim may have perceived as obstacles to endorsing James's account. We first considered the challenge of al-Ghazālī's scepticism which threatened to entirely undermine the enterprise of philosophy of religion. We engaged with al-Ghazālī's case for scepticism in Chapter 2 and discovered that his case was self-undermining, and that his strategy assumed that an attitude of trust could be justified only if there was no possibility of error. This assumption was shown to be problematic since there is the possibility of a fallibilist view of knowledge, and this involves trusting in our cognitive capacities while also acknowledging the possibility of error. The fallibilist does not view the possibility of error as precluding an attitude of trust. For these reasons, we set-aside al-Ghazālī's case for scepticism.

We also considered al-Ghazālī's Sufi account of faith. This account of faith, when aligned with Plantinga's model of Reformed epistemology, provided an answer to the question of entitlement to believe in God. The 'Reformed-Sufi' account of faith offered the believer epistemic certainty and knowledge. This response was in stark contrast to the Jamesian account which aims to accommodate, not eliminate epistemic uncertainty. The subsequent evaluation of the 'Reformed-Sufi' account of faith in Chapter 3 exposed a number of weaknesses of this account of faith. The major weakness was the fact that there are a number of individuals who subscribe to accounts of faith that parallel the 'Reformed-Sufi' account, yet such individuals at times have mutually incompatible beliefs, e.g., traditional Muslim concepts of monotheism vs. Trinitarian concepts monotheism. This observation suggests that the 'Reformed-Sufi' account of faith only serves to reinforce and does not resolve the question of entitlement to believe in God.

The final chapter considered the religious pluralism that is associated with the Jamesian account of faith. A proponent of James's account, we have noted, will have to endorse entitlements to a variety of theistic and naturalistic commitments, e.g., atheism, Christianity, Buddhism. This form of pluralism was open to challenge from a number of different perspectives. We considered three challenges, namely, the philosophical challenge as articulated by Plantinga, the psychological challenge, and the challenge of Muslim exclusivism. These three challenges, as we discovered, did not undermine the form of pluralism that is associated with the Jamesian account of faith. As with the challenge of evidentialism, we note that critiques of religious pluralism also turn on interpretation. For example, Plantinga construes the pluralist as someone who seeks to withhold judgment when there is internal epistemic parity. This is not the only way to construe the pluralist stance, and once we move beyond this construal, much of Plantinga's critique can easily be set aside. Similarly, the challenge of Muslim exclusivism presents us with an exclusivist reading of the Islamic tradition, but this reading is successful only if we constrain ourselves to a narrow range of interpretations. Once we move beyond these constraints and engage in a broader exploration of how key terms such as *ayah, fitra, kāfir* and *mu'min* have been understood and interpreted, we discover that the exclusivist's reading can be challenged and that a pluralist reading of the Islamic tradition is indeed viable.

We were initially concerned that the reflective Muslim may not endorse the Jamesian account on the grounds that it was undermined by considerations motivated from within the tradition of Islam. However, as we further explored the nature of these considerations, e.g., al-Ghazālī's scepticism, the 'Reformed-Sufi account, and the exclusivist reading of Muslim scripture, we discovered that we were able to overcome them. Accordingly, the reflective Muslim need not regard these considerations as an obstacle to embracing the Jamesian account. Importantly, we also presented a positive case for the reflective Muslim to welcome James's account. The positive case for embracing James was made in Chapter 4. We argued that the Jamesian account provided an interpretation of al-Ghazālī's illumination narrative that was philosophical and theologically superior to that provided by the Sufi account. The Jamesian account was also successfully applied to Muhammad's reported experience of divine commission. Given that the Jamesian account can be successfully applied to al-Ghazālī's narrative and the narrative of divine commission, we argued that James's account has a constructive role to play within the tradition of Islam. Accordingly, if the reflective Muslim is someone who is concerned with answering the question of entitlement to believe in God, then endorsing the Jamesian account of faith will achieve this goal.

Notes

Introduction

1. Brian Davies observes that 'much philosophy of religion focuses on the topic of God. He notes that all through the centuries philosophers have asked whether there is a reason to believe that God exists. See, *An Introduction to the Philosophy of Religion*, (Oxford University Press, 2004), p. 1.
2. This definition is derived from the John Bishop's understanding and construal of the thesis of religious ambiguity. See *Believing by Faith: An Essay in Epistemology and Ethics of Religious Belief* (Oxford University Press, 2007), p. 1. I also accept Bishop's view that 'classical philosophical theism specifies the nature of God as the omnipotent, omniscient, omnibenevolent, supernatural personal Creator *ex nihilo* of all that exists', p.7.
3. John L. Schellenberg argues that: 'the weakness and ambiguity of our evidence for the existence of God is not a sign that God is hidden; it is a revelation that God does not exist'. *Divine Hiddenness and Human Reason* (Ithaca, NY: Cornell University Press, 1993), p. 1. See also, Daniel Howard-Snyder and Paul K. Moser, *Divine Hiddenness: New Essays* (Cambridge University Press, 2002).
4. Keith Ward, 'Truth and the Diversity of Religions', in *The Philosophical Challenge of Religious Diversity* (eds.) Philip L. Quinn and Kevin Meeker (Oxford University Press, 2000).
5. John Hick, *An Interpretation of Religion* (London: Macmillan, 1989), pp.73–74. See also, John Hick, 'The Philosophy of World Religions', *Scottish Journal of Theology*, 1984, 37: 229–245.
6. Robert McKim has defended the view that neither the existence of God nor the nature of God is apparent or obvious. Such a view is consistent with, if not identical to, that of the ambiguity thesis. For a fuller discussion and defence of McKim's view, see *Religious Ambiguity and Religious Diversity* (Oxford University Press, 2001). See also, Graham Oppy, *Arguing About Gods* (Cambridge University Press, 2006). In this work Oppy argues that none of the contemporary arguments for and against the existence of God is powerful enough to change the minds of reasonable participants involved in the debate. This view is also in accordance with the ambiguity thesis.
7. Graham Oppy and Nick Trakakis, 'Religious Language Games', in *Realism and Religion: Philosophical and Theological* (eds.) Andrew Moore and Michael Scott (Ashgate Publishing, 2007), p. 123.
8. Ibid.
9. William James, *The Will to Believe, Human Immortality* (Dover Publications, 1956).
10. John Bishop, *Believing by Faith: An Essay in the Epistemology and Ethics of Religious Belief* (Oxford University Press, 2007).
11. I do, however, endorse Seyyed Hoessien Nasr's account of traditional Islam. Nasr's account turns on the following three terms, namely; *din, iman,* and

ihsan. The Arabic word *din* is defined by Nasr to mean 'religion', though it also describes an attitude whereby one 'humbles oneself before God', or the surrendering of oneself to the Divine. The term 'Islam' is said to 'refer to that universal surrender to the One and that primordial religion contained in the heart of all heavenly inspired religions'. The word *iman* is translated to mean 'faith'. Nasr also appeals to the Quran which defines the faithful as including, 'those who have faith [in what is revealed to Muhammad] and those who are Jews and Christians'. These verses suggest that whoever has faith in God and the Last Day and lives a virtuous life will be numbered amongst the faithful. The third term *ihsan* is said to mean 'beauty, goodness, and virtue'. Consequently, 'the goal of human life is to beautify the soul through goodness and virtue and to make it worthy of offering to God, Who is *the* beautiful'. Nasr suggests, 'the person who has realised *ihsan* is fully aware of the centrality of the qualities of compassion and love, peace and beauty in the Islamic spiritual universe'. Islamic theism, as seen by Nasr, represents an inclusive worldview and values all who pursue virtue while having faith in God. A true believer is a person who is humble before the Divine, and is inspired by faith to value and express compassion and love. Accordingly, the total religion that is traditional Islam can be understood to consist of the levels of *din* (surrender), *iman* (faith), and *ihsan* (spiritual beauty). See, *The Heart of Islam: Enduring Values for Humanity* (Harper SanFrancisco, 2002).

12. Frank Griffel, 'Al-Ghazālī', *Stanford Encyclopedia of Philosophy* (retrieved from http://plato.stanford.edu/entries/al-ghazali/#CumPosOccSecCau, 28/01/2009).

13. See Richard Frank, *Al-Ghazālī and the Ash'arite School* (Durham: Duke University Press, 1994); Frank Griffel, *Al-Ghazālī's Philosophical Theology: An Introduction to the Study of his Life and Thought* (New York: Oxford University Press, 2009); Farouk Mitha, *Al-Ghazālī and the Ismailis: A Debate on Reason and Authority in Medieval Islam* (I.B.Tauris, 2002); Ebrahim Moosa, *Ghazālī on the Poetics of Imagination* (The University of North Carolina Press, 2005); Eric Orsmby, *Ghazālī: The Revival of Islam* (Oneworld, Publications, 2008); and Montgomery Watt, *al-Ghazālī the Muslim Intellectual*, (Kazi publications, 2003).

1 A Jamesian Account of Faith

1. William James, *The Will to Believe. Human Immortality* (Dover Publications, 1956), p. 31.

2. John Bishop, 'Faith as Doxastic Venture', *Religious Studies*, 2002, 38(4): 474. A passional cause can be regarded as a broad category which captures all non-evidential causes of belief.

3. John Bishop, *Believing by Faith: An Essay in the Epistemology and Ethics of Religious Belief* (Oxford University Press, 2007), p. 24..

4. Bishop, *Believing by Faith*, pp. 125–126.

5. Within the tradition of Islam, the Mahdi is a person who will prefigure the return of Jesus. It is possible that James's example of belief in the Mahdi may have been inspired by Muhammad Ahmad ibn as Sayyid Abdallah, a religious

leader in Sudan who claimed to be the Mahdi in 1881. James's essay was published in 1896.

6. James, *The Will to Believe, Human Immortality*, p. 11.
7. William Clifford, 'The Ethics of Belief', reprinted in *Philosophy: The Big Question* (ed.) Ruth J. Sample, Charles W. Mills and James P. Sterba (Wiley-Blackwell, 2004), pp. 87.
8. Ibid., p. 83.
9. Ibid.
10. James, *The Will to Believe, Human Immortality*, p. 11.
11. Clifford, 'The Ethics of Belief', p. 86.
12. Ibid.
13. Bishop, 'Faith as Doxastic Venture', p. 477, see also Bishop, *Believing by Faith*, p. 165.
14. An ethical evaluation can have far-reaching consequences, especially with regard to the classical notions of God, providence and eschatology. A full discussion of these implications, however, would take me beyond the scope of this study.
15. In addition, the works already cited, e.g., Bishop's paper 'Faith as Doxastic Venture,' and his book *Believing by Faith*, there are two works that are relevant to assessing the viability of the Jamesian account of faith: the first is Anderi A. Buckareff, 'Can Faith be a Doxastic Venture?' *Religious Studies*, 2005, 41(4): 435–445; and the second is John Bishop, 'On the Possibility of Doxastic Venture: A Reply to Buckareff', *Religious Studies*, 2005, 41(4): 447–451.
16. John Hick, *Faith and Knowledge* (Ithaca, NY: Cornell University Press, 1966), pp. 35–46.
17. Ibid.
18. Gary Gutting, *Religious Belief and Religious Skepticism* (University of Notre Dame Press, c1982), pp. 106–107.
19. Robert McKim, *Religious Ambiguity and Religious Diversity* (Oxford University Press, 2001), pp. 182–183.
20. Ibid., p. 154.
21. Ibid., p. 184.
22. McKim, *Religious Ambiguity and Religious Diversity*, pp. 113–114.
23. Ibid.
24. Ibid.
25. McKim defines the Disaster Avoidance Principle as follows: God will arrange it so that we are not deprived by our circumstances of any good that is necessary for our long-term flourishing. *Religious Ambiguity and Religious Diversity*, p. 120.
26. Ibid., p. 114.
27. Bishop, 'Faith as Doxastic Venture', p. 474.
28. Bishop, *Believing by Faith*, p. 24.
29. Ibid., p. 195.
30. This argument is inspired by Hick, who suggests that, 'Belief in reality of Allah, Vishnu, Shiva, and of the non-personal Brahman, Dharmakaya, Tao, seem to be experientially well based as belief in the Holy Trinity...if only one of the many belief-systems based upon religious experience can be true, it follows that religious experience generally produces false beliefs, and that it is thus a generally unreliable basis for belief formation...'. See John Hick,

'The Epistemological Challenge of Religious Pluralism', *Faith and Philosophy*, 1997, 14: 277–278.

31. 'Trust in the Lord with all your heart. And do not lean on your own understanding. In all your ways acknowledge Him, and He will make your paths straight' (Proverbs 3: 5–6); 'And put your trust in the Ever-Living, Who never dies' (Quran 25: 58). These verses emphasise trust in God, and one may argue that in order to trust in God, a believer must also trust their inclinations that there is a God who is worthy of their trust.

32. A study which explores and responds to a wide range of critiques directed at James is authored by Robert J. O'Connell, *William James on the Courage to Believe* (Fordham University Press, 1997).

2   The Challenge of Al-Ghazālī's Scepticism

1. For a full biography, see Peter Adamson, *Al-Kindi* (Oxford University Press, 2007).

2. To trace the historical reception and development of philosophy within Islamic thought, see Shabbir Akhtar, 'The Possibility of a Philosophy of Islam', in *History of Islamic Philosophy* (ed.) Oliver Leaman and Seyyed Hossien Nasr (Routledge, 1996), pp. 1162–1169.

3. The quote is from al-Kindi's work entitled *On First Philosophy*, retrieved from http://plato.stanford.edu/entries/al-kindi/ 25/9/2007. An English translation of this work is available: see A. L. Ivry, *Al-Kindi's Metaphysics: A translation of Ya'qub ibn Ishaq al-Kindi's Treatise 'On First Philosophy'* (University of New York Press, 1974). In this work, he defines philosophy as: 'knowledge of the true nature of things, insofar as is possible for man' (p. 55).

4. For a full-blown Muslim critique of philosophical reasoning, see Muwaffaq al-Din `Abd Allah ibn Ahmad Ibn Qudama, *Censure of Speculative Theology*, Trans. George Makdisi (E.J.W. Gibb Memorial Series, 1962). For a summary of Ibn Qudama's arguments, see Binyamin Abrahamov, *Islamic Theology: Traditionalism and Rationalism* (Edinburgh University Press, 1998), pp. 24–24 and J. Pavlin, 'Sunni Kalam and Theological Controversies', in *History of Islamic Philosophy* (ed.) Oliver Leaman and Seyyed Hossien Nasr (Routledge. 1996), Vol. I, pp. 113–115.

5. Seyyed Hossein Nasr and Oliver Leaman (eds), *Islamic Philosophy from Its Origin to the Present: Philosophy in the Land of Prophecy* (State University of New York Press, 2006), p. 40.

6. Abrahamov, *Islamic Theology*, pp. 30–31.

7. Oliver Leaman, *A Brief Introduction to Islamic Philosophy* (Polity Press, 2001), p. 22.

8. For a Muslim defence of philosophical reasoning, see Abd Al-Jabbar, 'The Book of the Five Fundamentals', trans. by R. C. Martin, M. R. Woodward and D. S. Atmaja, *Defenders of Reason in Islam: Mutazilism from Medieval Schools to Modern Symbol* (Oneworld, 1997); Abu Hamid al-Ghazālī, *The Just Balance: al-Qistas al-Mustaqim*. Trans. by D. P Brewster (Ashraf Printing Press. Lahore. 1978); and, Abu al-Walid Muhammad ibn Ahmad Ibn Rushd, *Decisive Treatise & Epistle Dedicatory*, trans. by Charles E. Butterworth (Provo, Utah: Bringham Young University Press, 2001).

9. Brian Davies, *An Introduction to the Philosophy of Religion* (Oxford University Press, 2004), p. viii.
10. Beverley Clack and Brian R. Clack, *The Philosophy of Religion: A Critical Introduction* (Blackwell Publishers, 1998), p. 7.
11. Akhtar, 'The Possibility of a Philosophy of Islam', p. 1162.
12. Muhammad Iqbal, *Reconstruction of Religious Thought in Islam* (Lahore, 1960), p. 2. Asgar Ali Engineer offers a critical appraisal of Iqbal's philosophy of Islam; see 'Reconstruction of Religious Thought in Islam: A Critical Appraisal', *Social Scientist,* March 1980, 8(8): 52–63.
13. J. L. Mackie, *The Miracle of Theism: Arguments for and against the Existence of God* (Oxford, 1982), p. 1.
14. A. N. Whitehead, *Religion in the Making* (New York: The Macmillan Co., 1930), p. 85.
15. Abdullah Yusuf Ali, *The Meaning of Holy Quran* (Brentwood, MD., USA: Amana Corp., 1993), Chapter 31, Verse 20.
16. 'O you who have attained to faith! If you will remain conscious of God, he will endow you with a standard (*furqan*) by which to discern the true from the false...'. Ali, *The Meaning of Holy Quran,* Chapter 8, Verse 29. In a footnote on the Quranic use of the term *furqan*, Muhammad Asad writes: 'Muhammad Abduh amplifies the interpretation...of *al-furqan* (adopted by Tabari, Zamakshari and other great commentators) by maintaining that it applies also to 'human reason', which enables us to distinguish the true from the false...While the term *furqan* is often used in the Quran to describe one or another of the revealed scriptures...it has undoubtedly also the connotation pointed out by Abduh for instance, in (8:29), where it clearly refers to the faculty of moral valuation...' See, *The Message of the Quran* (Dar Al-Andalus, 1980), fn. 38, p. 12. The precise meaning of the Arabic term *furqan* is varied and at times contentious; see Fred M. Donner, 'Quranic Furqan', *Journal of Semitic Studies,* 2007, 55(2): 279–300.
17. Hannah Arendt viewed Adolf Eichmann – the architect of the Holocaust – as 'being constitutively incapable of exercising the kind of judgement that would have made his victims' suffering real or apparent for him. It was not the presence of hatred that enabled Eichmann to perpetrate the genocide, but the absence of the imaginative capacities that would have made the human and moral dimensions of his activities tangible for him. Eichmann failed to exercise his capacity of thinking, of having an internal dialogue with himself, which would have permitted self-awareness of the evil nature of his deeds. This amounted to a failure to use self-reflection as a basis for judgement, the faculty that would have required Eichmann to exercise his imagination so as to contemplate the nature of his deeds from the experiential standpoint of his victims'. See, Majid Yar, *The Internet Encyclopedia of Philosophy* (retrieved from http://www.iep.utm.edu/a/arendt.htm#H6, 9/02/2009).
18. Ali, *The Meaning of Holy Quran,* Chapter 86, Verses 5–14.
19. There are two key terms in relation to Islamic philosophical thought, *kalam* and *falsifa*. '*Kalam* is the common name of medieval Islamic, mostly rationalist, sometimes apologetic (or polemic) and religious philosophy. The literal meaning of the Arabic word is speaking, speech, things said, discussion. In the context of religious thought, it seems that around the middle of the eighth century, *kalam* came to denote a method of discussing matters relating

to religious doctrines, or to politico-religious questions... Those engaged in such arguments, or debates, and in reflection and speculation of them, were called *mutukallimun*. For them, the attainment of knowledge was not an end in itself, but rather a means in the service of religious doctrine and practice. The *mutakallimun* must be distinguished from thinkers (Muslims as well as Christians) who considered themselves committed to the legacy of Greek philosophy, mainly a Neoplatonic interpretation of Aristotelianism. These were the *falasifa*, and their systems and methods [referred to as] *falsifa*. The *falasifa*, who were, with few exceptions, observant members of their respective religious communities (Muslims, Christians and Jews), professed the attainment of true knowledge for its own sake, as the actual realization of perfection'. Haggai Ben-Shammai, '*Kalam* in Medieval Jewish Philosophy', in *History of Jewish Philosophy* (ed.) Daniel Frank and Oliver Leaman (Routledge, 1997), p. 115.

20. Al-Ghazālī, *The Incoherence of the Philosophers*, trans. by Michael M. Marmura (Bringham Young University Press, 1997), p. xxii.
21. Ibid., pp. 1–2.
22. Abu Yusuf al-Kindi, regarded as the first Muslim philosopher was an exception. Al-Kindi believed that the world could not be eternal and that it was created in time (*muhdath*). See 'Al-Kindi' in *History of Islamic Philosophy* (eds) Seyyed Hossein Nasr and Oliver Leaman (Routledge, 1996), p. 170)
23 For a consideration of al-Ghazālī's arguments and responses to them, see Oliver Leaman, *An Introduction to Medieval Islamic Philosophy* (Cambridge University Press, 1986), pp. 38–59.
24 Ibid., p. 20.
25 Al-Ghazālī, '*Al-Munqidh min al-dalal*', trans. by. W. M. Watt in *The Faith and Practice of Al-Ghazālī* (London, 1967), p. 36.
26 Frank Griffel notes the following with respect to al-Ghazālī's attitude toward reason: 'Al-Ghazālī follows Aristotle and the falasifa in their opinion that reason ('aql) is executed most purely and precisely by formulating demonstrative arguments, which reach a level at which their conclusion are beyond doubt. He remains true to the rationalist approach, which was shared by both Ash'arites as well as falasifa ...' *Al-Ghazali's Philosophical Theology: An Introduction to the Study of his Life and Thought* (New York: Oxford University Press, 2009), p. 116.
27 Al-Ghazālī also relates his observation to a tradition, where Muhammad, the prophet of Islam, is to have said, 'Everyone is born with a sound nature, it is one's parents who make one into a Jew, Christian or a Magian' – *Deliverance from Error and Mystical Union with the Almighty: Al-Munqidh Min Al- Dalāl*; English translation with introduction by Muhammad AbꞋulaylah Nurshif Abdul-Rahim Rifat; introduction and notes, George F. McLean (Washington, D.C.: Council for Research in Values and Philosophy, 2001), p. 62.
28 Ibid., pp. 62–63.
29 Eric Ormsby, *Ghazali: The Revival of Islam* (Oneworld Publications, 2007, p. 1.
30. He uses scepticism as a foil against which he develops his Sufi epistemology of religious belief. In the chapter to follow, I will also elaborate on the complementary relationship between scepticism and the Sufi path.
31. Al-Ghazālī, *Deliverance from Error and Mystical Union with the Almighty*, p. 65.
32. Ibid., p. 66.

33. Ibid., pp. 66–68.
34. W. Doney (ed.), *Descartes: A Collection of Critical Essays* (Macmillan, 1968), pp. 145–146. Tamara Albertini observes that while the similarities between al-Ghazālī and Descartes are striking, they in fact pursue very different philosophical aims. See 'Crisis and Certainty of Knowledge in Al-Ghazali (1058–1111) and Descartes (1596–1650)', *Philosophy East & West*, January 2005, 1–14.
35. Al-Ghazālī's crisis involves a loss of trust in the deliverances of human rational capacities. The Quranic verses quoted earlier, however, suggest that human rational capacities can be trusted. Accordingly, we may interpret al-Ghazālī's crisis as one of religious faith, since his inability to trust in reason runs counter to the ethos of the Quran.
36. Jeffery Whitman, *The Power and Value of Skepticism* (Rowman & Littlefield Publishers, 1996), p. 16.
37. Stewart Cohen, 'Contextualism, Skepticism, and the Structure of Reasons', *Noûs*, 1999, 33 (Supplement); *Philosophical Perspectives*, 13; *Epistemology*, 58.
38. Ibid.
39. A full defence of fallibilism is beyond the scope of this study, although it is a view that is endorsed by a majority of epistemologists. See Baron Reed, 'How to Think About Fallibilism', *Philosophical Studies*, 2002, 107(2): 143–157.
40. Baron Reed makes this point with reference to Descartes, and I think it is equally applicable to al-Ghazālī. See 'A New Argument for Skepticism', *Philosophical Studies*, 2009, 142(1): 92.
41. Our response to al-Ghazālī's case for scepticism should not be seen as a definitive answer to scepticism. At best, the evaluation of al-Ghazālī's scepticism suggests that it is self-undermining. There are a variety of ways to refine and defend a sceptical stance. See Reed, 'A New Argument for Skepticism', pp. 91–104. A deeper study of scepticism would, however, extend us beyond the scope of this study.

3   Al-Ghazālī's Sufi Account of Faith

1. The broader argument views human reason as fallible and therefore unsuitable as foundation for 'certain knowledge'. The case for scepticism aims to demonstrate the limits of human reason.
2. Abu Hamid Al-Ghazālī, *Deliverance from Error and Mystical Union with the Almighty: Al-Munqidh Min Al- Dalā*; English translation with introduction by Muhammad Ab⁻ulaylah Nurshif Abdul-Rahim Rifat; introduction and notes. George F. McLean (Washington. D.C.: Council for Research in Values and Philosophy, 2001), p. 67.
3. I have adapted this argument from Immanuel Kant. See Paul Guyer. 'Immanuel Kant', (ed.) E. Craig, *Routledge Encyclopedia of Philosophy* (London: Routledge, 1998; 2004). Retrieved from http://www.rep.routledge.com/article/DB047SECT5, 27/05/2009.
4. Abdullah Yusuf Ali, *The Meaning of the Holy Quran* (Brentwood. MD: Amana Corp., 1993), Chapter 4, Verse 163.
5. I have compared and contrasted al-Ghazālī's metaphysics with the aesthetics of Arthur Schopenhauer, See 'Al-Ghazālī and Schopenhauer on Knowledge and Suffering', *Philosophy East and West*, 2007, 57(4): 409–419.

6. Abu Hamid Al-Ghazālī, *The Niche of Lights: Mishkat al-anwar*, trans., introd., and annot. by David Buchman (Brigham Young University Press, 1998), p. 12.
7. Ibid.
8. Ibid., p. xvii.
9. Ibid., p. xxxiii.
10. Ibid.
11. Ibid.
12. Ibid., pp. 39–41.
13. Ibid., pp. 42–43.
14. Ibid.
15. Ibid.
16. Ibid.
17. Ibid.
18. Ibid., p. 44.
19. Ibid., p. 45.
20. Ibid., p. 52.
21. Al-Ghazālī, *Deliverance from Error and Mystical Union with the Almighty*, p. 67.
22. This point suggests that the Sufi account can be consistent with the Jamesian account.
23. Michael Sudduth, 'Reformed Epistemology and Christian Apologetics', *Religious Studies*, 2003, 39: 303.
24. Alvin Plantinga, *Warranted Christian Belief* (Oxford University Press, 2001), p. 95.
25. Ibid., p. 98.
26. Ibid.
27. There are other approaches to Reformed epistemology; for example, William Alston defends the view that Christian Mystical Practice is a reliable source of beliefs about God. See William Alston, *Perceiving God, Perceiving God: The Epistemology of Religious Experience* (Cornell University Press, 1991).
28. Ibid., p. 172.
29. Ibid., p. 73.
30. Ibid., p. 175.
31. Ibid., p. 176.
32. Michael Sudduth, 'Reformed Epistemology and Christian Apologetics', p. 303.
33. John Bishop and Imran Aijaz, 'How to Answer the *de jure* Question about Christian Belief', *International Journal for the Philosophy of Religion*, 2004, 56: 116. I have altered the quote slightly, replacing the word 'Christian' with the word 'theistic'.
34. Plantinga maintains that if God does indeed exist, then basic beliefs about God will be warranted. He notes, 'that theistic belief produced by the *sensus divinitatis* can also be *properly basic with respect to warrant*. It isn't just that the believer in God is within her epistemic rights in accepting theistic belief in the basic way. That is indeed so; more than that, however, this belief can have warrant for the person in question, warrant that is often sufficient for knowledge. The *sensus divinitatis* is a belief-producing faculty (or power, or mechanism) that under the right conditions produces belief that isn't evidentially based on other beliefs. On this model, our cognitive faculties

have been designed and created by God; the design plan, therefore, is a design plan in the literal and paradigmatic sense. It is a blueprint or plan for our ways of functioning, and it has been developed and instituted by a conscious, intelligent agent. The purpose of the *sensus divinitatis* is to enable us to have true beliefs about God; when it functions properly, it ordinarily *does* produce true beliefs about God. These beliefs therefore meet the conditions for warrant; if the beliefs produced are strong enough, then they constitute knowledge'. *Warranted Christian Belief,* (Oxford University Press. 2001), pp. 178–179.

35. Ibid., p. 109.
36. The evidentialist principle is the thesis that a person can take *p* to be true if and only if they are evidentially justified in holding *p* to be true.
37. Ibid., p. 110.
38. Ibid., p. 119.
39. Ibid., p. 121.
40. Ibid.
41. Ibid., pp. 121–122.
42. Ibid.
43. Duncan Pritchard, 'Reforming Reformed Epistemology', *International Philosophical Quarterly*, 2003, 43: 43–66.
44. 'John and Aijaz, 'How to Answer the *de jure* Question about Christian Belief', p. 122.
45. One may suggest that proponents of PRE might be concerned that their account of how to set aside the *de jure* question could apply only to a minority of theists.

4 A Jamesian Reading of Al-Ghazālī

1. We may construe al-Ghazālī's illumination experience as involving a passional cause of a belief. A passional cause, or a non-evidential cause of a belief, to recall, is defined as being any cause of a belief other than a cause that provides the believer with evidence for its truth.
2. Abu Hamid Al-Ghazālī, *Deliverance from Error and Mystical Union with the Almighty: Al-Munqidh Min Al- Dalāl*; English translation with introduction by Muhammad Abʿulaylah Nurshif Abdul-Rahim Rifat; introduction and notes. George F. McLean. (Washington. D.C.: Council for Research in Values and Philosophy. 2001), p. 67.
3. Kojiro Nakamura, *Al-Ghazālī and Prayer* (Islamic Book Trust, 2001), p. 10.
4. Al-Ghazālī writes, 'what I seek is knowledge of the true meaning of things. Of necessity, therefore, I must inquire into just what the true meaning of knowledge is. Then it became clear to me that *sure* and *certain* knowledge is that in which the thing known is made manifest that no doubt clings to it, nor is it accompanied by the possibility of error and deception...'. Richard McCarthy, *Freedom and Fulfilment* (Twayne Publishers, 1980), p. 63.
5. Imran Aijaz, *Islamic Philosophy of Religion: Reflections on Fideism, Rationalism and Religious Ambiguity* (Ph.D. Dissertation, 2009), p. 150.
6. Paul Moser, *The Elusive God* (Cambridge University Press, 2008), p. 102.
7. Ibid.

8. Paul Sands, *The Justification of Religious Faith in Soren Kierkegaard, John Henry Newman, and William James* (Gorgias Press, 2003), p. 257.
9. 'Muslim spirituality as we have said, is demanding and, through the Islamic teaching, touches all the dimensions of life…The return to one's self gives birth to a feeling of humility that characterises the human being before God. This humility should spread wide and deep through all the areas of life: at every stage of working on one's self there will be a struggle against complacency, pride and the pretentious human desire to succeed alone, using one's own resources (on the social, professional, political, or intellectual level)'. Tariq Ramadan, *Western Muslims and the Future of Islam* (Oxford University Press, 2005), p. 122. See also Abdulaziz Sachedina, *The Islamic Roots of Democratic Pluralism* (Oxford University Press, 2001) and Vincent Cornell, *Voices of Islam* (Praeger Publishers, 2007).
10. Osman Bakar notes that al-Ghazālī understands certainty (*yaqin*) in two distinct ways: 'the term *yaqin* can be employed to signify lack or negation of doubt, in the sense that the knowledge or the truth in question is established from evidence which leaves no place for any possibility of doubt. The second meaning of the term *yaqin*… refers to the intensity of religious faith or fervour which involves both the acceptance, by the soul, of that which prevails over the heart and takes hold of it and the submission of the soul to that thing in question'. Bakar also suggests that: 'For al-Ghazālī, both kinds of *yaqin* need to be strengthened, but it is the second kind of *yaqin* which is the nobler of the two, since without it serving as an epistemological basis for the first kind of *yaqin,* the latter would definitely lack epistemic substance and value. Moreover, it fosters religious and spiritual obedience, and praiseworthy habits. In other words, philosophical certainty is of no value if it is not accompanied by submission to the truth and by the transformation of one's being in conformity with that truth'. *The History and Philosophy of Islamic Science* (Islamic Texts Society, 1999), pp. 55–56.
11. Muhammad Muhsin Khan, *The Translations of the Meanings of Sahih al-Bukhari*, 9 vols. (Beirut, 1405/1985), I, p. 3. This account of the Prophet's first meeting with the Angel is a Sunni account, and thus accepted by the majority of Muslims.
12. Muhammad's response also suggests that disobeying the commission was not a possibility that he has seriously considered, that is, it was not a live hypothesis.
13. Tim Winter, 'Pluralism from a Muslim Perspective', in *Abraham's Children: Jews, Christians and Muslims in Conversation* (ed.) Norman Solomon et al. (T. & T. Clark Publishers, 2006), p. 203.
14. Abdulaziz Sachedina, 'The Quran and Other Religions', in *The Cambridge Companion to the Qur'an* (ed.) Jane Dammen McAuliffe (Cambridge University Press, 2006), p. 293.
15. Bruce Waller, *Critical Thinking: Consider the Verdict* (4th ed.) (Upper Saddle River, NJ: Prentice Hall, 2001), p. 14.
16. *A Common Word Between Us and You*, retrieved from http://www.acommonword.com/index.php?lang=en&page=option1, 26/11/2008.
17. The number of signatories has now grown close to 300.
18. *A Common Word Between Us and You.*

19. Ibid.
20. Ibid.
21. Ibid.
22. Ibid. The document also notes that the three faculties are also acknowledged in the Old and New Testament: 'Mark 12:32...contain the three terms *kardia* ("heart"), *dianoia* ("mind"), and *ischus* ("strength")...In the *Shema* of Deuteronomy 6:4–5 (*Hear, O Israel: The LORD our God, the LORD is one! / You shall love the LORD your God with all your heart, and with all your soul, and with all your strength*). In Hebrew the word for "heart" is *lev*, the word for "soul" is *nefesh*, and the word for "strength" is *me'od*.'
23. Ibid.
24. Ibid.
25. Admittedly, a proponent of al-Ghazālī's account, or its 'Reformed' counterpart, can also claim that their accounts of faith also have these three components, namely: *understanding, willing,* and *feeling* are also consistent with their accounts of faith. However, as we have already discovered, al-Ghazālī's account and its Reformed counterpart are deeply problematic from a philosophical and theological point of view. Although, we will need to concede that having the components of *understanding, willing,* and *feeling* is a necessary but not a sufficient conditions of an Islamic account of faith.
26. Abdullah Saeed, 'The Need to Rethink Apostasy Laws', in *Freedom of Religion, Apostasy and Islam* (ed.) Abdullag Saeed and Hassan Saeed (Ashgate Publishing, 2004), p. 172.
27. Muhammad Asad, *The Message of the Quran* (Dar Al-Andalus. 1980), pp. 3–4.
28. D. B. Macdonald-[L. Gardet], 'al-Ghayb', in *Encyclopaedia of Islam*, by H. A. R. Gibb et al. (Leiden: E.J. Brill, 1960– [i.e., 1954–]–2001), pp. 1025–1026.
29. Ibn Kathir, *Tafsir Ibn Kathir Juz' 1 (Part 1): Al-Fatihah 1 To Al-Baqarah 141* (2nd edn) (ed.) Muhammad Saed Abdul-Rahman (MSA Publication Limited, 2009), p. 65.
30. Asad, *The Message of the Quran*, fn. 3, p. 4.
31. The 'will of God' can also be considered to be *al-ghayb*, as opposed to the existence of God. I do not think alternative definitions of *al-ghayb* undercut my argument, since the exegesis I offer is an accepted reading of the term. My argument, if correct, also establishes the possibility that belief in God is a case of believing in *al-ghayb*, and this seems compatible with the ambiguity thesis.

5   The Challenge of Contemporary Evidentialism

1. Jonathan E. Adler, *Belief's Own Ethics* (Cambridge, Mass.: MIT Press, 2002), p. 52.
2. Ibid., p. 26.
3. Ibid.
4. Jonathan E. Adler, 'William James and What Cannot Be Believed', *The Harvard Review of Philosophy*, 2005, XII(1): 70.
5. Ibid., p. 73.
6. Ibid., p. 74.
7. William James, 'The Will to Believe', in *Essays in Pragmatism* (Holloway Press, 2007), p. 90.

8. Adler, 'William James and What Cannot be Believed', p. 68.
9. Ibid., p. 69.
10. Ibid., p. 72.
11. Ibid.
12. Ibid., p. 116.
13. Adler, *Belief's Own Ethics*, p. 105.
14. Ibid., p. 118.
15. Ibid., p. 120.
16. Ibid., p. 119.
17. John L. Schellenberg, *Divine Hiddenness and Human Reason* (Cornell University Press, 1993), p. 10.
18. Ibid.
19. Richard Swinburne, *The Existence of God* (Oxford University Press, 1979), p. 153.
20. Ibid.
21. Adler, 'William James and What Cannot be Believed', pp. 66–67.
22. Ibid., refer to p. 78, n. 8.
23. William James, *The Will to Believe, Human Immortality* (Dover Publications, 1956), p. 11.
24. Also see p. 19, where I use the example of the mountaineer to explain the claim of epistemic parity.
25. See Bishop, 'Faith as Doxastic Venture', *Religious Studies*, 2002, 38(4): 471–487.
26. Adler, 'William James and What Cannot be Believed', p. 72.
27. Adler, *Belief's Own Ethics*, p. 29.
28. Ibid., p. 27.
29. Ibid.
30. Ibid.
31. Ibid., p. 28.
32. Ibid., p. 31.
33. Adler, 'William James and What Cannot be Believed', p. 70. Adler explains that 'overtness' signals that nothing of the agent's epistemic position – in particular, his evidence, his relevant beliefs, that the propositional-attitude involved is belief, and his essential commitments in regard to belief – is hidden. Full awareness suggests a methodological idealisation as opposed to a psychological state. In *Belief's Own Ethics* (p. 29), Adler articulates the test in the following terms: '*p* is incoherently believed by anyone X just in case *p* is believed by X, but, if X became fully aware of his epistemic position in regard to *p* (his believing that *p* is true, and his assessment of his evidence of reasons to believe it), X could not continue to believe that *p* (since the corresponding thought would be an overt contradiction)'.
34. Adler, *Belief's Own Ethics*, p. 30.
35. Ibid., p. 74.
36. Ibid., p. 52.
37. Peter Strawson, 'Freedom and Resentment', *Proceedings of the British Academy*, 1962, 48: 187–211.
38. Adler, *Belief's Own Ethics*, p. 216.
39. Ibid., p. 220.
40. Ibid., p. 219.

41. Ibid., p. 216.
42. Ibid., p. 220.
43. Ibid., p. 223.
44. Ibid., p. 224.
45. Adler, 'William James and What Cannot be Believed', p. 69.
46. Adler, *Belief's Own Ethics*, p. 36.
47. Ibid.
48. To defend the view that 'one should assert *p* only if one knows *p*', Adler cites Timothy Williamson's *Knowledge and its Limits* (Oxford University Press, 2002). According to Williamson, there are reasons to think that: (a) knowledge is purely a mental state, and (b) that one's total evidence is simply one's total knowledge. For a response to these claims, see Adam Leite, 'On Williamson's Arguments that Knowledge is a Mental State', *Ratio* (new series), June 2005, XVIII(2): 165–175.
49. Even if we accept that properly believing also entails knowing, we encounter the issue of subjectivity, since knowing, given Adler's account, assumes that the reasons we have for believing have been judged by us to be adequate. If judgments do vary, then there will be differences on whether reasons for believing will be judged as being adequate or sufficient, and these differences will carry over into claims pertaining to knowledge. The concern here is that Adler is using the term 'knowledge' in a way that presumes it to be a common agreed-upon standard, but the subjective element means the concept will turn out to mean different things to different people.

6 Challenges to Religious Pluralism

1. Imran Aijaz, 'Belief, Providence and Eschatology: Some Philosophical Problems in Islamic Theism', *Philosophy Compass*, 2008, 3(1): 231–253.
2. Ibid., p. 233.
3. Ibid.
4. Alvin Plantinga, 'Pluralism: A Defense of Religious Exclusivism', in *The Philosophical Challenge of Religious Diversity* (ed.) Philip Quinn and Kevin Meeker (Oxford University Press, 1999), p. 174.
5. Alvin Plantinga, 'Ad Hick', *Faith and Philosophy*,1997, 14(3): 296.
6. Ibid., pp. 296–297.
7. Robert McKim, *Religious Ambiguity and Religious Diversity* (Oxford University Press, 2001), p. 136.
8. Ibid.
9. Plantinga, 'Pluralism: a Defense of Religious Exclusivism', p. 190.
10. Ibid., p. 176.
11. The atheist can also be an exclusivist, since they can also deny absolute epistemic parity, i.e., belief in God can be portrayed as the product of: (a) ignorance and fear in the face of the hostile forces of nature (Hume); (b) an inequitable social order (Marx); or, (c) an immature infantile psychology (Freud). See Graham Oppy and Nick Trakakis, 'Religious Language Games', in *Realism and Religion: Philosophical and Theological Perspectives* (ed.) Andrew Moore and Michael Scott (Ashgate, 2007), p. 125.

12. Ibid., p. 182.
13. Plantinga may argue that he does have *good reason* to doubt overall epistemic parity, thus he is entitled to an exclusivist stance. However, as I have already noted, Plantinga's exclusivist strategy can also be employed by a Muslim or Jew. Accordingly, there would be multiple and mutually exclusive claims of epistemic superiority. This state of affairs indicates that if we are to doubt overall epistemic parity, then we need reasons that are independent from a given theological framework, i.e., reasons which do not first presuppose the truth of a given theological framework.
14. John Hick notes the following distinction between pluralism and exclusivism: 'Pluralism is ... not another historical religion making an exclusive religious claim, but a meta-theory about the relation between the historical religions. Its logical status as a second-order philosophical theory or hypothesis is different in kind from that of a first-order religious creed or gospel. And so the religious pluralist does not, like the traditional religious exclusivist, consign non-believers to perdition, but invites them to try to produce a better explanation of the data'. 'The Possibility of Religious Pluralism', *Religious Studies*, 1997, 33(2): 163.
15. Kelly James Clark, 'Perils of Pluralism', *Faith and Philosophy*, 1997, 14(3): 318.
16. In an autobiographical work entitled *From Fundamentalist to Freethinker*, Ray Bradley summarises his negative childhood experiences with religion as follows: 'Given what I've told you of my story so far, you could be forgiven for supposing that my struggles to free myself from the bondage of Baptist beliefs occurred in an atmosphere of sweetness and light. How about the darker side that we normally associate with the term "fundamentalism"? Condemnation of films, dancing, immodest clothing, lipstick, alcohol, and the like? Prohibitions against work – even homework – on the Lord's Day? Blasphemy-charges? Book-burnings? Beating those who dared to differ? Sad to say, I experienced all these at the hands of those who most sincerely sought to save my soul from perdition: my parents. The book-burnings occurred when my Biology teacher, Peter Ohms, lent me a textbook outlining evolutionary theory and a novel depicting St. Paul as a misogynist who occasionally sought relief in the warm flesh of a woman of the night. Both books disappeared mysteriously from my shelves. It was only when questioned that my parents revealed the fate of both. They had been thrown into a bonfire along with "other garbage." My teacher was magnanimous. But that didn't erase my shame and outrage'. Retrieved from http://www.sfu.ca/philosophy/bradley/Fundamentalist%20to%20Free-thinker.pdf, 29/10/2008.
17. Robert Wicks, 'Arthur Schopenhauer', *Stanford Encyclopedia of Philosophy* (retrieved from http://plato.stanford.edu/entries/schopenhauer/, 25/02/2009).
18. Aijaz, 'Belief, Providence and Eschatology', pp. 231–253.
19. Aijaz notes that *tawhīd*, which is often translated as belief in 'Islamic monotheism', and also understood to mean believing that nothing has the right to be worshipped apart from God alone, and believing that certain names and attributes are unique to God (so that there is nothing in creation that is like God).
20. I am grateful to Imran Aijaz for helping me in formulating a presentation of his argument in standard form.

21. Abdullah Yusuf Ali, *The Meaning of the Holy Quran* (Brentwood. MD: Amana Corp., 1993), Chapter 7, Verse 172.
22. Aijaz, 'Belief, Providence and Eschatology', p. 244.
23. Aijaz notes that 'the language used by the Qur'ān, in those particular narratives in which the *kāfir* is accused of rejecting religious truth, makes sense only if the *kāfir* actually has knowledge of the relevant religious truth and literally 'covers up' or 'conceals' that knowledge and truth' (p. 238).
24. Aijaz, 'Belief, Providence and Eschatology', p. 239. The quote itself is from, Toshihiko Izutsu, *The Concept of Belief in Islamic Theology* (Basingstoke: Yurindo, 1965), pp. 7–8.
25. Ibid., p.242.
26. D. B. Macdonald, 'Fitra', in *Encyclopaedia of Islam* (ed.) H. A. R. Gibb [et al.] (Leiden: E.J. Brill, 1960– [i.e., 1954–]–2001), pp. 931–932.
27. Ibid.
28. Ibid.
29. Ibid.
30. This definition of *fitrah* is provided in *Islam Key Concepts* by Kecia Ali and Oliver Leaman (Routledge, 2007).
31. Abdullah Yusuf ali,*The Meaning of the Holy Quran (Brentwood. MD: Amana Corp., 1993) Chapter (Surah) 45, Verses 3-4*.
32. J. J. G. Jansen, 'Mu'Min', in *Encyclopaedia of Islam,* by H.A.R. Gibb [et al.] (Leiden: E.J. Brill, 1960- [i.e.1954-] – <2001), pp. 554–555.
33. Ibid.
34. W. Bjorkman, 'Kāfir', in *Encyclopaedia of Islam* (ed.) H. A. R. Gibb [et al.] (Leiden: E.J. Brill, 1960– [i.e., 1954–]–2001), pp. 407–408.
35. Ibid.
36. Ibid.
37. Ibid.
38. Muhammad Asad, *The Message of the Quran* (Dar Al-Andalus. 1980), p. 907.
39. Ibid., Chapter 4, Verses 97–99.
40. Ibid., p.124.
41. Ibid.
42. Ibid.
43. The tradition is quoted by Muhammad Saed Abdul-Rahman, *Islam: Questions and Answers Volume 1* (MSA Publication Limited, 2003), p. 465.
44. Sherman Jackson, *On the Boundaries of Theological Tolerance in Islam : Abu Ḥamid al-Ghazālī's Fayṣal al-Tafriqa Bayna al-Islām wa al-Zandaqa* (Oxford University Press, 2002), p. 126.
45. Ibid., p. 128.
46. A recent paper on the work of Ibn Qayyim al-Jawziyya suggests that universal salvation may be compatible with an exclusivist perspective. Ibn al-Qayyim argues that every person will eventually be encompassed by God's mercy. He maintains that hell is not merely punitive, but also therapeutic, i.e., a person will be cleansed from their sins, including the sin of non-belief. See Jon Hoover, 'Islamic Universalism: Ibn Qayyim al-Jawziyya's Salafī Deliberations on the Duration of Hell-Fire', *The Muslim World*, January 2009, 99(1): 181–201.
47. *The Translations of the Meanings of Sahih al-Bukhari,* Vol. 8, Bk. 73, No. 116.

Bibliography

A Common Word between Us and You (Retrieved from www.acommonword.com).

Abdul-Rahman, Muhammad Saed. *Islam: Questions and Answers Volume 1* (MSA Publication Limited, 2003).

Abrahamov, Binyamin. *Islamic Theology: Traditionalism and Rationalism Polity* (Edinburgh University Press, 1998).

Abu Yusuf, 'Al Kindi', in *History of Islamic Philosophy* (eds) Seyyed Hossein Nasr and Oliver Leaman (Routledge, 1996), p. 170.

Adamson, Peter. *Al-Kindi* (Oxford University Press, 2007).

Adler, Jonathan E. *Belief's Own Ethis* (Cambridge, Mass.: MIT Press, 2002).

—— 'William James and What Cannot be Believed', *The Harvard Review of Philosophy*, 2005, XII(1): 65–79.

Aijaz, Imran. 'Belief, Providence and Eschatology: Some Philosophical Problems in Islamic Theism', *Philosophy Compass*, 2008, 3(1): 231–253.

Aijaz, Imran. *Islamic Philosophy of Religion: Reflections on Fideism, Rationalism and Religious Ambiguity* (Ph.D. Dissertation, 2009) – 'Belief, Providence and Eschatology: Some Philosophical Problems in Islamic Theism', Philosophy Compass, 2008, 3(1): 231-253.

Akhtar, Shabbir. 'The Possibility of a Philosophy of Islam', in *History of Islamic Philosophy* (ed.) Oliver Leaman and Seyyed Hossien Nasr (Routledge. 1996), pp. 1162–1169.

Albertini, Tamara. 'Crisis and Certainty of Knowledge in Al-Ghazali (1058–1111) and Descartes (1596–1650)', *Philosophy East & West*, January 2005, pp. 1–14.

Al-Ghazālī, Abu Hamid. *The Foundations of the Articles of Faith : Kitab Qawa 'id al Aqa 'id*, trans. by Sabih Amin Faris (Lebanon: American University of Beirut, 1963).

—— *Al-Munqidh Min Al-dalal,* trans. by W. M. Watt. in *The Faith and Practice of Al-Ghazāli* (London, 1967).

—— *The Just Balance: Al-Qistas al-Mustaqim,* trans. by D. P. Brewster (Lahore: Ashraf Printing Press, 1978).

—— *The Incoherence of the Philosophers,* trans. by Michael M. Marmura (Bringham Young University Press, 1997).

—— *The Niche of Lights: Mishkat Al-anwar,* trans., introd. and annot. by David Buchman (Brigham Young University Press, 1998).

—— *Deliverance from error and mystical union with the Almighty: Al-Munqidh Min Al-Dalāl;* English translation with introduction by Muhammad Ab⁻ulaylah Nurshif Abdul-Rahim Rifat; introduction and notes. George F. McLean (Council for Research in Values and Philosophy, 2001).

—— *The Alchemy of Happiness,* trans. Henry A. Homes (Forgotten Books, 2008).

Ali, Abdullah Yusuf. *The Meaning of the Holy Quran* (Amana Corp., 1993).

Ali, Kecia and Oliver Leaman. *Islam Key Concepts* (Routledge, 2007).

Ali, Zain. 'Al-Ghazālī and Schopenhauer on Knowledge and Suffering', *Philosophy East and West*, 2007, 57(4): 409–419.

Al-Jabbar, Abd. 'The Book of the Five Fundamentals', trans. R. C. Martin, M. R. Woodward and D. S.Atmaja, *Defenders of Reason in Islam: Mutazilism from Medieval Schools to Modern Symbol* (Oneworld, 1997).

Alston,William. *Perceiving God, Perceiving God: The Epistemology of Religious Experience* (Cornell University Press, 1991)

Asad, Muhammad. *The Message of the Quran* (Dar Al-Andalus, 1980).

Bakar, Osman. *The History and Philosophy of Islamic Science* (Islamic Texts Society, 1999).

Ben-Shammai, Haggai. '*Kalam* in Medieval Jewish Philosophy', *History of Jewish Philosophy* (eds) Daniel Frank and Oliver Leaman (Routledge, 1997), pp. 115–148.

Bishop, John. 'Faith as Doxastic Venture', *Religious Studies*, 2002, 38(4): 471–487.

——. and Imran Aijaz. 'How to Answer the *de jure* Question About Christian Belief', *International Journal for the Philosophy of Religion*, 2004, 56: 109–129.

——. 'On the Possibility of Doxastic Venture: A Reply to Buckareff', *Religious Studies*, 2005, 41(4): 447–451.

——— *Believing by Faith: An Essay in the Epistemology and Ethics of Religious Belief* (Oxford University Press, 2007).

Bjorkman, W. 'Kāfir', in *Encyclopaedia of Islam*, by H. A. R. Gibb [et al.] (Leiden: E.J. Brill, 1960– [i.e., 1954–]–2001), pp. 407–408.

Bradley, Ray. *From Fundamentalist to Freethinker* (Retrieved from http://www.sfu.ca/philosophy/bradley/Fundamentalist%20to%20Free-thinker.pdf).

Buckareff, Anderi A. 'Can Faith Be a Doxastic Venture?' *Religious Studies*, 2005, 41(4): 435–445.

Clack, Beverley and Brian R. Clack. *The Philosophy of Religion: A Critical Introduction* (Blackwell Publishers, 1998).

Clark, Kelly James. 'Perils of Pluralism', *Faith and Philosophy*, 1997, 14(3): 303–320.

Clifford, William. 'The Ethics of Belief', reprinted in *Philosophy: The Big Question* (ed.) Ruth J. Sample, Charles W. Mills and James P. Sterba (Wiley-Blackwell, 2004), pp. 83–87.

Cohen, Stewart. 'Contextualism, Skepticism and the Structure of Reasons', *Noûs*, 1999, 33 (Supplement); Philosophical Perspectives, 13; Epistemology, 57–89.

Cornell, Vincent. *Voices of Islam* (Praeger Publishers, 2007).

Davies, Brian. *An Introduction to the Philosophy of Religion.* (Oxford University Press, 2004).

Doney, W. (ed.) *Descartes: A Collection of Critical Essays* (Macmillan, 1968).

Donner, Fred M. 'Quranic Furqan', *Journal of Semitic Studies*, 2007, 55(2): 279–300.

Engineer, Asgar Ali. 'Reconstruction of Religious Thought in Islam: A Critical Appraisal', *Social Scientist,* March 1980, 8(8): 52–63.

Frank, Richard. *Al-Ghazali and the Ash'arite School* (Duke University Press, 1994).

Griffel, Frank. 'Al-Ghazali', *Stanford Encyclopedia of Philosophy* (Retrieved from http://plato.stanford.edu/entries/al-ghazali/#CumPosOccSecCau).

——— *Al-Ghazali's Philosophical Theology: An Introduction to the Study of his Life and Thought* (New York: Oxford University Press, 2009).

Gutting, Gary. *Religious Belief and Religious Skepticism* (University of Notre Dame Press: 1982c).

Guyer, Paul. 'Immanuel Kant', In E. Craig (ed.) *Routledge Encyclopedia of Philosophy* (London: Routledge, 2004) (Retrieved from http://www.rep.routledge.com/article/DB047SECT5).

Hick, John. *Faith and Knowledge* (Ithaca, NY: Cornell University Press, 1966).

———'The Philosophy of World Religions', *Scottish Journal of Theology*, 1984, 37: 229-245.

——— *An Interpretation of Religion* (London: Macmillan, 1989)

——— 'The Epistemological Challenge of Religious Pluralism', *Faith and Philosophy*, 1997, 14: 77–286

——— 'The Possibility of Religious Pluralism: A Reply to Gavin D'Costa', *Religious Studies*, 1997, 33(2): 161–166.

Hoover, Jon. 'Islamic Universalism: Ibn Qayyim al-Jawziyya's Salafī Deliberations on the Duration of Hell-Fire', *The Muslim World*, January 2009, 99(1): 181–201.

Howard-Snyder, Daniel and Paul K. Moser *Divine Hiddenness: New Essays* (Cambridge University Press, 2002).

Ibn Kathir, *Tafsir Ibn Kathir Juz' 1 (Part 1): Al-Fatihah 1 To Al-Baqarah 141* (2nd edn) by Muhammad Saed Abdul-Rahman (MSA Publication Limited, 2009).

Ibn Qudama, Muwaffaq al-Din `Abd Allah ibn Ahmad. *Censure of Speculative Theology*, trans. George Makdisi (E.J.W. Gibb Memorial Series, 1962).

Ibn Rushd, Abu al-Walid Muhammad ibn Ahmad. *Decisive Treatise & Epistle Dedicatory*, trans. Charles E. Butterworth (Provo, Utah: Bringham Young University Press, 2001).

Iqbal, Muhammad. *Reconstruction of Religious Thought in Islam* (Lahore, 1960).

Ivry, A. L. *Al-Kindi's Metaphysics: A Translation of Ya'qub ibn Ishaq al-Kindi's Treatise 'On First Philosophy'* (University of New York Press, 1974).

Izutsu, Toshihiko. *The Concept of Belief in Islamic Theology* (Basingstoke: Yurindo, 1965).

James, William. *The Will to Believe. Human Immortality* (Dover Publications, 1956).

Jackson, Sherman. *On the Boundaries of Theological Tolerance in Islam: Abu HamidAl-Ghazali's Faysal al-Tafriqa Bayna al-Islam wa al-Zandaqa* (Oxford University Press,2002).

——— 'The Will to Believe', in *Essays in Pragmatism* (Holloway Press, 2007).

Jansen, J. J. G. 'Mu'Mim', in *Encyclopaedia of Islam*, by H. A. R. Gibb [et al.] (Leiden: E.J. Brill, 1960– [i.e., 1954–]–2001). pp. 554–555.

Khan, Muhammad Muhsin. *The Translations of the Meanings of Sahih al-Bukhari*, 9 vols. (Beirut, 1405/1985).

Leaman, Oliver. *An Introduction to Medieval Islamic Philosophy* (Cambridge University Press, 1986).

——— *A Brief Introduction to Islamic Philosophy* (Polity Press, 2001).

Leite, Adam. 'On Williamson's Arguments that Knowledge is a Mental State', *Ratio* (new series), June 2005, XVIII(2): 165–175.

Macdonald, D. B. 'Fitra', in *Encyclopaedia of Islam*, by H. A. R. Gibb [et al.] (Leiden: E.J. Brill, 1960– [i.e., 1954–]–2001). pp. 931–932.

———. and L. Gardet. 'Al-Ghayb', in *Encyclopaedia of Islam*, by H. A. R. Gibb [et al.] (Leiden: E.J. Brill, 1960– [i.e., 1954–]–2001). pp. 1025–1026.

Mackie, J. L. *The Miracle of Theism: Arguments for and against the Existence of God* (Oxford, 1982).

McCarthy, Richard. *Freedom and Fulfilment* (Twayne Publishers, 1980).
McKim, Robert. *Religious Ambiguity and Religious Diversity* (Oxford University Press, 2001).
Mitha, Farouk. *Al-Ghazālī and the Ismailis: A Debate on Reason and Authority in Medieval Islam* (I.B.Tauris, 2002).
Moosa, Ebrahim. *Ghazali on the Poetics of Imagination* (The University of North Carolina Press, 2005).
Moser, Paul. *The Elusive God* (Cambridge University Press, 2008).
Muslim, Abul Husayn Muslim ibn al-Hajjaj Qushayri al-Nisapuri. *Shahi Muslim* (Retrieved from http://www.usc.edu/schools/college/crcc/engagement/resources/texts/muslim/hadith/bukhari/).
Nakamura, Kojiro. *Al-Ghazālī and Prayer* (Islamic Book Trust, 2001).
Nasr, Seyyed Hossien and Oliver, Leaman (eds) *History of Islamic Philosophy* (Routledge, 1996).
——*The Heart of Islam: Enduring Values for Humanity* (Harper SanFrancisco, 2002).
——*Islamic Philosophy from its origin to the Present: Philosophy in the Land of Prophecy* (State University of New York Press, 2006).
O'Connell, Robert J. *William James on the Courage to Believe* (Fordham University Press, 1997).
Oppy, Graham. *Arguing About Gods* (Cambridge University Press, 2006).
——. and Nick Trakakis. 'Religious Language Games', in *Realism and Religion: Philosophical and Theological Perspectives* (ed.) Andrew Moore and Michael Scott (Ashgate, 2007).
Ormsby, Eric. *Ghazali: The Revival of Islam* (Oneworld Publications, 2007).
Pavlin, J. 'Sunni Kalam and Theological Controversies', in *History of Islamic Philosophy* (ed.) Oliver Leaman and Seyyed Hossien Nasr (Routledge, 1996), Vol. I. pp. 105–118.
Plantinga, Alvin. 'Ad Hick', *Faith and Philosophy*, 1997, 14(3): 295–302.
—— 'Pluralism: A Defense of Religious Exclusivism', in *The Philosophical Challenge of Religious Diversity* (ed.) Philip Quinn and Kevin Meeker (Oxford University Press, 1999), pp. 172–192.
—— *Warranted Christian Belief* (Oxford University Press, 2001).
Prichard, Duncan. 'Reforming Reformed Epistemology', *International Philosophical Quarterly*, 2003, 43(169): 43–66.
Ramadan, Tariq. *Western Muslims and the Future of Islam* (Oxford University Press, 2005).
Reed, Baron. 'How to Think About Fallibilism', *Philosophical Studies*, 2002, 107(2): 143–157.
——'A New Argument for Skepticism', *Philosophical Studies*, 2009, 142(1): 91–104.
Sachedina, Abdulaziz. *The Islamic Roots of Democratic Pluralism* (Oxford University Press, 2001).
—— 'The Quran and Other Religions', in *The Cambridge Companion to the Qur'an* (ed.) Jane Dammen Mcauliffe (Cambridge University Press, 2006), pp. 291–309.
Saeed, Abdullah. 'The Need to Rethink Apostasy Laws', in *Freedom of Religion: Apostasy and Islam.* by Abdullag Saeed and Hassan Saeed (Ashgate Publishing, 2004), pp. 167–173.
Sahih al-. Bukhari, and Muhammad Muhsin Khan. *The translation of the meanings of Sahih al-Bukhari: Arabic-English* (Al Maktabat al Salafiat, Al Madinato al Monawart, 1979).

Sands, Paul. *The Justification of Religious Faith in Soren Kierkegaard, John Henry Newman, and William James* (Gorgias Press, 2003).

Schellenberg, John. L. *Divine Hiddeness and Human Reason* (Cornell University Press, 1993).

Strawson, Peter. 'Freedom and Resentment', *Proceedings of the British Academy*, 1962, 48: 187–211.

Sudduth, Michael. 'Reformed Epistemology and Christian Apologetics', *Religious Studies*, 2003, 39(3): 299–321.

Swinburne, Richard. *The Existence of God* (Oxford University Press, 1979).

Trakakis, Nick. 'The Evidential Problem of Evil', *The Internet Encyclopedia of Philosophy* (Retrieved from http://www.iep.utm.edu/e/evil-evi.htm).

Waller, Bruce. *Critical thinking: Consider the Verdict* (4th edn) (Upper Saddle River, NJ: Prentice Hall, 2001).

Ward, Keith. 'Truth and the Diversity of Religions', in Philip L. Quinn and Kevin Meeker (eds) *The Philosophical Challenge of Religious Diversity*. (Oxford University Press, 2000), pp. 109–125.

Watt, Montgomery. *Al-Ghazali the Muslim Intellectual* (Kazi Publications, 2003).

Whitehead, A. N. *Religion in the Making* (New York: The Macmillan Co., 1930).

Whitman, Jeffery. *The Power and Value of Skepticism* (Rowman & Littlefield Publishers, 1996).

Wicks, Robert. 'Arthur Schopenhauer', *Stanford Encyclopedia of Philosophy* (Retrieved from http://plato.stanford.edu/entries/schopenhauer/).

Winter, Tim. 'Pluralism from A Muslim Perspective', in *Abraham's Children: Jews. Christians and Muslims in Conversation*, (ed.) Norman Solomon et al. (T. &T. Clark Publishers, 2006), pp. 202–211.

Yar, Majid. 'Hannah Arendt (1906–1975)', *The Internet Encyclopedia of Philosophy* (Retrieved from http://www.iep.utm.edu/a/arendt.htm#H6).

Index

Adler, Jonathan
  argument for evidentialism, 116;
    see also evidentialism
  concept of belief, 102
  critique of William James,
    102–3, 108
  Moore's paradox, 102–3
  reactive attitudes, 117–19
  reading of James, 109
Aijaz, Imran, 88
  exclusivism, 138
Akhtar, Shabbir
  on the philosophy of religion, 38–9
al-ghayb, 97–8
Al-Ghazālī, Abu Hamid, 4–5
  argument from dreams, 47
  case for a supra-rational faculty, 56
  case for scepticism, 49
  certainty and knowledge, 45
  critique of the *falasifa*
    (philosophers), 42–4
  divine mercy, 55
  enlightenment experience, 63
  epistemological and existential
    crisis, 45–6
  and the Jamesian account of
    faith, 80–5
  and reformed epistemology, 70
  Sufi account of faith, 56–7
ambiguity thesis (defined), 1
  and divine hiddenness, 155n3
ayah (signs of God), 140–3

Bishop, John, 3
  ethical constraint, 21
  passional inclinations, 28

Descartes, Rene, 47

evidentialism
  in William Clifford, 15–16
  see also Adler

exclusivism
  Muslim exclusivism, 138–9
  see also Plantinga

fallibilism, 51
fasik, 144
fitrah (inborn disposition), 139,
  141–3
foundationalism, challenge to
  religious belief, 66

God, 1
  ambiguity thesis, 1
  concept of, 155n2
  momentousness of believing in,
    26–8
  the reflective Muslim, 10
  the Sufi account of faith, 6

Hick, John, 2, 157n30

Ibn Qayyim, 169n46
inculpable non-belief, 147–50
Iqbal, Muhammad, on rationalising
  faith, 39
Islam, 155n11

James, William, 3
  believing beyond the evidence,
    11–14
  critique of Clifford's evidentialism,
    16–18
  Jamesian account of faith (defined),
    32–3
  applied to al-Ghazali, 80–5
  applied to Muhammad's
    experience of divine
    commission, 90–2
  charge of doxastic voluntarism,
    106–7

kāfir, 140–4

176   *Index*

Muhammad
divine commission, 90–1
see also Jamesian account of faith
mu'min, 140, 143–4

passional causes of belief
(defined), 13
passional nature, 14
trusting in, 30–1
Plantinga, Alvin
critique of pluralism, 131
defence of Christian exclusivism,
125–6
and his conception of reformed
epistemology, 68–9

question of entitlement (defined), 2
Quran
divine inspiration, 59
human faculties, 96
parable of darkness, 62
parable of light, 61
passional cause, 13
use of reason, 40

reflective Muslim (defined), 3–4
Reformed epistemology, *see*
al-Ghazali; Plantinga
religious pluralism
and the Common Word document,
95–7
and the Jamesian account of faith,
93, 123
Muslim views of, 94–6
psychological challenge of, 133
see also Plantinga

subjective principle of sufficient
reason
as define by Adler, 115
Swinburne, Richard, 107

tawhīd, 138
and the exclusivist argument,
139–40
tentative belief, 24
and non-dogmatic commitment,
25–6

Ward, Keith, 1
Whitehead, Alfred North, 40
Wittgenstein, Ludwig, 3

Printed and bound in the United States of America